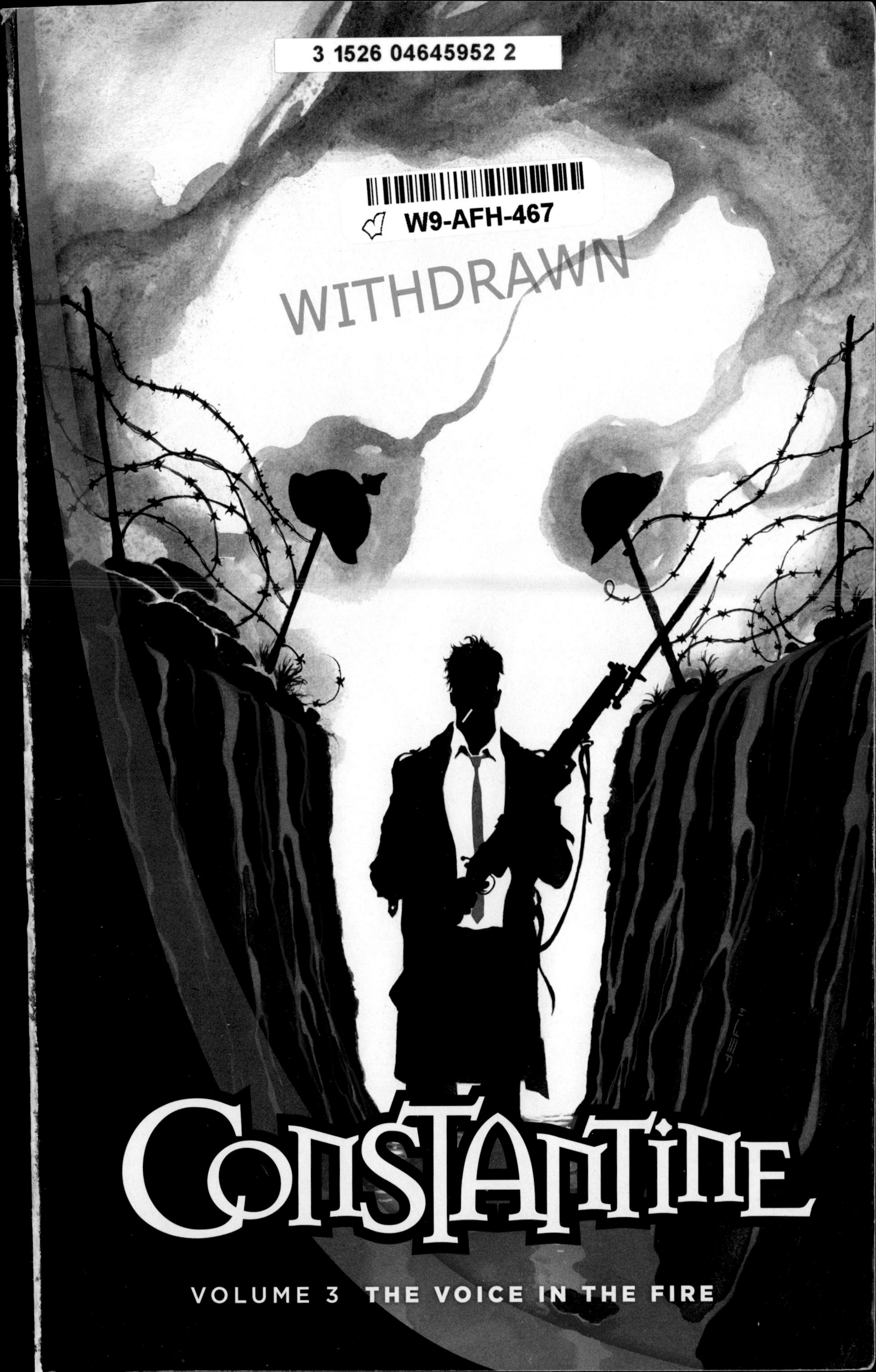

CONSTANTINE

VOLUME 3 THE VOICE IN THE FIRE

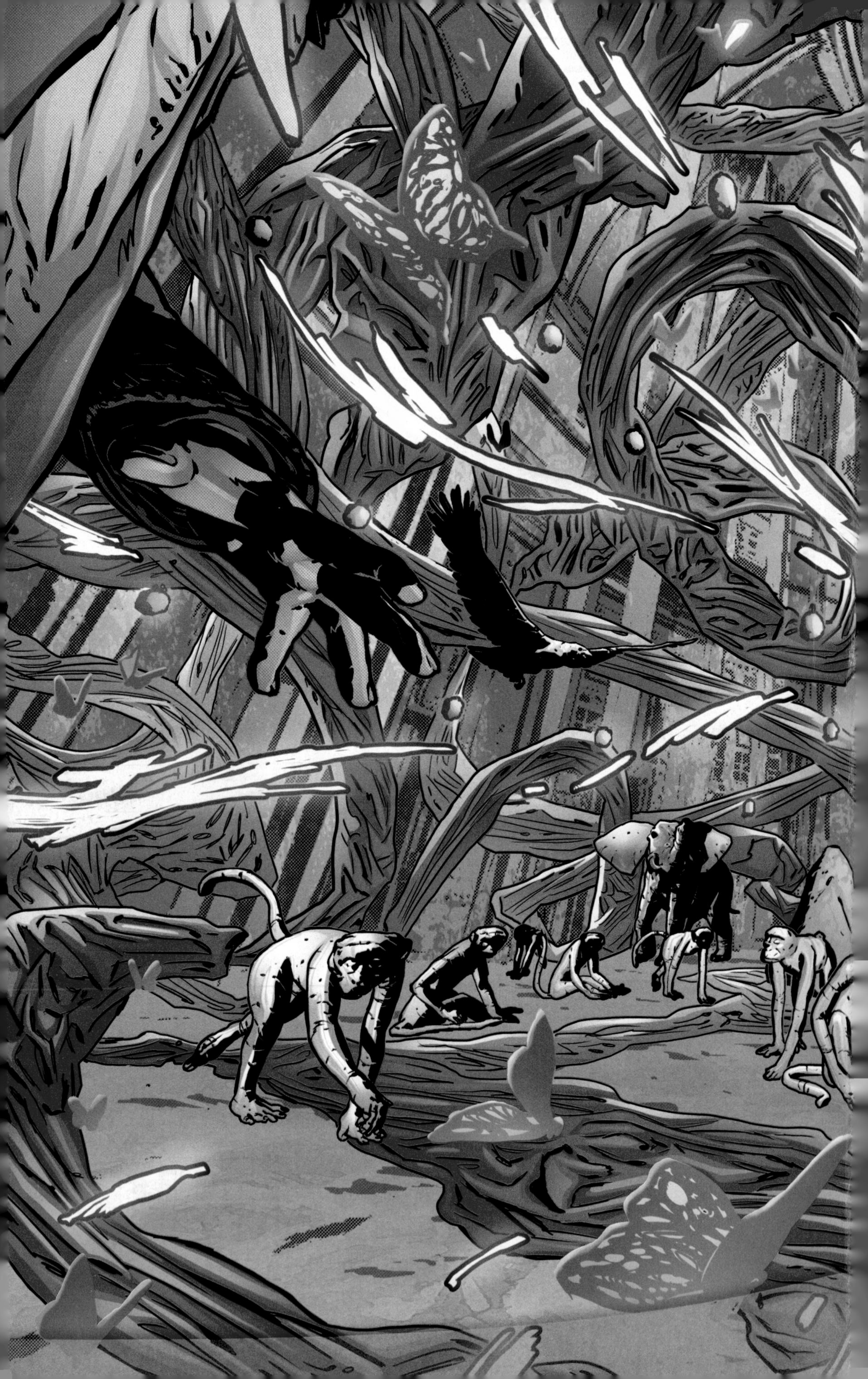

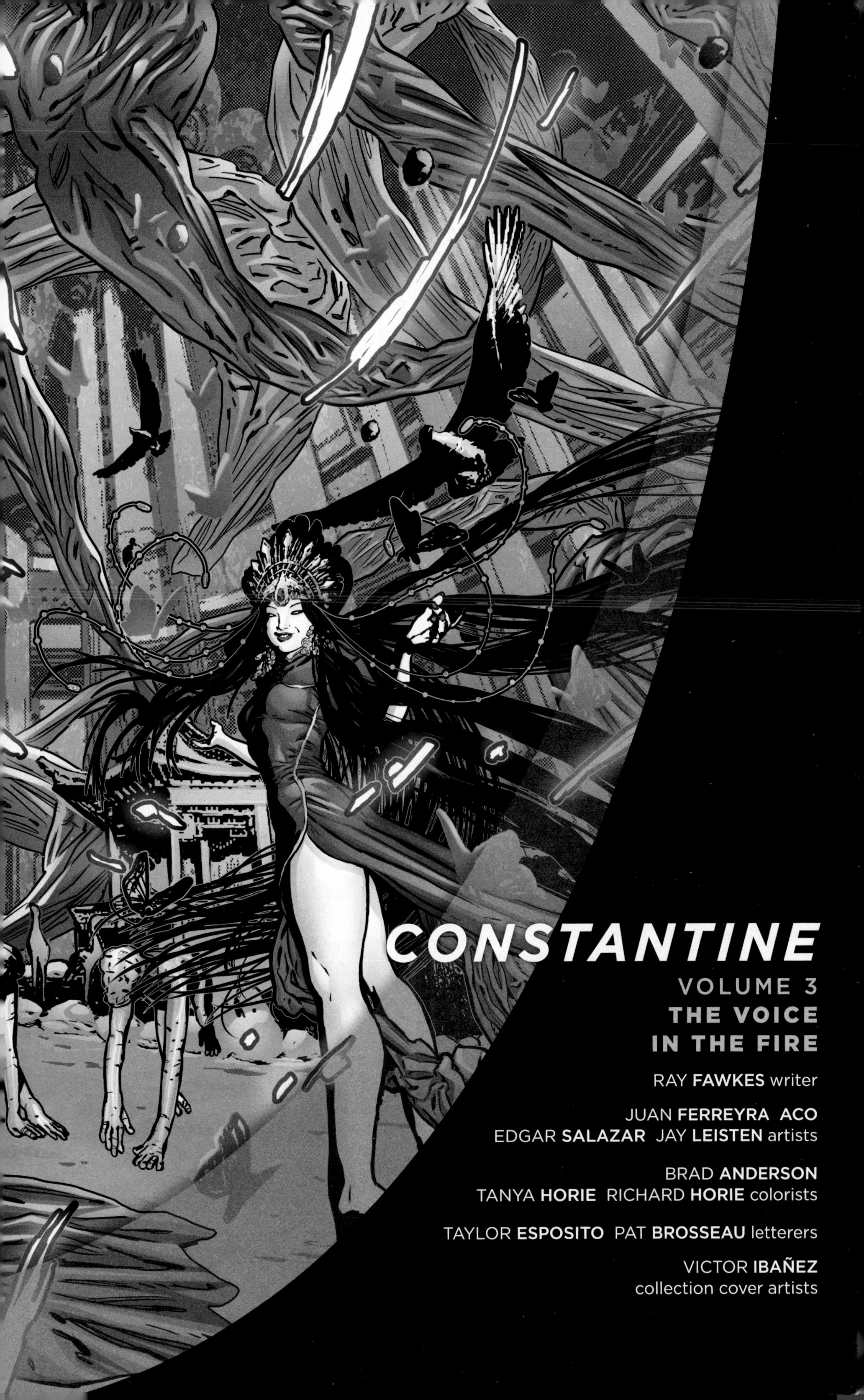

CONSTANTINE

VOLUME 3
THE VOICE IN THE FIRE

RAY **FAWKES** writer

JUAN **FERREYRA** **ACO**
EDGAR **SALAZAR** JAY **LEISTEN** artists

BRAD **ANDERSON**
TANYA **HORIE** RICHARD **HORIE** colorists

TAYLOR **ESPOSITO** PAT **BROSSEAU** letterers

VICTOR **IBAÑEZ**
collection cover artists

BRIAN CUNNINGHAM CHRIS CONROY RACHEL GLUCKSTERN Editors – Original Series
HARVEY RICHARDS Associate Editor – Original Series
KATE DURRÉ AMEDEO TURTURRO DAVE WIELGOSZ Assistant Editors – Original Series ROWENA YOW Editor
ROBBIN BROSTERMAN Design Director – Books ROBBIE BIEDERMAN Publication Design

BOB HARRAS Senior VP – Editor-in-Chief, DC Comics

DIANE NELSON President DAN DIDIO and JIM LEE Co-Publishers GEOFF JOHNS Chief Creative Officer
AMIT DESAI Senior VP – Marketing and Franchise Management
AMY GENKINS Senior VP – Business and Legal Affairs NAIRI GARDINER Senior VP – Finance
JEFF BOISON VP – Publishing Planning MARK CHIARELLO VP – Art Direction and Design
JOHN CUNNINGHAM VP – Marketing TERRI CUNNINGHAM VP – Editorial Administration
LARRY GANEM VP – Talent Relations and Services ALISON GILL Senior VP – Manufacturing and Operations
HANK KANALZ Senior VP – Vertigo and Integrated Publishing JAY KOGAN VP – Business and Legal Affairs, Publishing
JACK MAHAN VP – Business Affairs, Talent NICK NAPOLITANO VP – Manufacturing Administration SUE POHJA VP – Book Sales
FRED RUIZ VP – Manufacturing Operations COURTNEY SIMMONS Senior VP – Publicity BOB WAYNE Senior VP – Sales

CONSTANTINE VOLUME 3: THE VOICE IN THE FIRE

DC Comics, 1700 Broadway, New York, NY 10019
A Warner Bros. Entertainment Company.
Printed by RR Donnelley, Owensville, MO, USA. 1/16/15. First Printing.
ISBN: 978-1-4012-5085-0

Library of Congress Cataloging-in-Publication Data

Fawkes, Ray, author.
Constantine. Volume 3, The voice in the fire / Ray Fawkes ; [illustrated by].
pages cm. — (The New 52!)
ISBN 978-1-4012-5085-0 (pbk.)
1. Graphic novels. I. illustrator. II. Title. III. Title: Voice in the fire.

PN6728.H383F394 2015
741.5'973—dc23

2014039176

SUSTAINABLE
FORESTRY
INITIATIVE

Certified Chain of Custody
20% Certified Forest Content,
80% Certified Sourcing
www.sfiprogram.org
SFI-01042
APPLIES TO TEXT STOCK ONLY

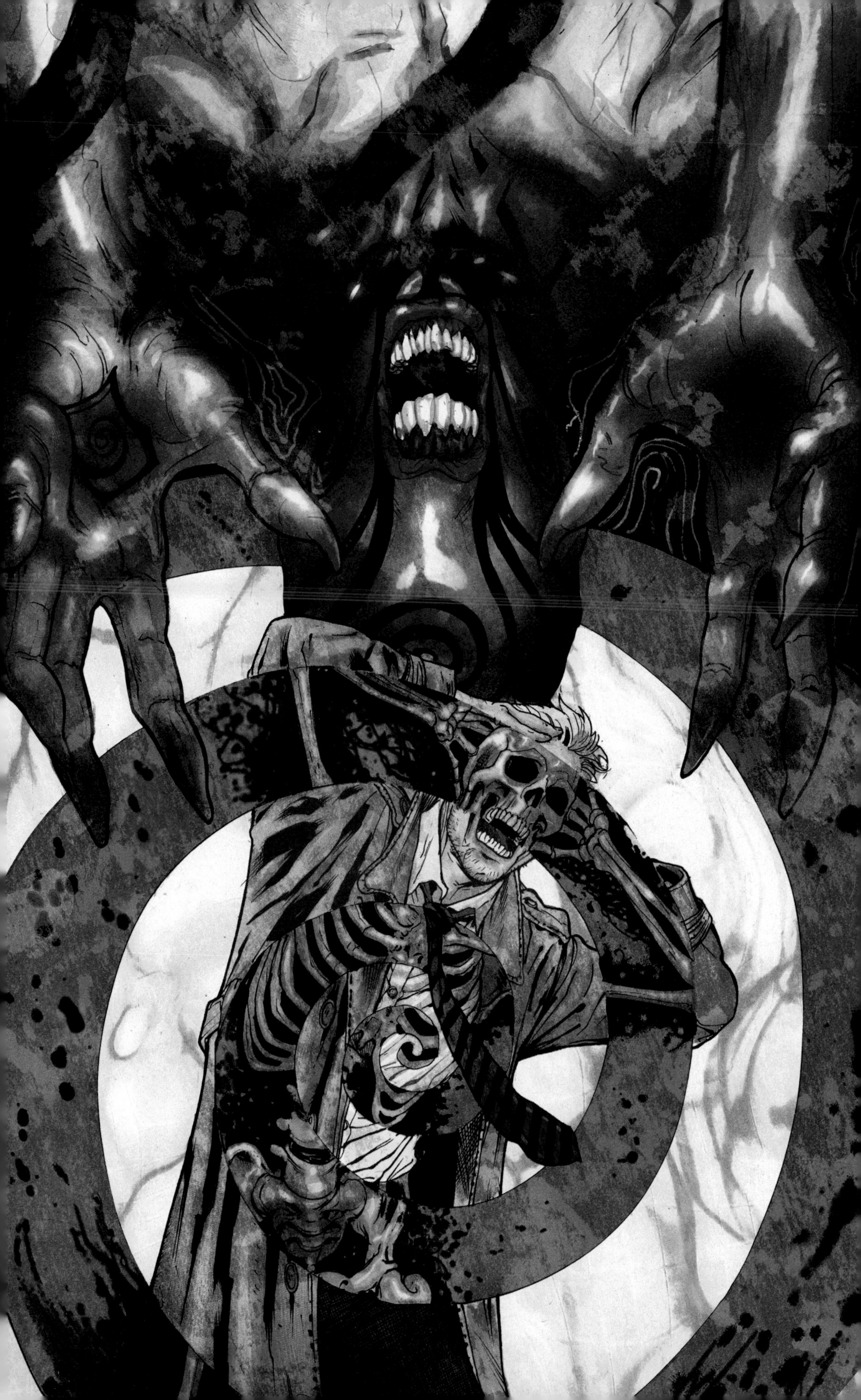

SPELLBOUND

RAY FAWKES
writer

ACO
artist

BRAD ANDERSON
colorist

TAYLOR ESPOSITO
letterer

cover art by
VICTOR IBAÑEZ

MOSCOW.

KNOCK KNOCK

JOHN CONSTANTINE. I COULD ASK HOW YOU GOT PAST MY *WARDS*, BUT WHAT'S THE POINT?

VIKTOR MIRONOV. *SPELLBINDER.* YOU'VE GOT A HELL OF A REPUTATION, MATE. PUTTING MIND-CONTROLLED WORLD *LEADERS* ON THE BLACK MARKET, ENSLAVED TO ORDER.

STANDARD FEE FOR STARTING A *WAR* OR STACKING A NATION'S *SUPREME COURT* IS A BILLION DOLLARS, YEAH?

WE NEED TO TALK.

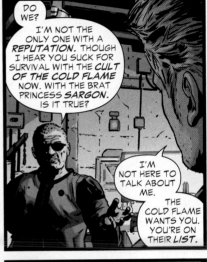

DO WE?

I'M NOT THE ONLY ONE WITH A *REPUTATION.* THOUGH I HEAR YOU SUCK FOR SURVIVAL WITH THE *CULT OF THE COLD FLAME* NOW. WITH THE BRAT PRINCESS *SARGON.* IS IT TRUE?

I'M NOT HERE TO TALK ABOUT ME.

THE COLD FLAME WANTS YOU. YOU'RE ON THEIR *LIST.*

THEY *CONSUME* EVERY MAGE TOO FOOLISH OR TOO WEAK TO FIGHT *BACK.* CLAIM THEIR POWER. BUT I AM A *REAL* MYSTIC. IF THEY COME FOR ME, I MAKE REAL *TROUBLE* FOR THEM.

I HAVE NO DOUBT OF THAT, GUV.

AND YET HERE YOU ARE ON THEIR BEHALF.

SURELY YOU KNOW BETTER THAN TO RISK CONFRONTING ME IN PERSON. UNLESS THERE'S SOME *OTHER* PLAY. SOMETHING *WORTH* THE RISK.

WHAT ARE YOU *DOING* HERE, CONSTANTINE?

TELL YOU WHAT, VIKTOR. THE ANSWER'S IN *HERE.*

WHY DON'T YOU COME IN AND SEE?

YOUR *FUNERAL.*

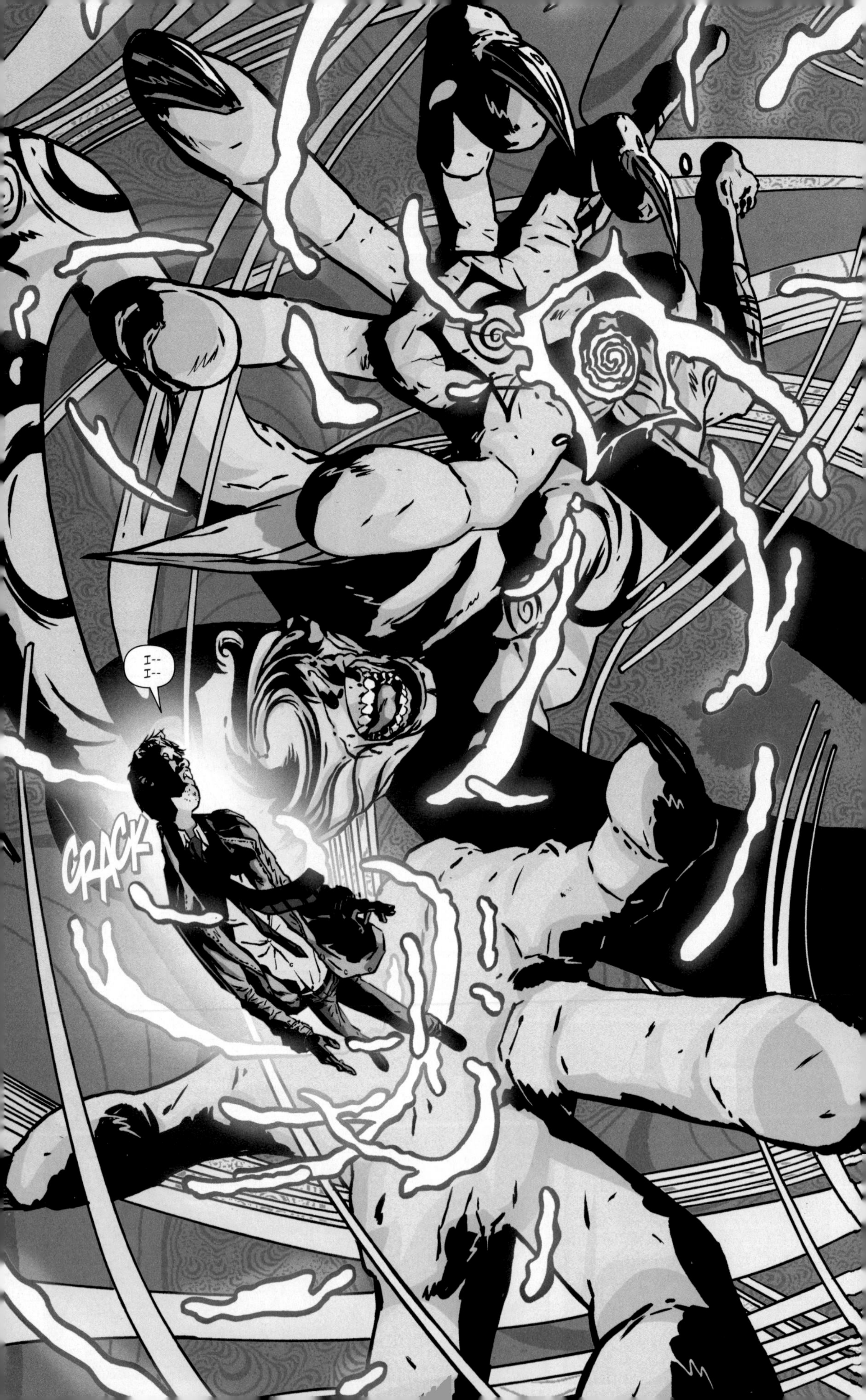
I--
I--
CRACK

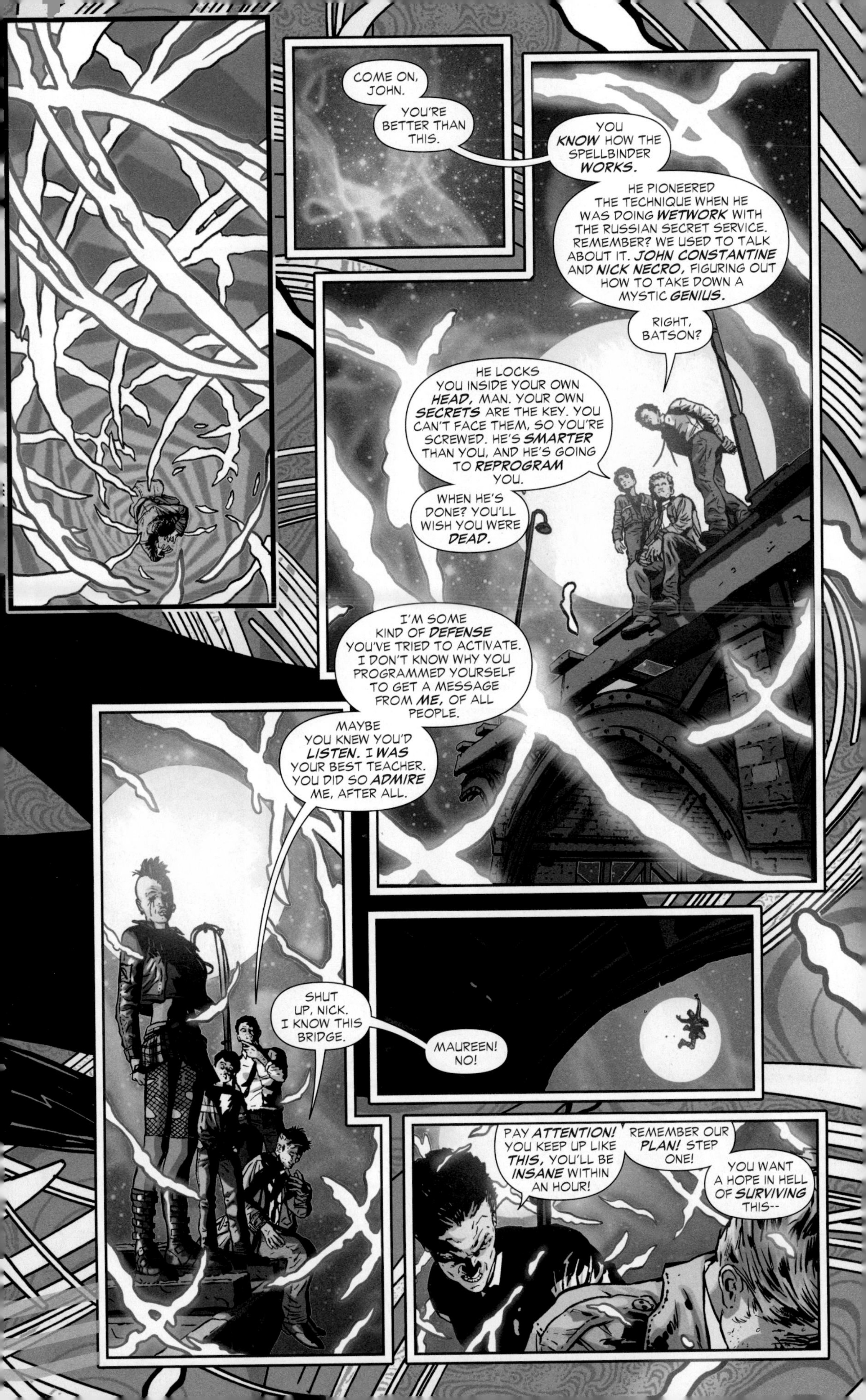
COME ON, JOHN.
YOU'RE BETTER THAN THIS.
YOU KNOW HOW THE SPELLBINDER WORKS.
HE PIONEERED THE TECHNIQUE WHEN HE WAS DOING WETWORK WITH THE RUSSIAN SECRET SERVICE. REMEMBER? WE USED TO TALK ABOUT IT. JOHN CONSTANTINE AND NICK NECRO, FIGURING OUT HOW TO TAKE DOWN A MYSTIC GENIUS.
RIGHT, BATSON?
HE LOCKS YOU INSIDE YOUR OWN HEAD, MAN. YOUR OWN SECRETS ARE THE KEY. YOU CAN'T FACE THEM, SO YOU'RE SCREWED. HE'S SMARTER THAN YOU, AND HE'S GOING TO REPROGRAM YOU.
WHEN HE'S DONE? YOU'LL WISH YOU WERE DEAD.
I'M SOME KIND OF DEFENSE YOU'VE TRIED TO ACTIVATE. I DON'T KNOW WHY YOU PROGRAMMED YOURSELF TO GET A MESSAGE FROM ME, OF ALL PEOPLE.
MAYBE YOU KNEW YOU'D LISTEN. I WAS YOUR BEST TEACHER. YOU DID SO ADMIRE ME, AFTER ALL.
SHUT UP, NICK. I KNOW THIS BRIDGE.
MAUREEN! NO!
PAY ATTENTION! YOU KEEP UP LIKE THIS, YOU'LL BE INSANE WITHIN AN HOUR!
REMEMBER OUR PLAN! STEP ONE!
YOU WANT A HOPE IN HELL OF SURVIVING THIS--

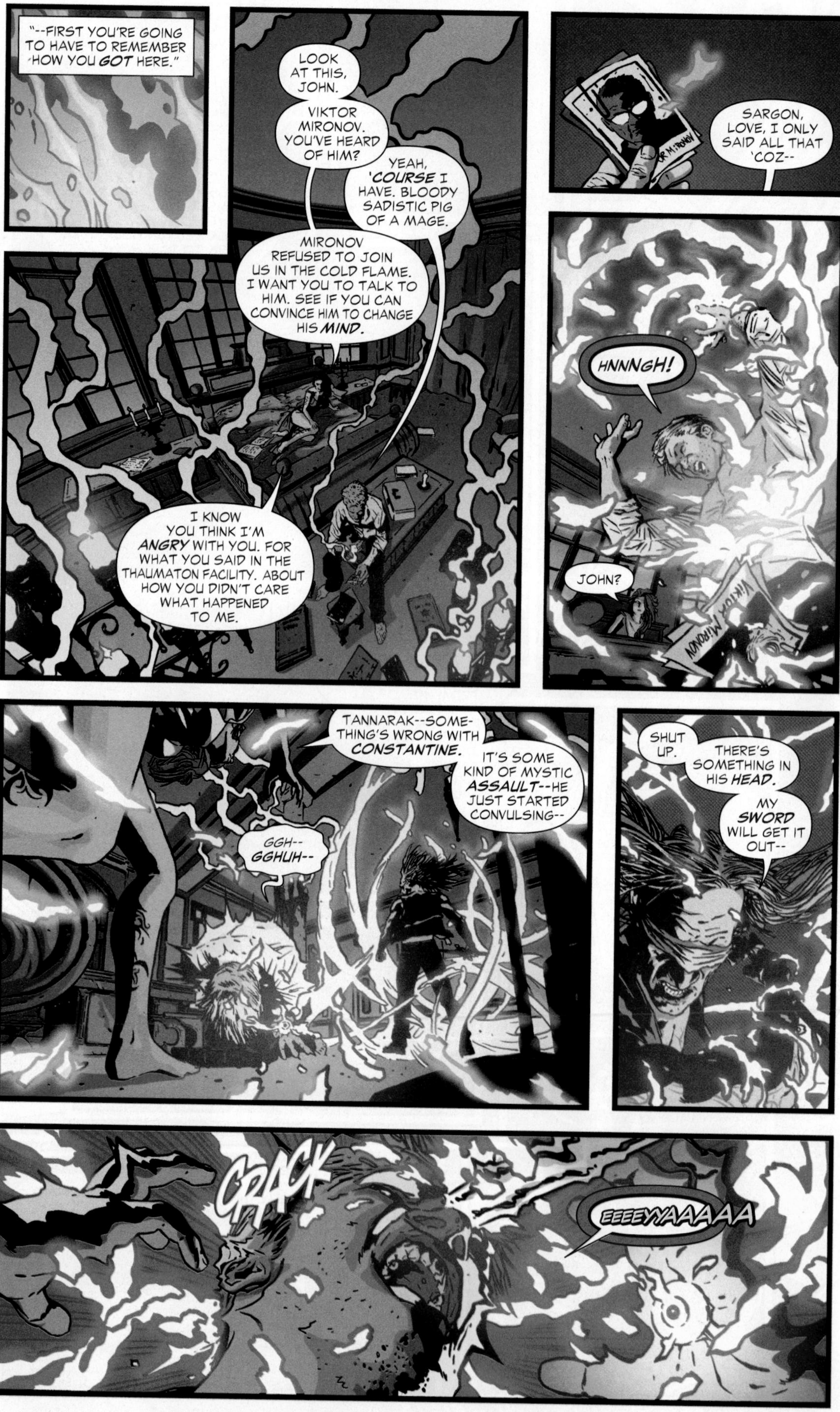
"--FIRST YOU'RE GOING TO HAVE TO REMEMBER HOW YOU GOT HERE."
LOOK AT THIS, JOHN.
VIKTOR MIRONOV. YOU'VE HEARD OF HIM?
YEAH, 'COURSE I HAVE. BLOODY SADISTIC PIG OF A MAGE.
MIRONOV REFUSED TO JOIN US IN THE COLD FLAME. I WANT YOU TO TALK TO HIM. SEE IF YOU CAN CONVINCE HIM TO CHANGE HIS MIND.
I KNOW YOU THINK I'M ANGRY WITH YOU. FOR WHAT YOU SAID IN THE THAUMATON FACILITY. ABOUT HOW YOU DIDN'T CARE WHAT HAPPENED TO ME.
SARGON, LOVE, I ONLY SAID ALL THAT 'COZ--
HNNNGH!
JOHN?
VIKTOR MIRONOV
TANNARAK--SOMETHING'S WRONG WITH CONSTANTINE.
IT'S SOME KIND OF MYSTIC ASSAULT--HE JUST STARTED CONVULSING--
GGH-- GGHUH--
SHUT UP.
THERE'S SOMETHING IN HIS HEAD.
MY SWORD WILL GET IT OUT--
CRACK
EEEEYYAAAAAA

KAFF.

HNH!

JESUS. WHAT A *NIGHTMARE.*

KKUGH.

BLOODY HELL...WHY DO I FEEL SO...

--OLD?!

THERE'S SOMETHING IN YOUR HEAD

HUH? WHAT THE--

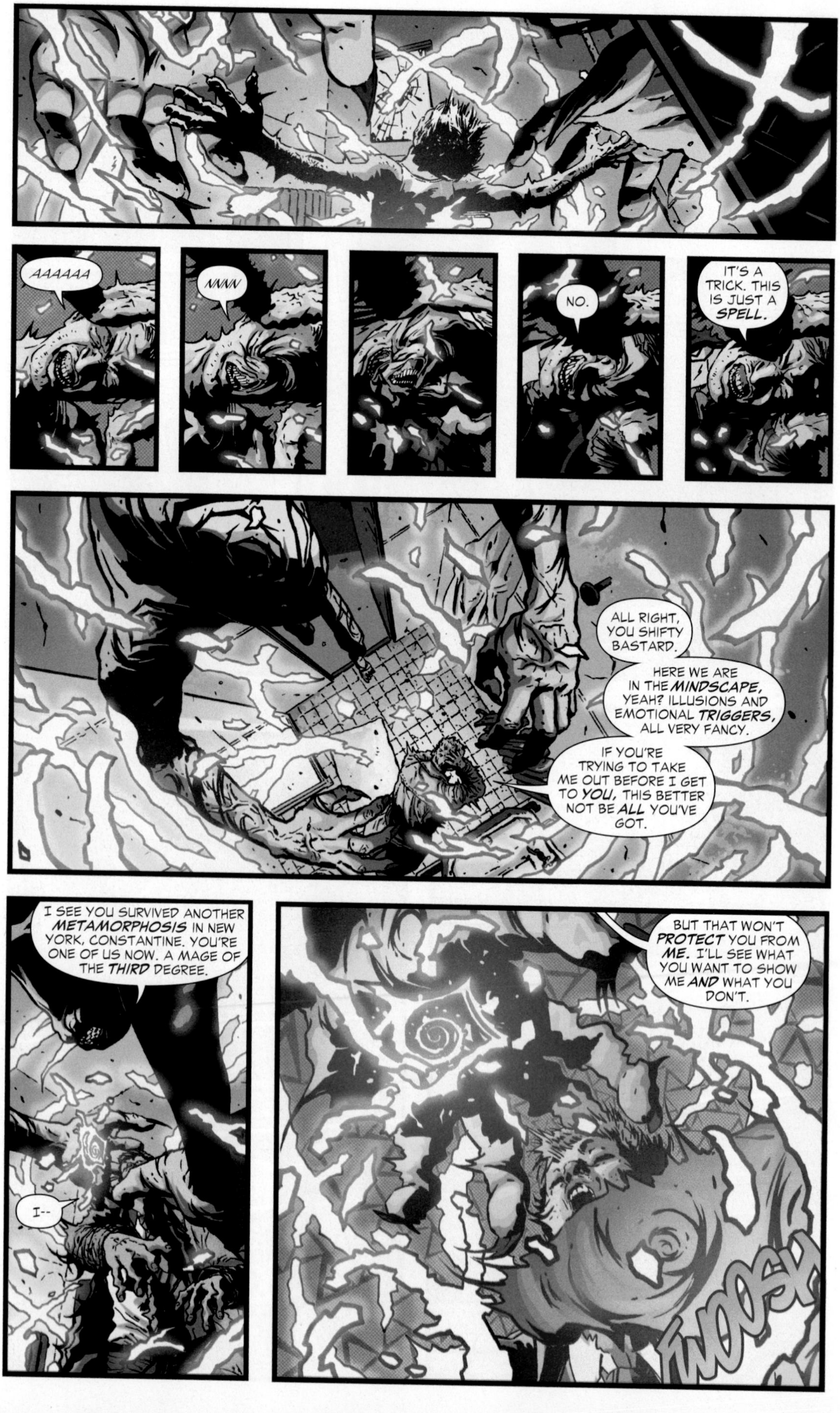
AAAAAA
NNNN
NO.
IT'S A TRICK. THIS IS JUST A *SPELL.*
ALL RIGHT, YOU SHIFTY BASTARD.
HERE WE ARE IN THE *MINDSCAPE,* YEAH? ILLUSIONS AND EMOTIONAL *TRIGGERS,* ALL VERY FANCY.
IF YOU'RE TRYING TO TAKE ME OUT BEFORE I GET TO *YOU,* THIS BETTER NOT BE *ALL* YOU'VE GOT.
I SEE YOU SURVIVED ANOTHER *METAMORPHOSIS* IN NEW YORK, CONSTANTINE. YOU'RE ONE OF US NOW. A MAGE OF THE *THIRD* DEGREE.
I--
BUT THAT WON'T *PROTECT* YOU FROM *ME.* I'LL SEE WHAT YOU WANT TO SHOW ME *AND* WHAT YOU DON'T.
WOOSH

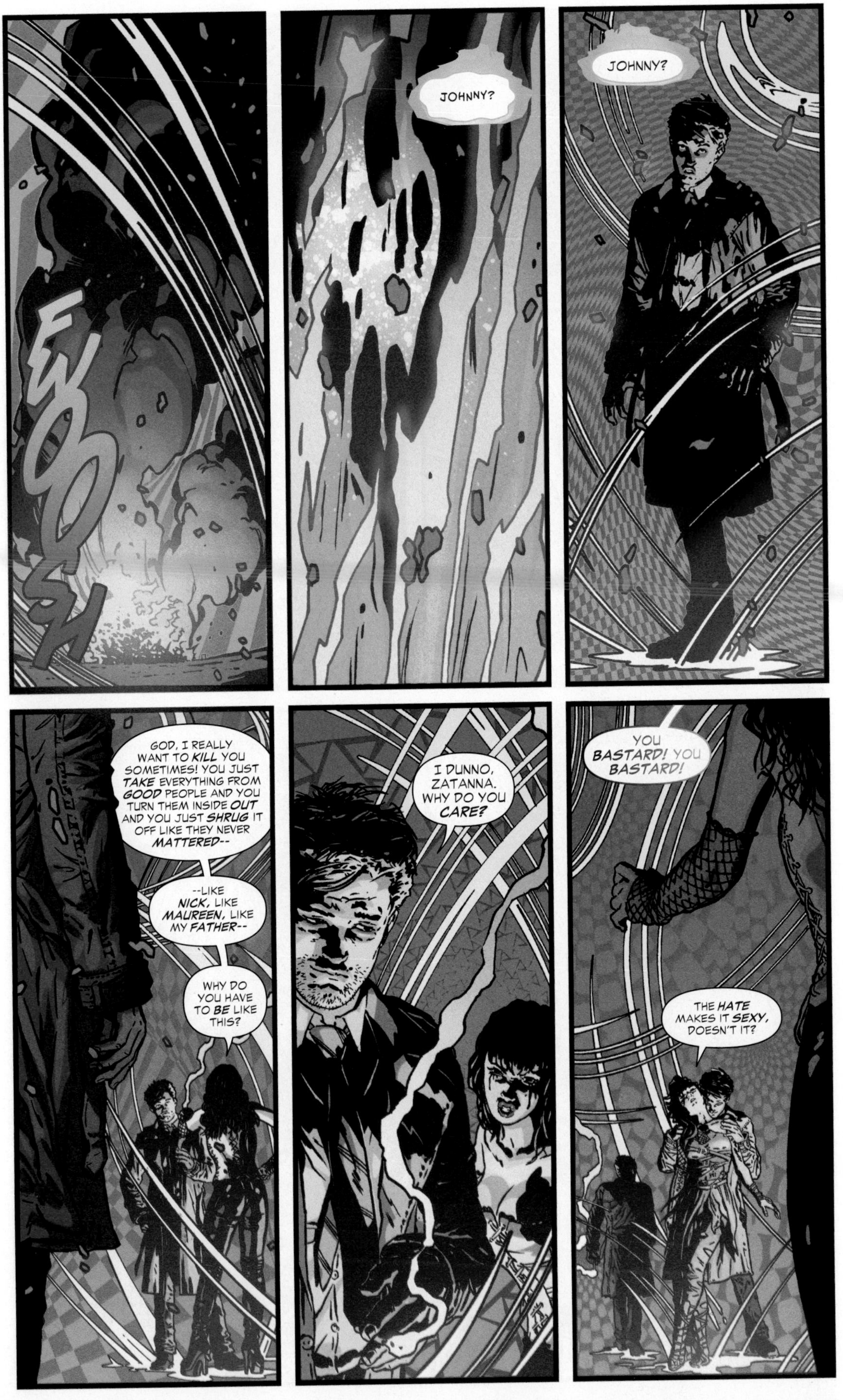
FWOOSH
JOHNNY?
JOHNNY?
GOD, I REALLY WANT TO KILL YOU SOMETIMES! YOU JUST TAKE EVERYTHING FROM GOOD PEOPLE AND YOU TURN THEM INSIDE OUT AND YOU JUST SHRUG IT OFF LIKE THEY NEVER MATTERED--
--LIKE NICK, LIKE MAUREEN, LIKE MY FATHER--
WHY DO YOU HAVE TO BE LIKE THIS?
I DUNNO, ZATANNA. WHY DO YOU CARE?
YOU BASTARD! YOU BASTARD!
THE HATE MAKES IT SEXY, DOESN'T IT?

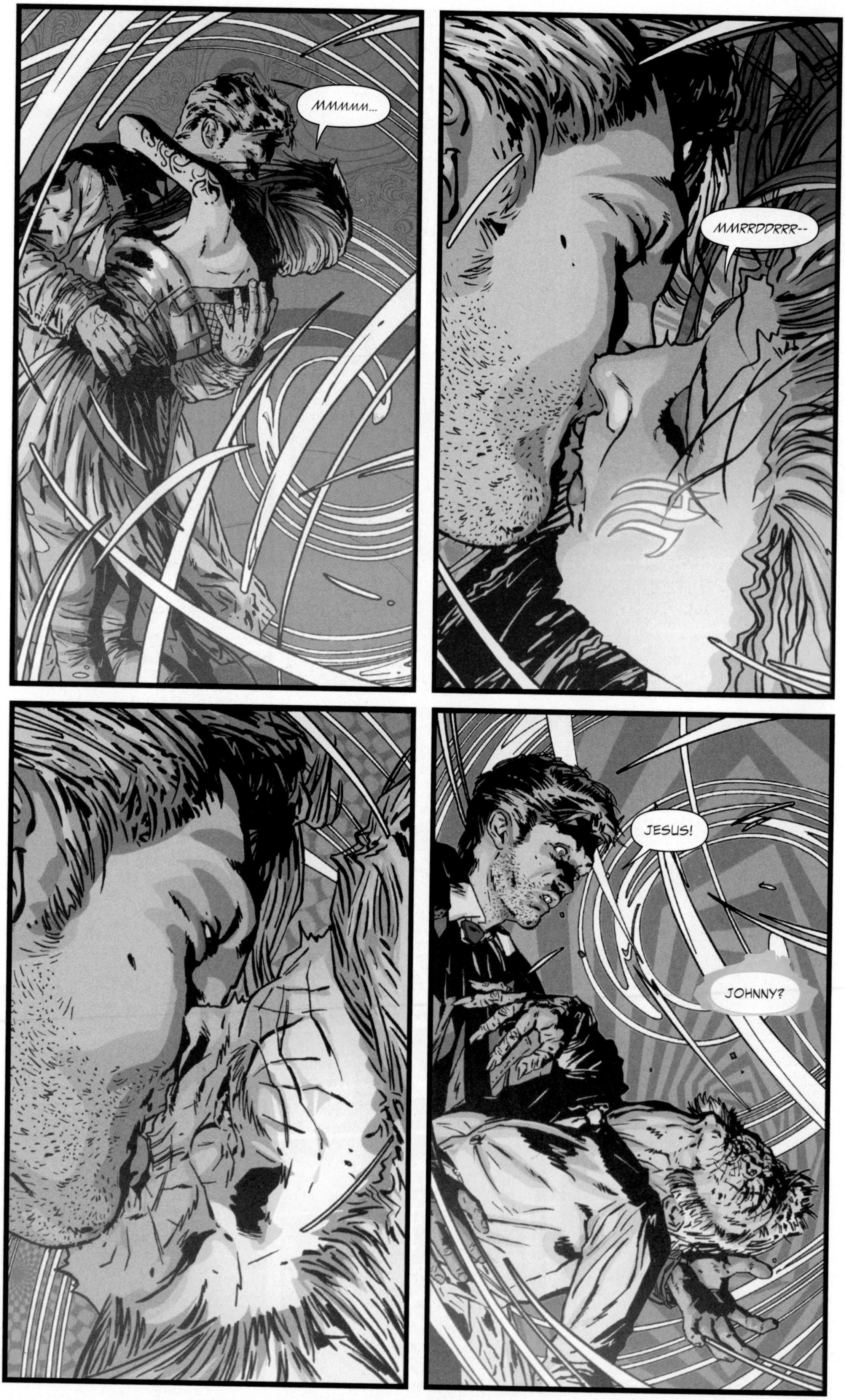
MMMMM...
MMRRDDRRR--
JESUS!
JOHNNY?

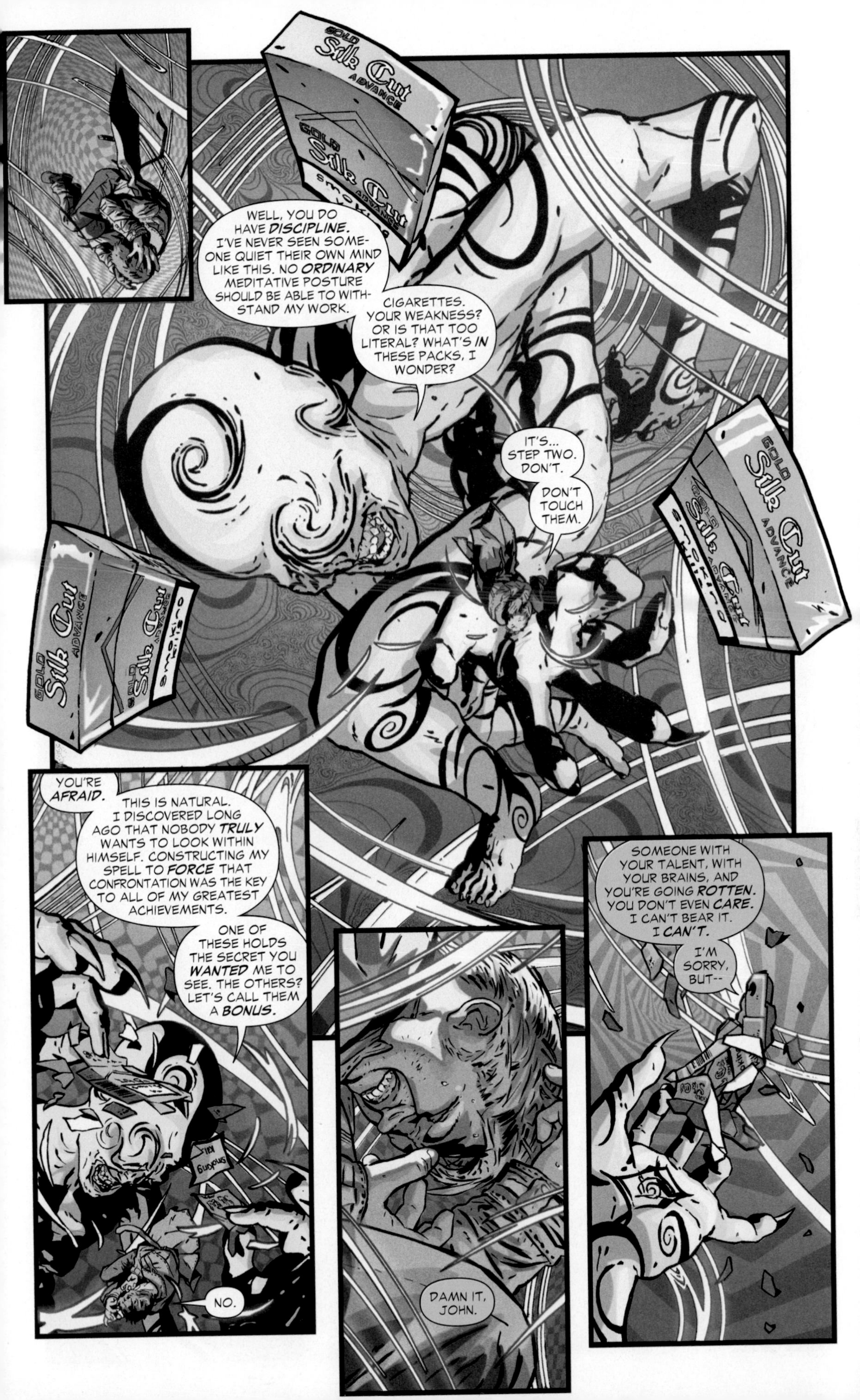
GOLD
Silk Cut
ADVANCE
WELL, YOU DO HAVE *DISCIPLINE.* I'VE NEVER SEEN SOME-ONE QUIET THEIR OWN MIND LIKE THIS. NO *ORDINARY* MEDITATIVE POSTURE SHOULD BE ABLE TO WITH-STAND MY WORK.
CIGARETTES. YOUR WEAKNESS? OR IS THAT TOO LITERAL? WHAT'S *IN* THESE PACKS, I WONDER?
IT'S... STEP TWO. DON'T.
DON'T TOUCH THEM.
YOU'RE *AFRAID.*
THIS IS NATURAL. I DISCOVERED LONG AGO THAT NOBODY *TRULY* WANTS TO LOOK WITHIN HIMSELF. CONSTRUCTING MY SPELL TO *FORCE* THAT CONFRONTATION WAS THE KEY TO ALL OF MY GREATEST ACHIEVEMENTS.
ONE OF THESE HOLDS THE SECRET YOU *WANTED* ME TO SEE. THE OTHERS? LET'S CALL THEM A *BONUS.*
NO.
DAMN IT, JOHN.
SOMEONE WITH YOUR TALENT, WITH YOUR BRAINS, AND YOU'RE GOING *ROTTEN.* YOU DON'T EVEN *CARE.* I CAN'T BEAR IT. *I CAN'T.*
I'M SORRY, BUT--

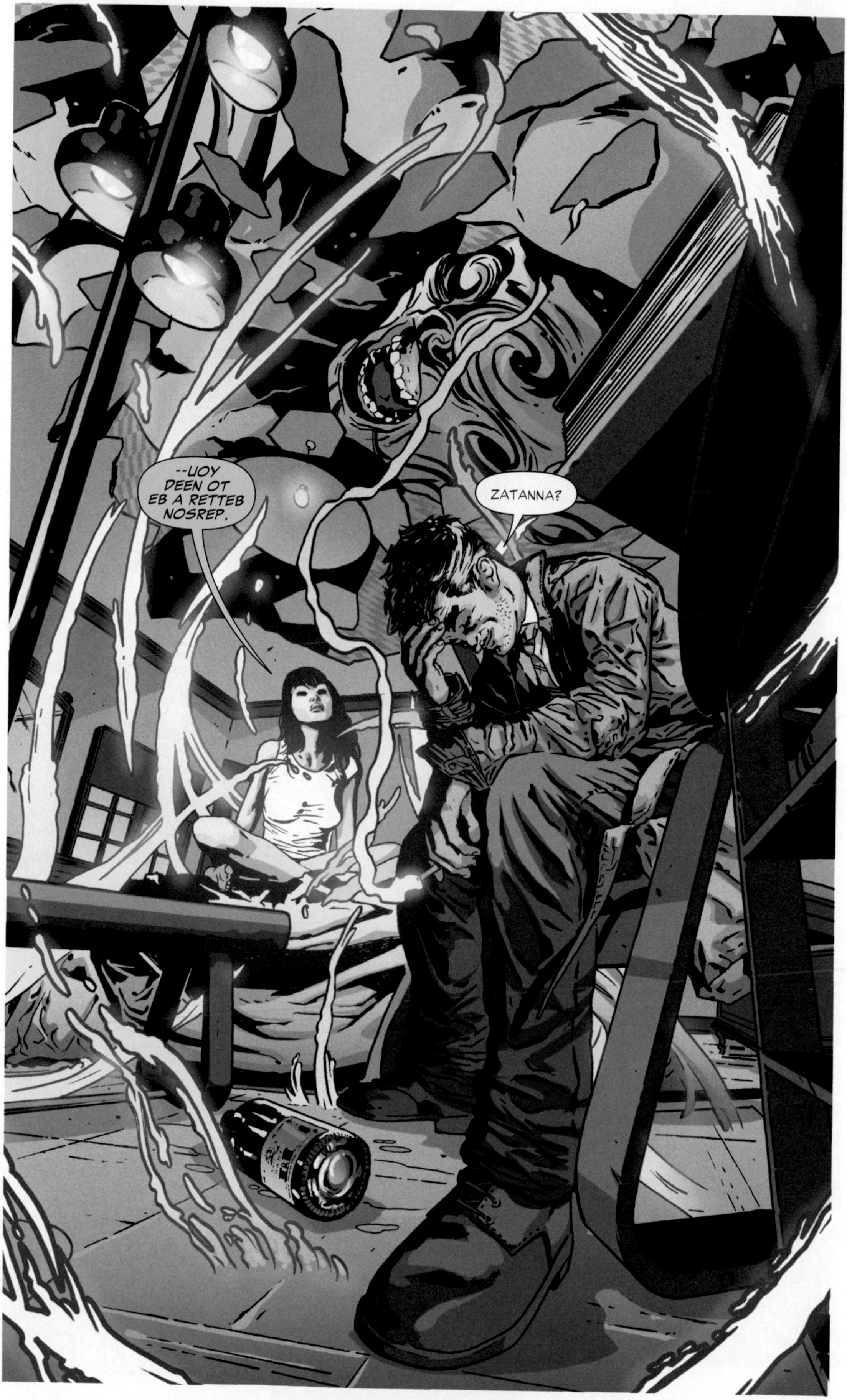
--UOY DEEN OT EB A RETTEB NOSREP.
ZATANNA?

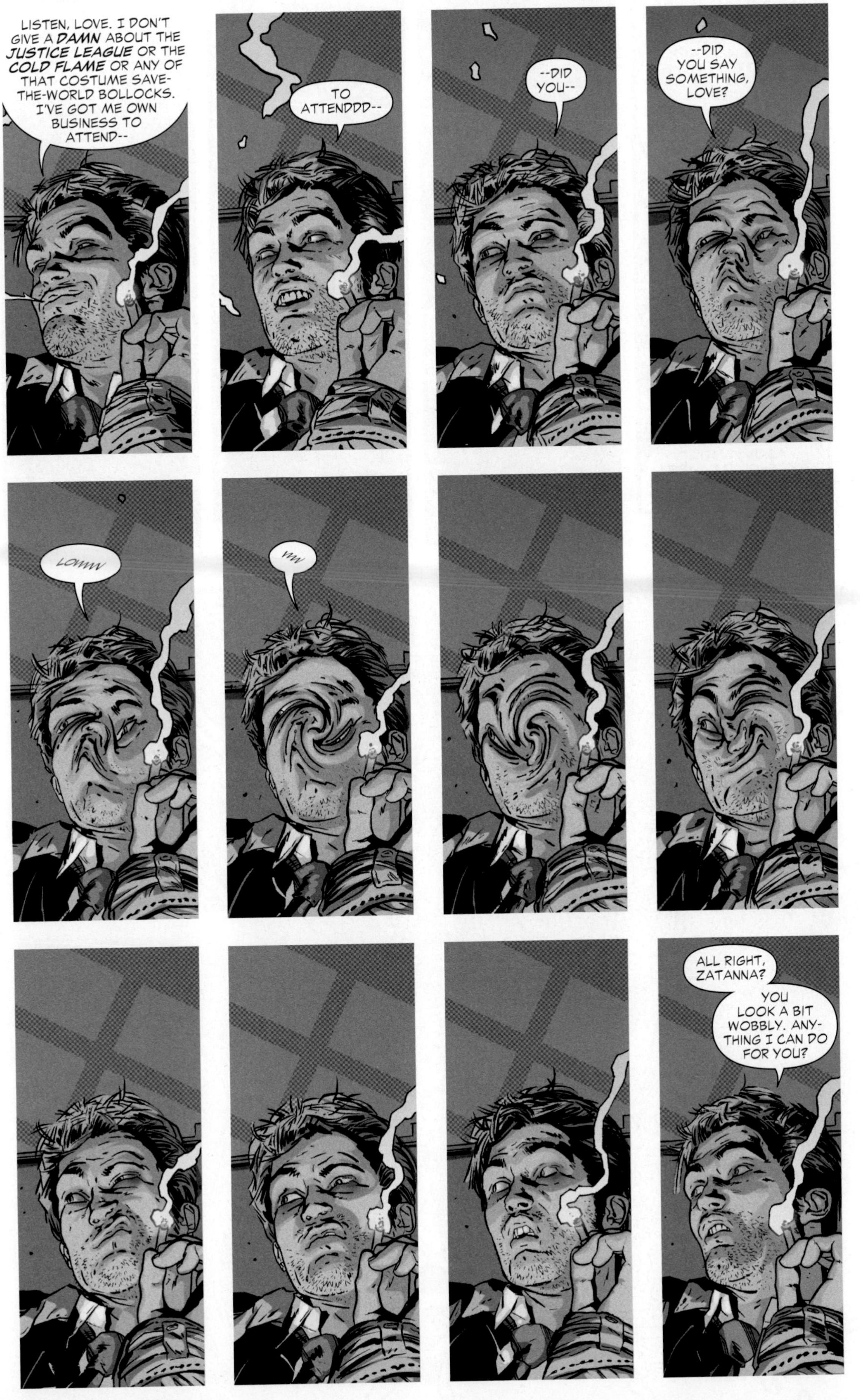
LISTEN, LOVE. I DON'T GIVE A DAMN ABOUT THE JUSTICE LEAGUE OR THE COLD FLAME OR ANY OF THAT COSTUME SAVE-THE-WORLD BOLLOCKS. I'VE GOT ME OWN BUSINESS TO ATTEND--
TO ATTENDDD--
--DID YOU--
--DID YOU SAY SOMETHING, LOVE?
ALL RIGHT, ZATANNA?
YOU LOOK A BIT WOBBLY. ANYTHING I CAN DO FOR YOU?

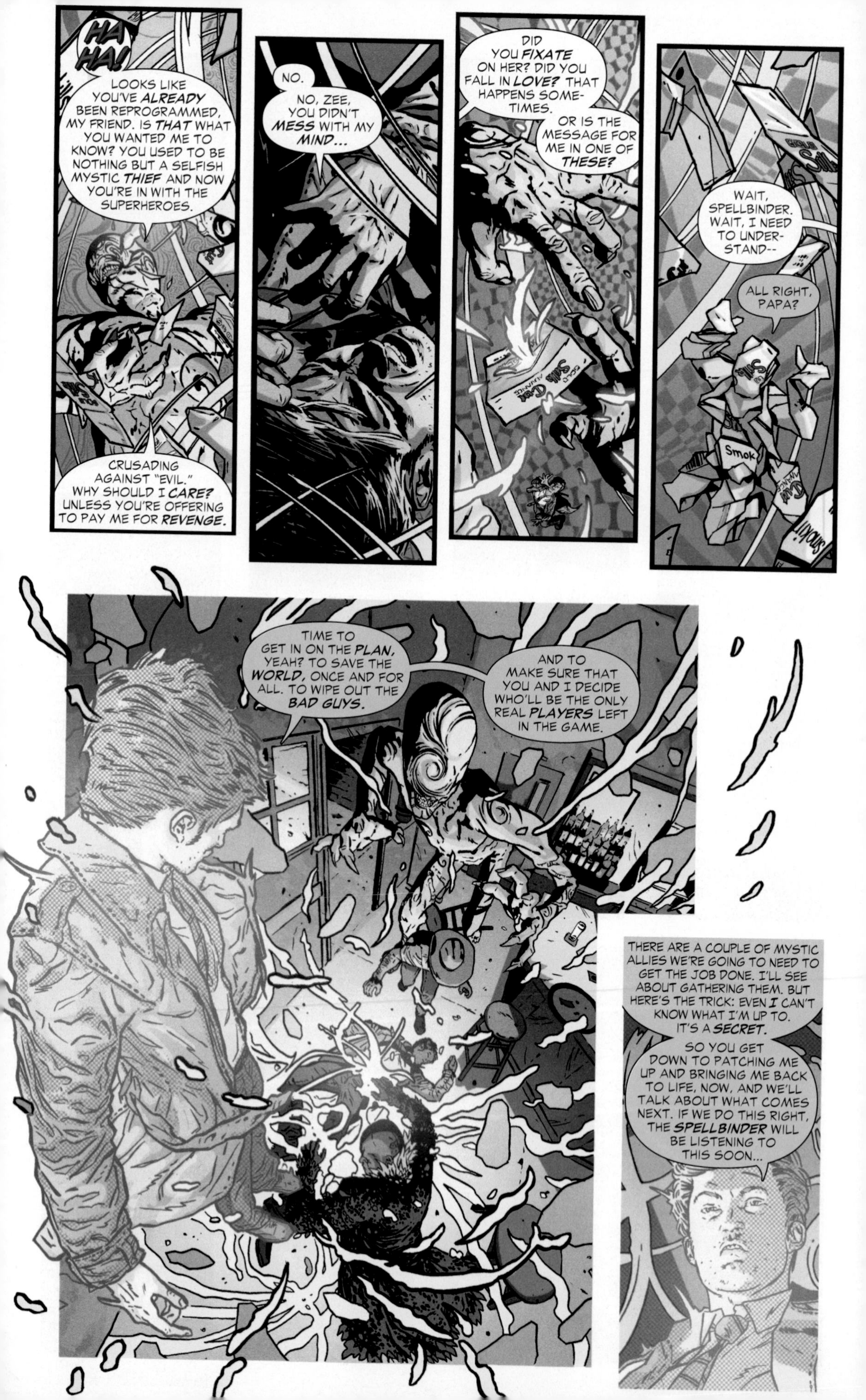
HA HA!
LOOKS LIKE YOU'VE ALREADY BEEN REPROGRAMMED, MY FRIEND. IS THAT WHAT YOU WANTED ME TO KNOW? YOU USED TO BE NOTHING BUT A SELFISH MYSTIC THIEF AND NOW YOU'RE IN WITH THE SUPERHEROES.
CRUSADING AGAINST "EVIL." WHY SHOULD I CARE? UNLESS YOU'RE OFFERING TO PAY ME FOR REVENGE.
NO.
NO, ZEE, YOU DIDN'T MESS WITH MY MIND...
DID YOU FIXATE ON HER? DID YOU FALL IN LOVE? THAT HAPPENS SOMETIMES.
OR IS THE MESSAGE FOR ME IN ONE OF THESE?
WAIT, SPELLBINDER. WAIT, I NEED TO UNDERSTAND--
ALL RIGHT, PAPA?
Smok
TIME TO GET IN ON THE PLAN, YEAH? TO SAVE THE WORLD, ONCE AND FOR ALL. TO WIPE OUT THE BAD GUYS.
AND TO MAKE SURE THAT YOU AND I DECIDE WHO'LL BE THE ONLY REAL PLAYERS LEFT IN THE GAME.
THERE ARE A COUPLE OF MYSTIC ALLIES WE'RE GOING TO NEED TO GET THE JOB DONE. I'LL SEE ABOUT GATHERING THEM. BUT HERE'S THE TRICK: EVEN I CAN'T KNOW WHAT I'M UP TO. IT'S A SECRET.
SO YOU GET DOWN TO PATCHING ME UP AND BRINGING ME BACK TO LIFE, NOW, AND WE'LL TALK ABOUT WHAT COMES NEXT. IF WE DO THIS RIGHT, THE SPELLBINDER WILL BE LISTENING TO THIS SOON...

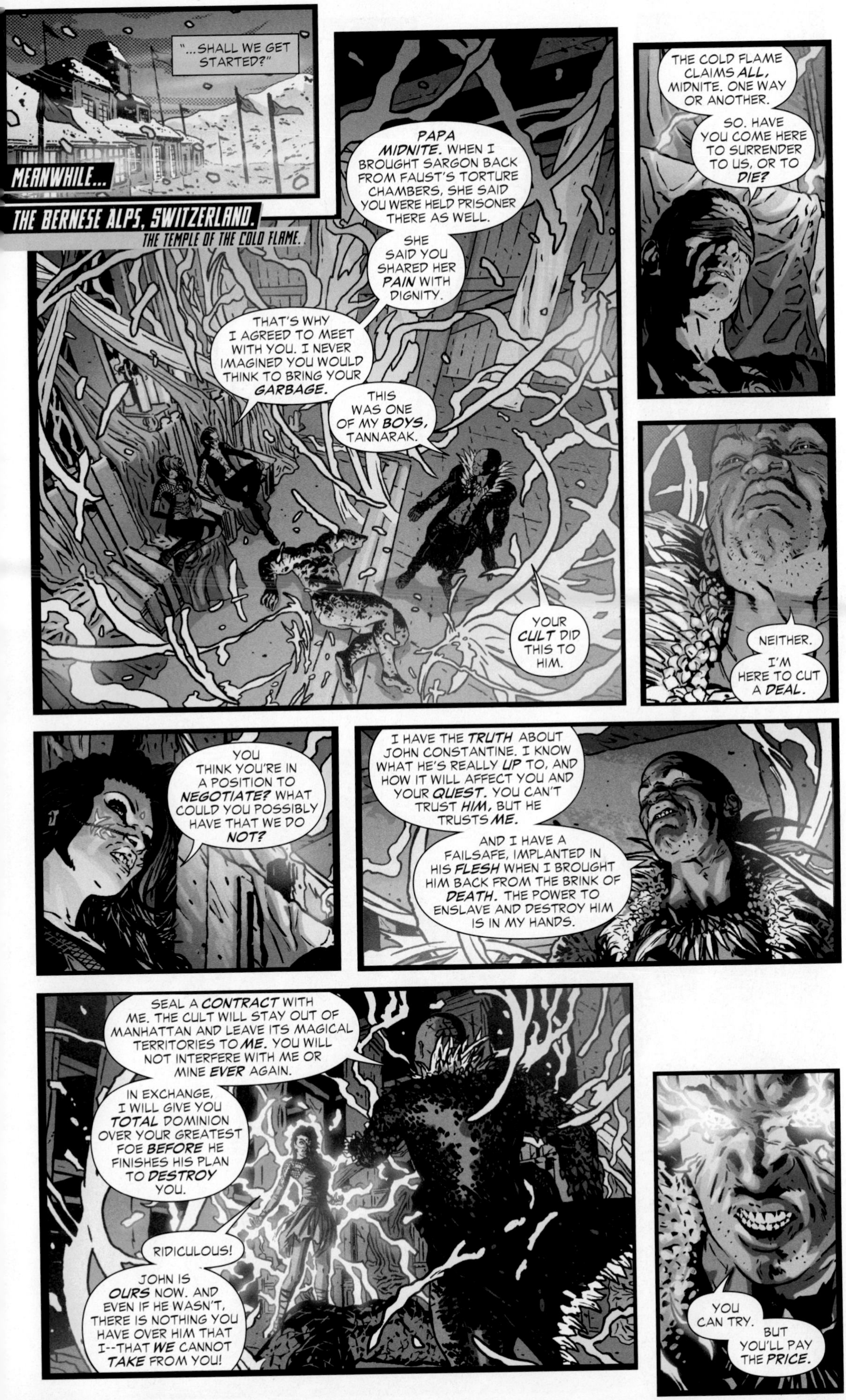

"...SHALL WE GET STARTED?"
MEANWHILE...
THE BERNESE ALPS, SWITZERLAND.
THE TEMPLE OF THE COLD FLAME.
PAPA MIDNITE. WHEN I BROUGHT SARGON BACK FROM FAUST'S TORTURE CHAMBERS, SHE SAID YOU WERE HELD PRISONER THERE AS WELL.
SHE SAID YOU SHARED HER PAIN WITH DIGNITY.
THAT'S WHY I AGREED TO MEET WITH YOU. I NEVER IMAGINED YOU WOULD THINK TO BRING YOUR GARBAGE.
THIS WAS ONE OF MY BOYS, TANNARAK.
YOUR CULT DID THIS TO HIM.
THE COLD FLAME CLAIMS ALL, MIDNITE. ONE WAY OR ANOTHER.
SO. HAVE YOU COME HERE TO SURRENDER TO US, OR TO DIE?
NEITHER.
I'M HERE TO CUT A DEAL.
YOU THINK YOU'RE IN A POSITION TO NEGOTIATE? WHAT COULD YOU POSSIBLY HAVE THAT WE DO NOT?
I HAVE THE TRUTH ABOUT JOHN CONSTANTINE. I KNOW WHAT HE'S REALLY UP TO, AND HOW IT WILL AFFECT YOU AND YOUR QUEST. YOU CAN'T TRUST HIM, BUT HE TRUSTS ME.
AND I HAVE A FAILSAFE, IMPLANTED IN HIS FLESH WHEN I BROUGHT HIM BACK FROM THE BRINK OF DEATH. THE POWER TO ENSLAVE AND DESTROY HIM IS IN MY HANDS.
SEAL A CONTRACT WITH ME. THE CULT WILL STAY OUT OF MANHATTAN AND LEAVE ITS MAGICAL TERRITORIES TO ME. YOU WILL NOT INTERFERE WITH ME OR MINE EVER AGAIN.
IN EXCHANGE, I WILL GIVE YOU TOTAL DOMINION OVER YOUR GREATEST FOE BEFORE HE FINISHES HIS PLAN TO DESTROY YOU.
RIDICULOUS!
JOHN IS OURS NOW. AND EVEN IF HE WASN'T, THERE IS NOTHING YOU HAVE OVER HIM THAT I--THAT WE CANNOT TAKE FROM YOU!
YOU CAN TRY.
BUT YOU'LL PAY THE PRICE.

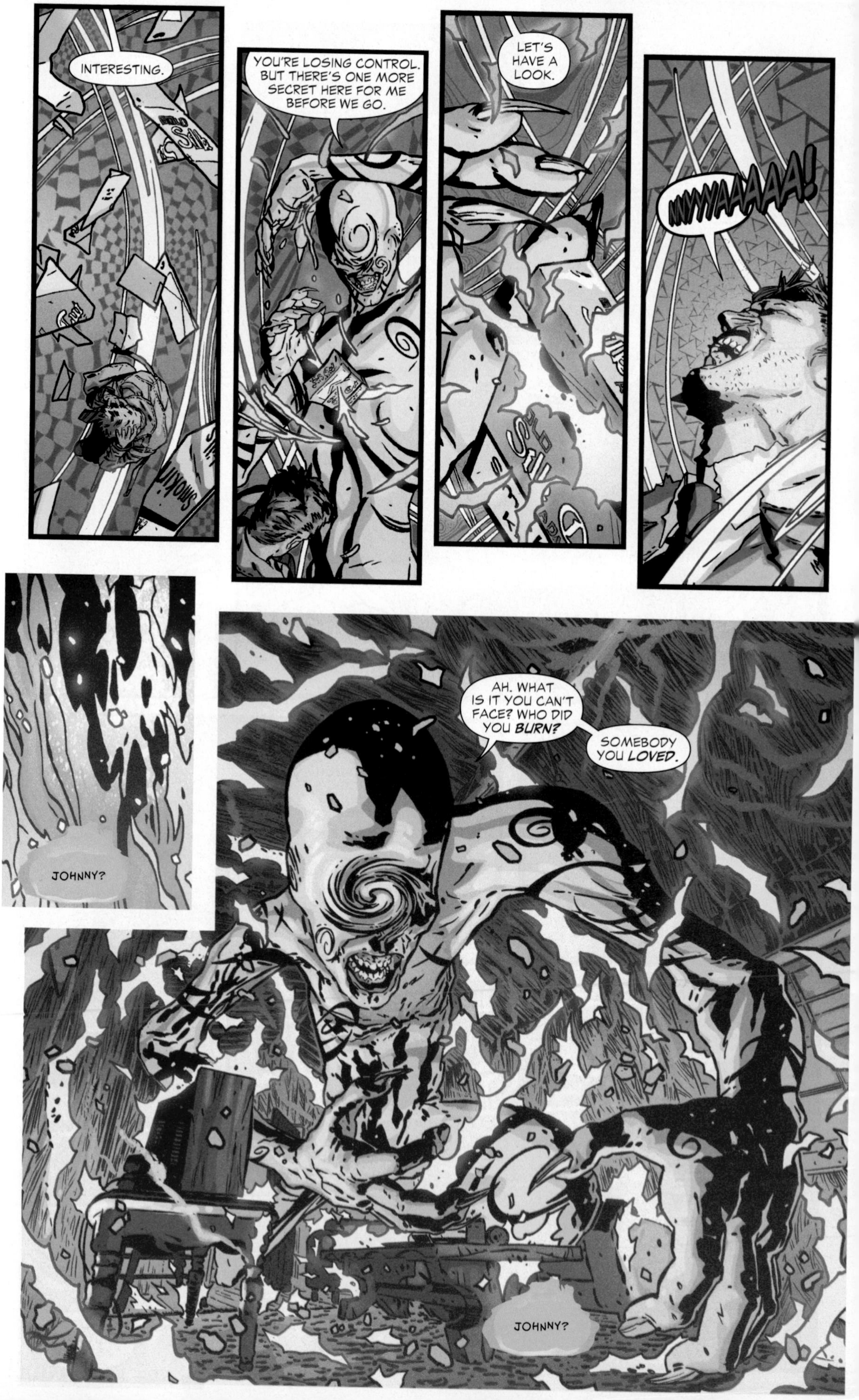
INTERESTING.
YOU'RE LOSING CONTROL. BUT THERE'S ONE MORE SECRET HERE FOR ME BEFORE WE GO.
LET'S HAVE A LOOK.
NNNYYYAAAAAA!
JOHNNY?
AH. WHAT IS IT YOU CAN'T FACE? WHO DID YOU BURN?
SOMEBODY YOU LOVED.
JOHNNY?

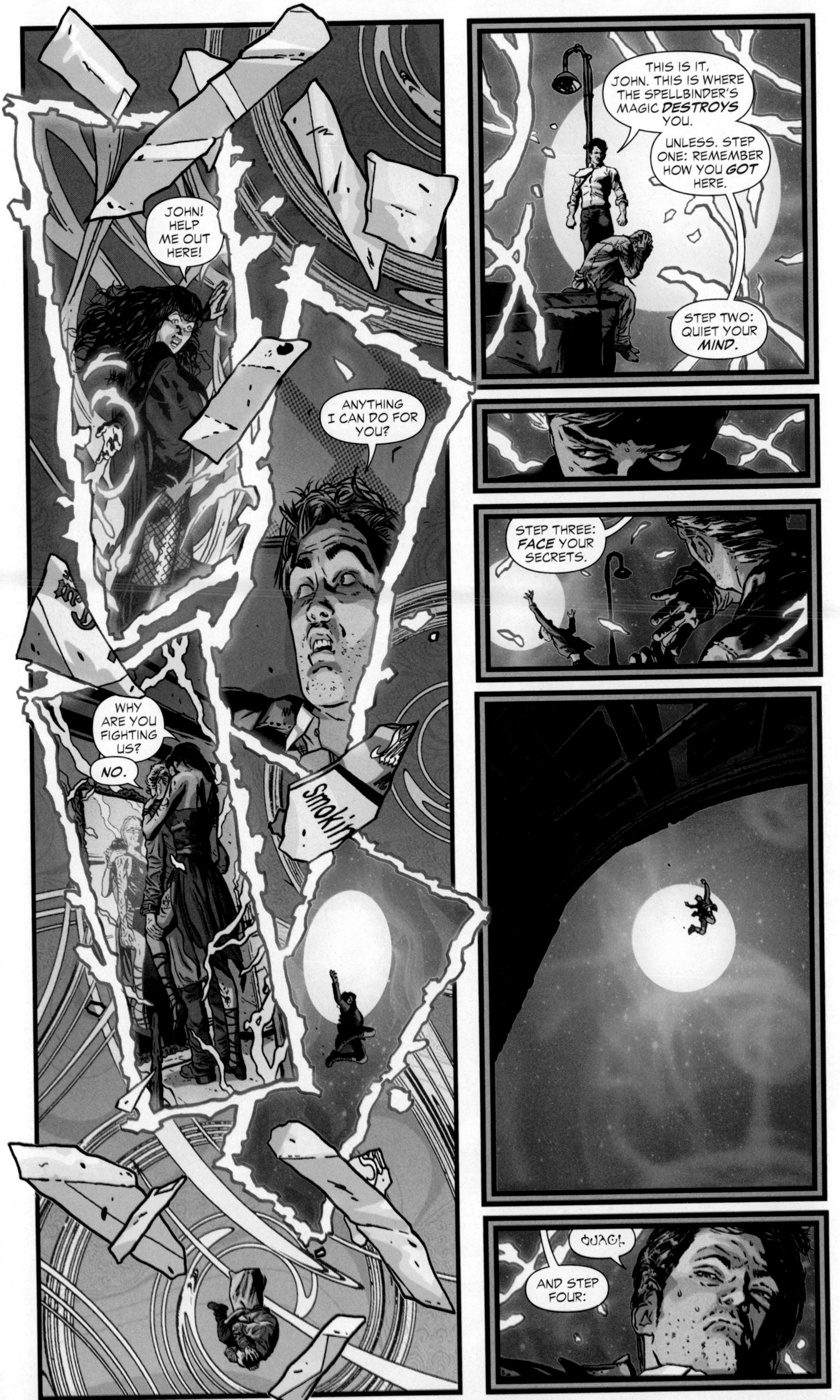
JOHN! HELP ME OUT HERE!
ANYTHING I CAN DO FOR YOU?
WHY ARE YOU FIGHTING US?
NO.
THIS IS IT, JOHN. THIS IS WHERE THE SPELLBINDER'S MAGIC **DESTROYS** YOU.
UNLESS. STEP ONE: REMEMBER HOW YOU **GOT** HERE.
STEP TWO: QUIET YOUR **MIND**.
STEP THREE: **FACE** YOUR SECRETS.
AND STEP FOUR:

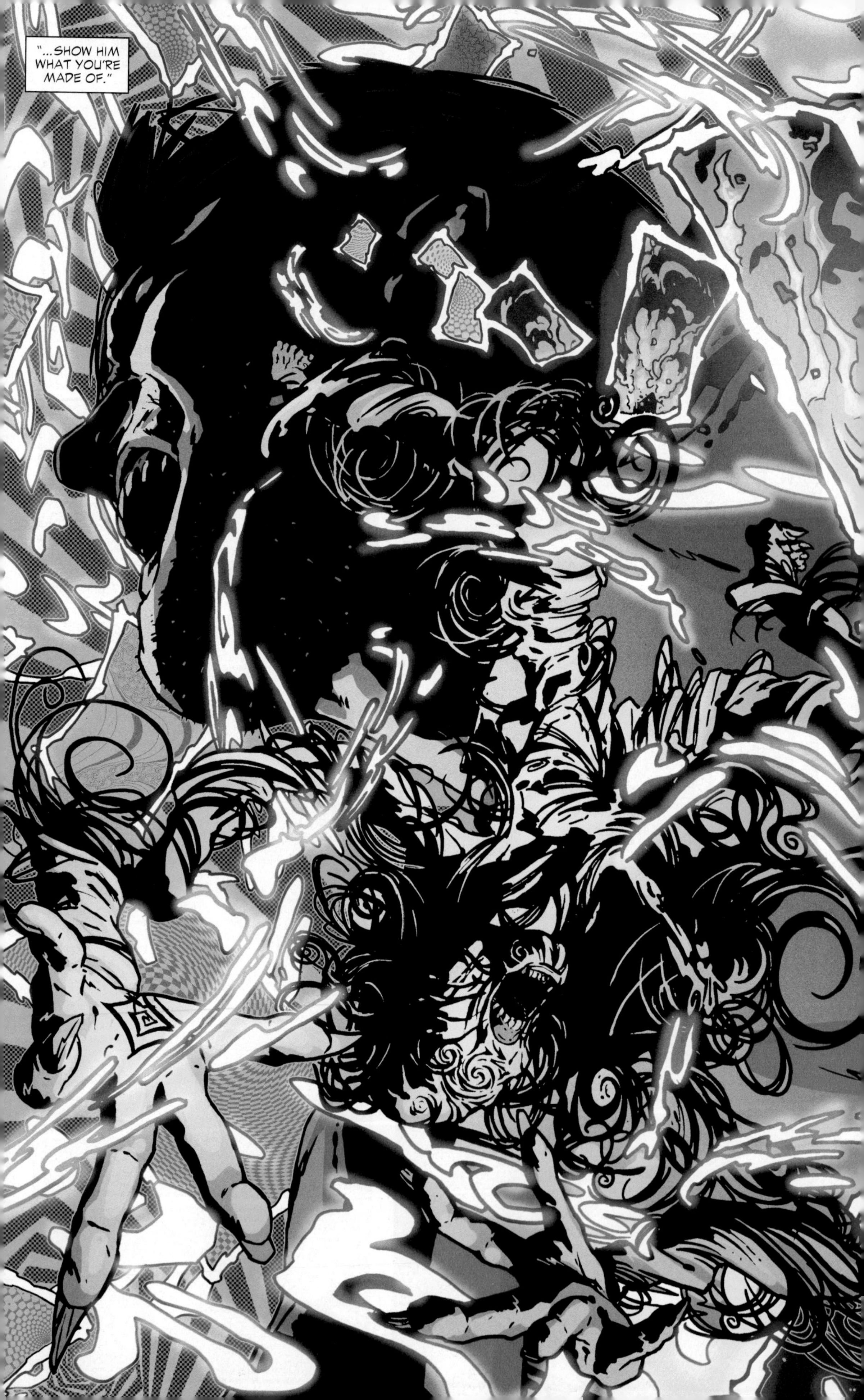
"...SHOW HIM WHAT YOU'RE MADE OF."

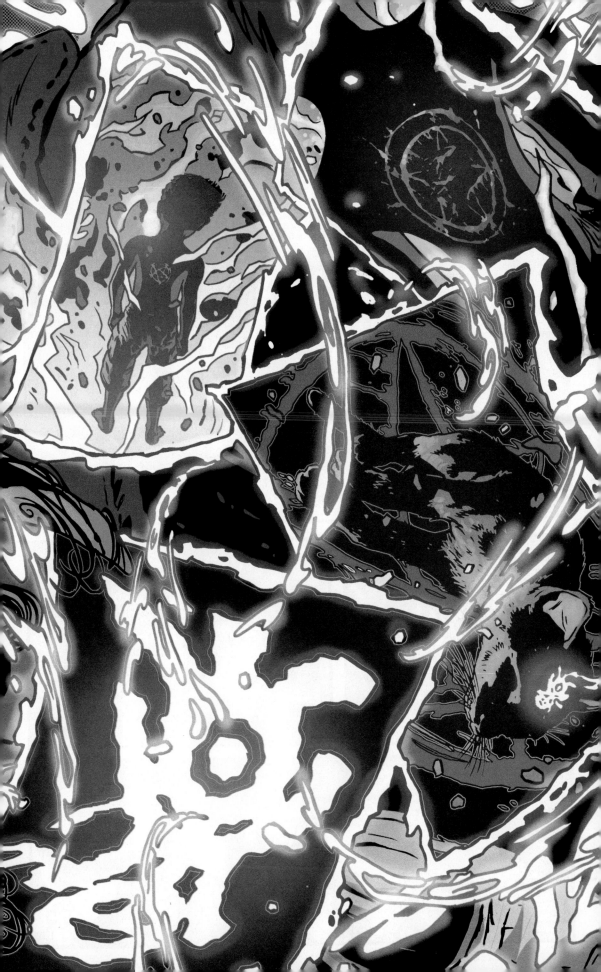

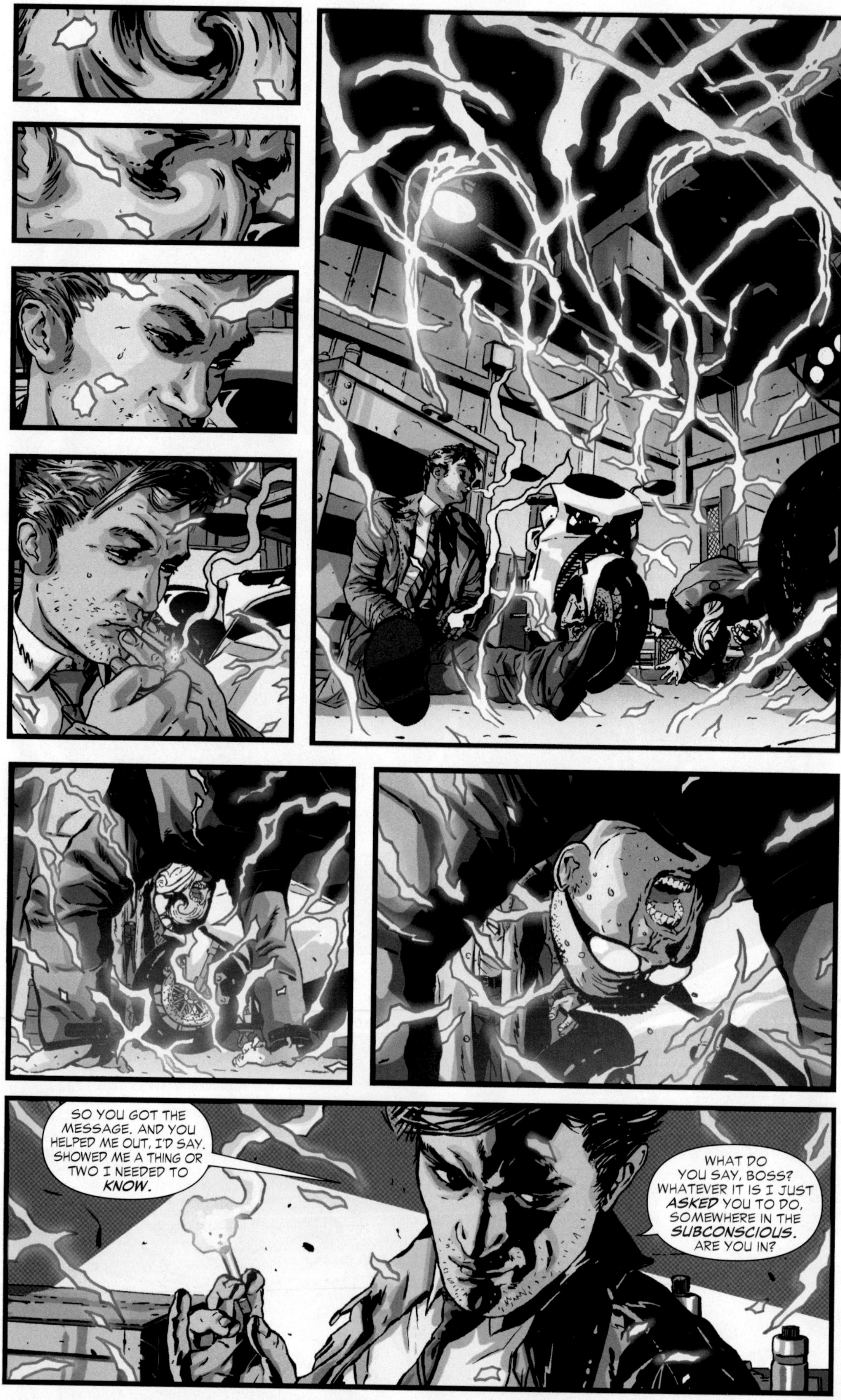
SO YOU GOT THE MESSAGE. AND YOU HELPED ME OUT, I'D SAY. SHOWED ME A THING OR TWO I NEEDED TO **KNOW**.
WHAT DO YOU SAY, BOSS? WHATEVER IT IS I JUST **ASKED** YOU TO DO, SOMEWHERE IN THE **SUBCONSCIOUS**. ARE YOU IN?

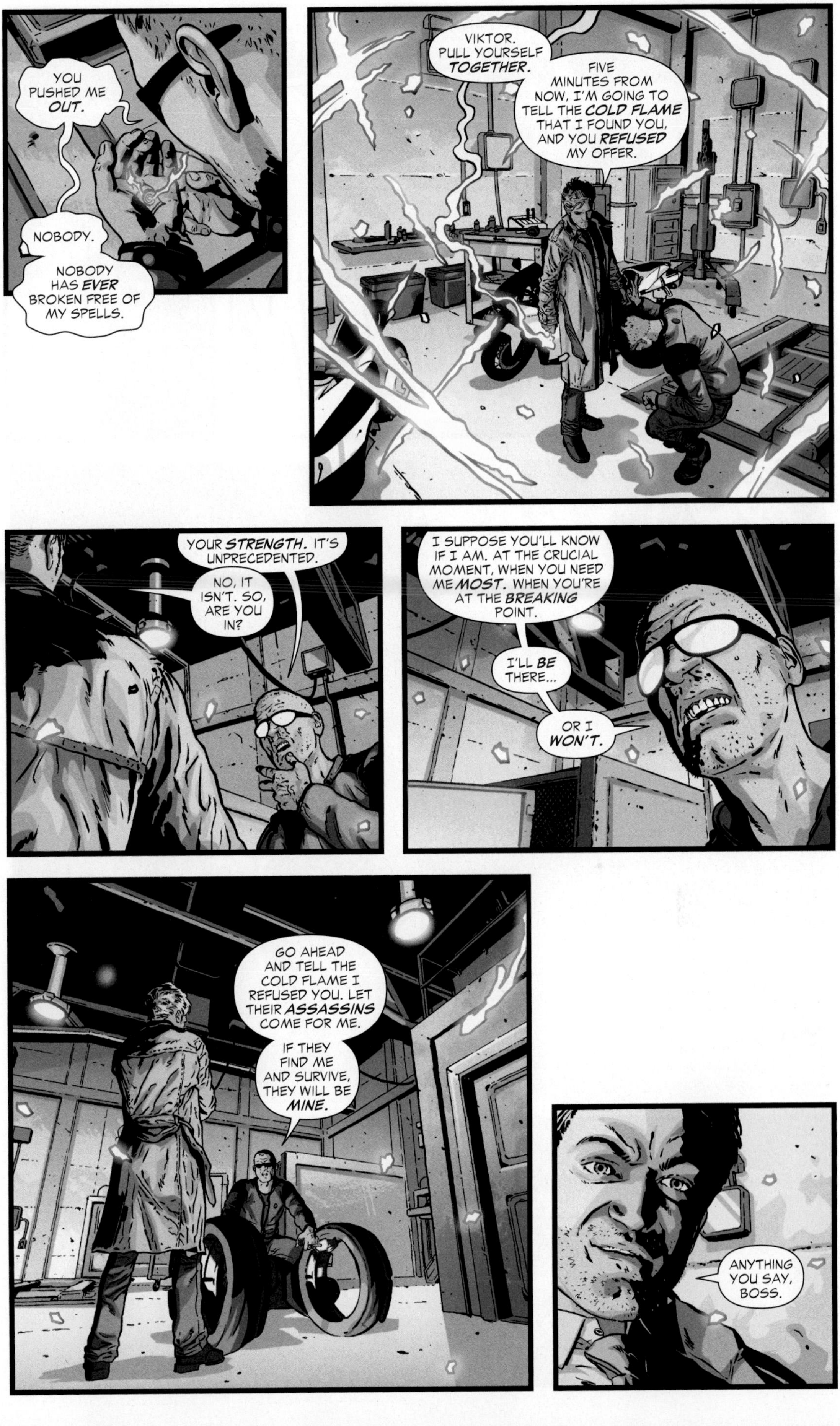
YOU PUSHED ME OUT.
NOBODY.
NOBODY HAS EVER BROKEN FREE OF MY SPELLS.
VIKTOR. PULL YOURSELF TOGETHER.
FIVE MINUTES FROM NOW, I'M GOING TO TELL THE COLD FLAME THAT I FOUND YOU, AND YOU REFUSED MY OFFER.
YOUR STRENGTH. IT'S UNPRECEDENTED.
NO, IT ISN'T. SO, ARE YOU IN?
I SUPPOSE YOU'LL KNOW IF I AM. AT THE CRUCIAL MOMENT, WHEN YOU NEED ME MOST. WHEN YOU'RE AT THE BREAKING POINT.
I'LL BE THERE...
OR I WON'T.
GO AHEAD AND TELL THE COLD FLAME I REFUSED YOU. LET THEIR ASSASSINS COME FOR ME.
IF THEY FIND ME AND SURVIVE, THEY WILL BE MINE.
ANYTHING YOU SAY, BOSS.

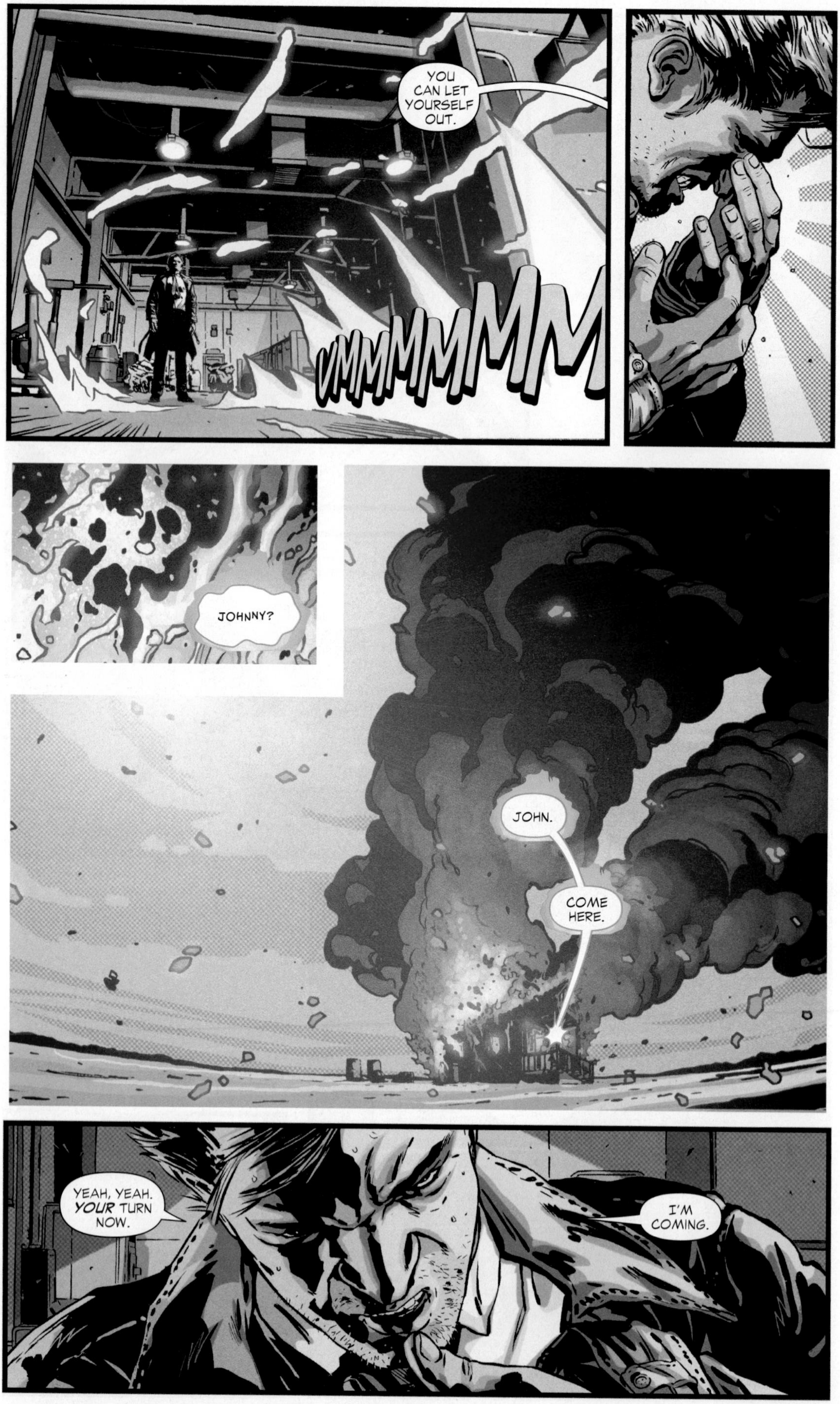
YOU CAN LET YOURSELF OUT.
VMMMMMMMM
JOHNNY?
JOHN.
COME HERE.
YEAH, YEAH. YOUR TURN NOW.
I'M COMING.

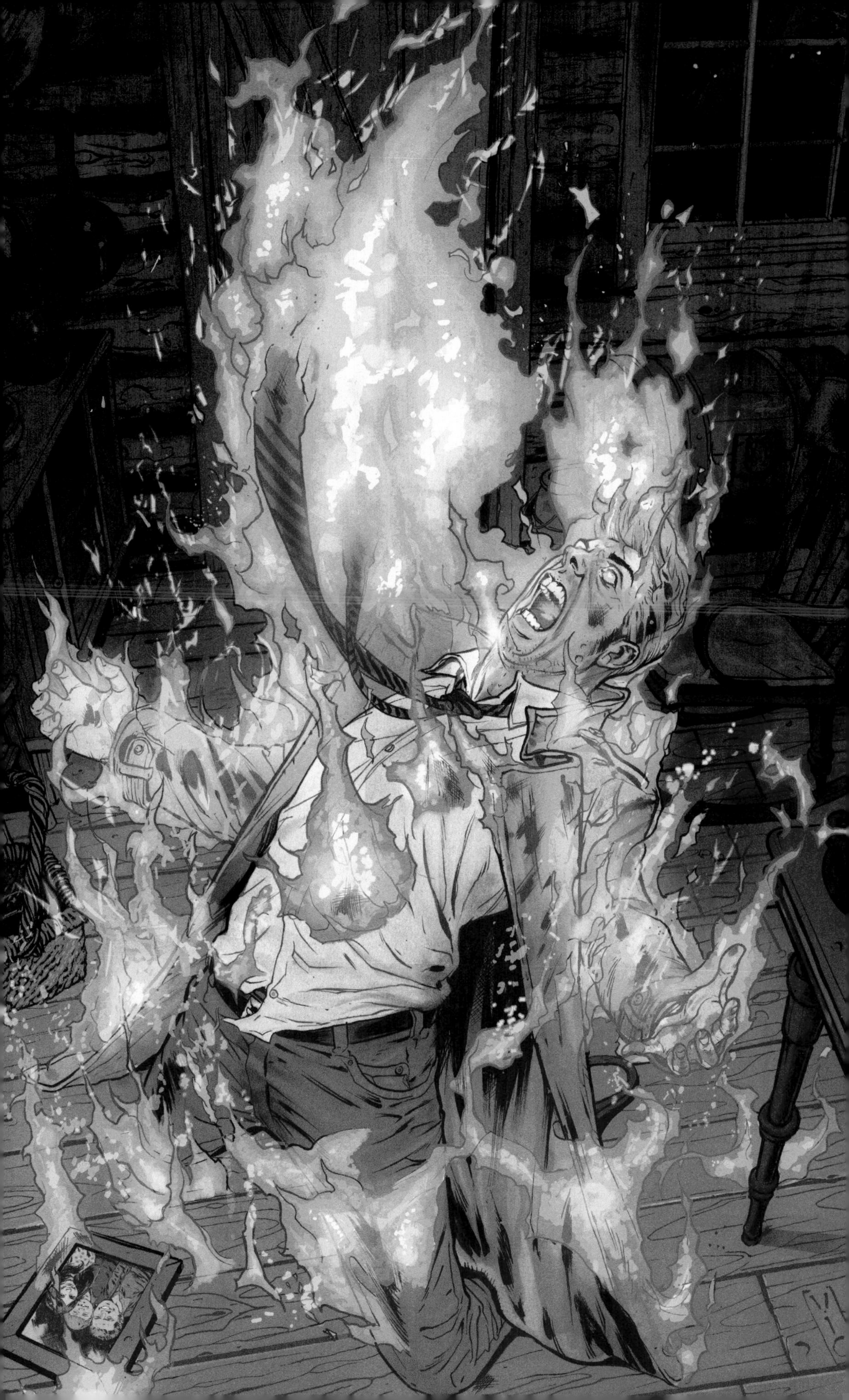

THE VOICE IN THE FIRE

RAY FAWKES
writer

EDGAR SALAZAR
penciller

JAY LEISTEN
inker

BRAD ANDERSON
colorist

TAYLOR ESPOSITO
letterer

cover art by
VICTOR IBAÑEZ

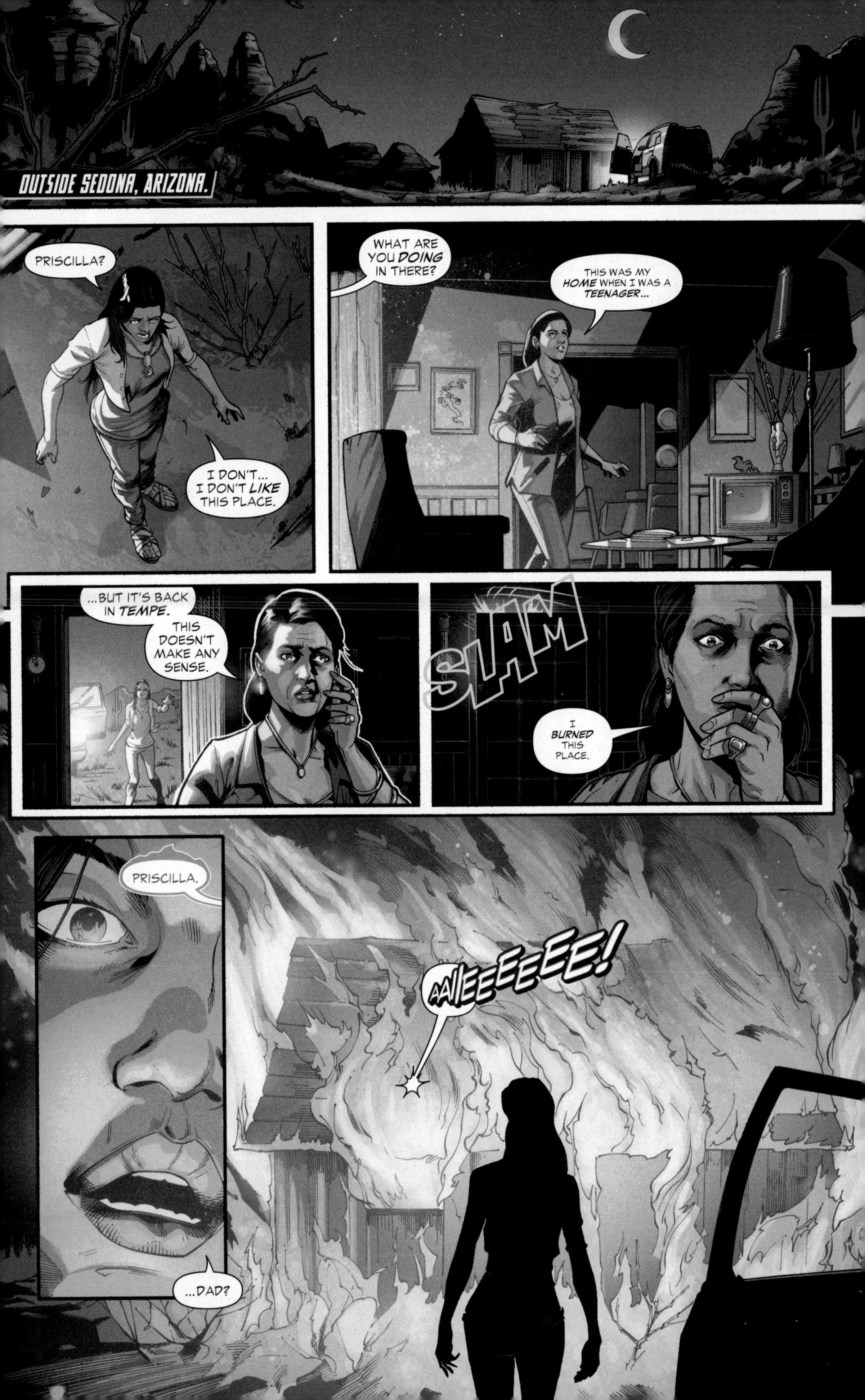
OUTSIDE SEDONA, ARIZONA.
PRISCILLA?
I DON'T... I DON'T LIKE THIS PLACE.
WHAT ARE YOU DOING IN THERE?
THIS WAS MY HOME WHEN I WAS A TEENAGER...
...BUT IT'S BACK IN TEMPE.
THIS DOESN'T MAKE ANY SENSE.
SLAM
I BURNED THIS PLACE.
PRISCILLA.
AAIIEEEEEEE!
...DAD?

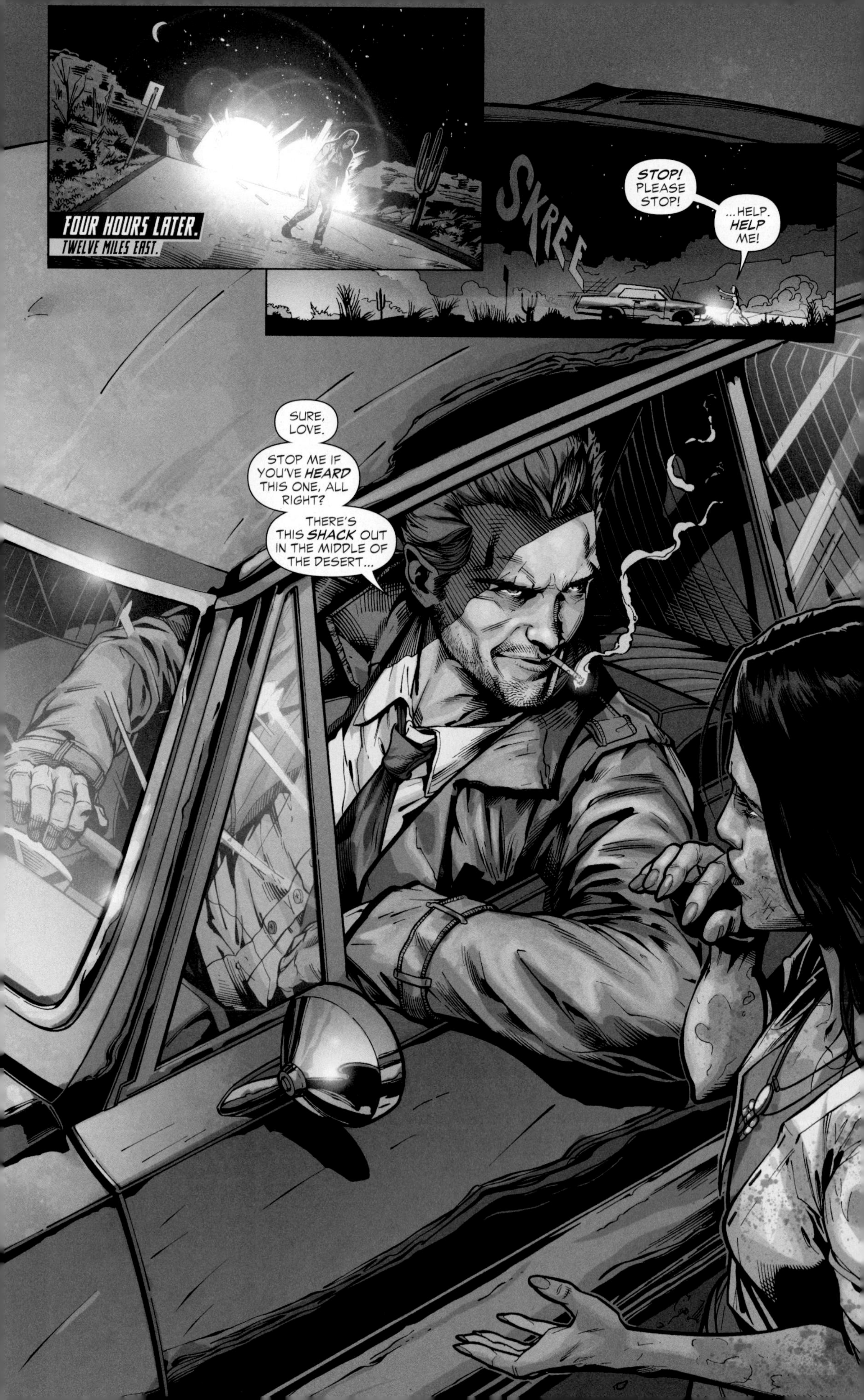
FOUR HOURS LATER.
TWELVE MILES EAST.
SKREE
STOP! PLEASE STOP!
...HELP. HELP ME!
SURE, LOVE.
STOP ME IF YOU'VE HEARD THIS ONE, ALL RIGHT?
THERE'S THIS SHACK OUT IN THE MIDDLE OF THE DESERT...

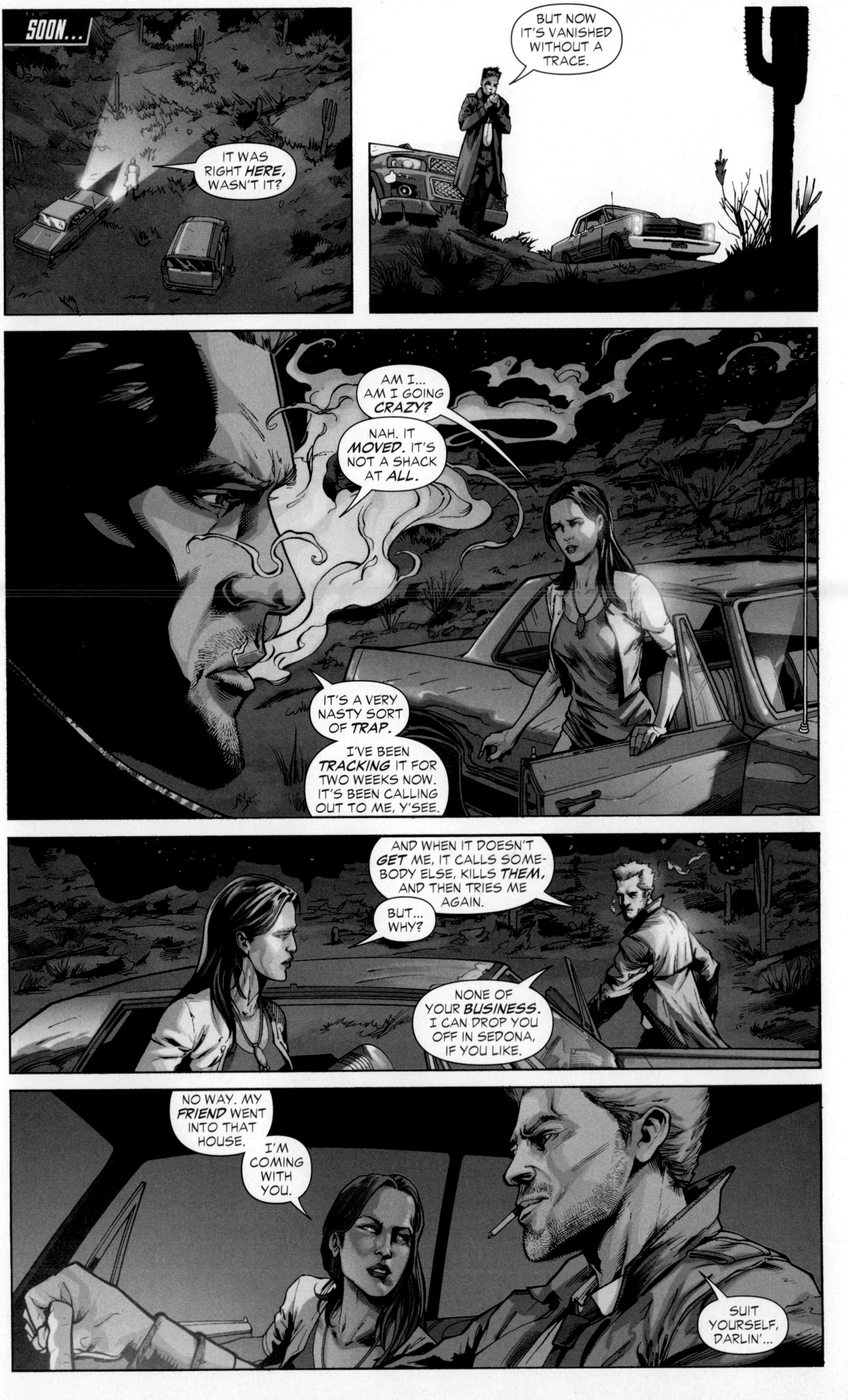
SOON...
IT WAS RIGHT HERE, WASN'T IT?
BUT NOW IT'S VANISHED WITHOUT A TRACE.
AM I... AM I GOING CRAZY?
NAH. IT MOVED. IT'S NOT A SHACK AT ALL.
IT'S A VERY NASTY SORT OF TRAP.
I'VE BEEN TRACKING IT FOR TWO WEEKS NOW. IT'S BEEN CALLING OUT TO ME, Y'SEE.
AND WHEN IT DOESN'T GET ME, IT CALLS SOME-BODY ELSE, KILLS THEM, AND THEN TRIES ME AGAIN.
BUT... WHY?
NONE OF YOUR BUSINESS. I CAN DROP YOU OFF IN SEDONA, IF YOU LIKE.
NO WAY. MY FRIEND WENT INTO THAT HOUSE.
I'M COMING WITH YOU.
SUIT YOURSELF, DARLIN'...

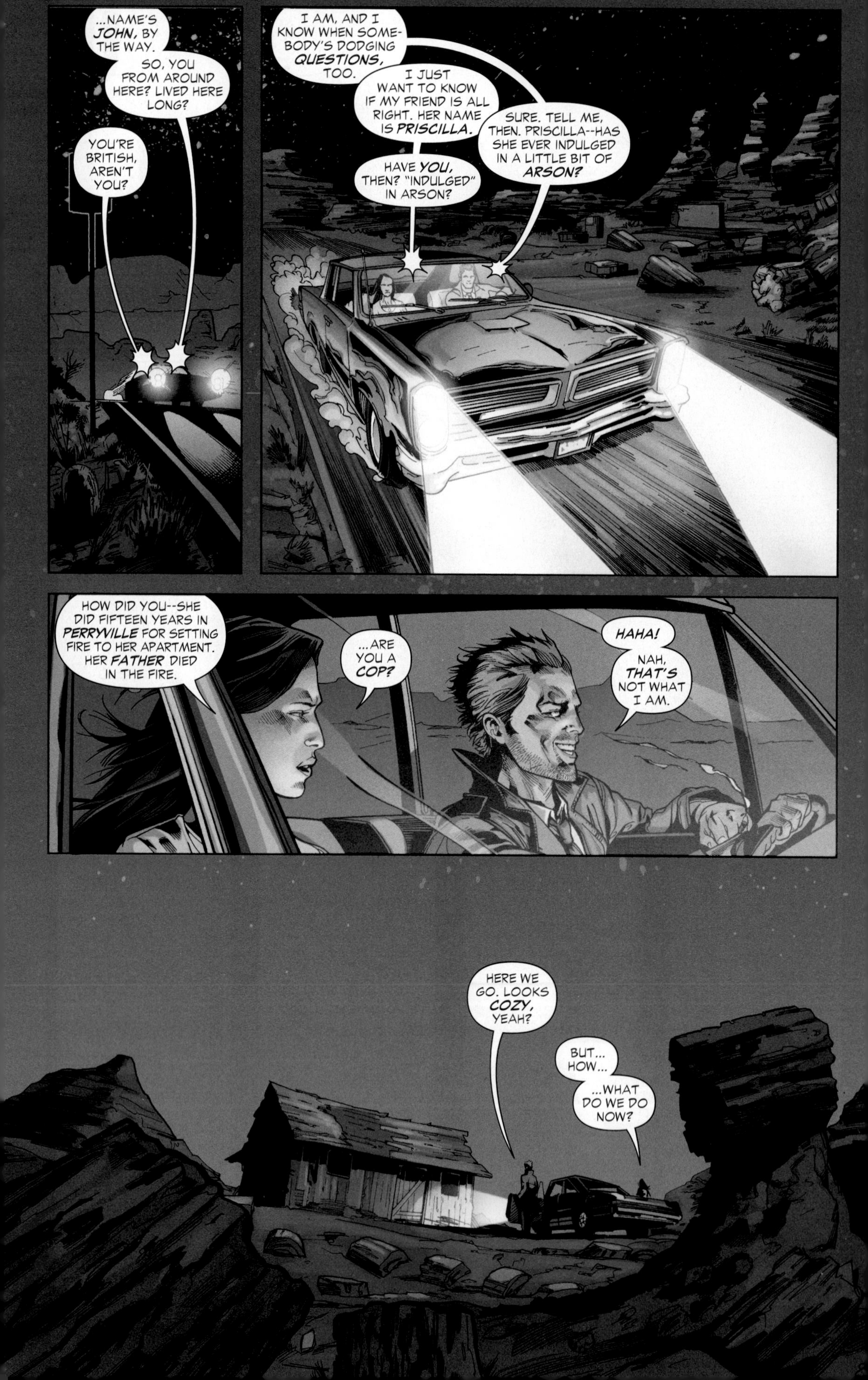
...NAME'S JOHN, BY THE WAY.
SO, YOU FROM AROUND HERE? LIVED HERE LONG?
YOU'RE BRITISH, AREN'T YOU?
I AM, AND I KNOW WHEN SOMEBODY'S DODGING QUESTIONS, TOO.
I JUST WANT TO KNOW IF MY FRIEND IS ALL RIGHT. HER NAME IS PRISCILLA.
SURE. TELL ME, THEN. PRISCILLA--HAS SHE EVER INDULGED IN A LITTLE BIT OF ARSON?
HAVE YOU, THEN? "INDULGED" IN ARSON?
HOW DID YOU--SHE DID FIFTEEN YEARS IN PERRYVILLE FOR SETTING FIRE TO HER APARTMENT. HER FATHER DIED IN THE FIRE.
...ARE YOU A COP?
HAHA!
NAH, THAT'S NOT WHAT I AM.
HERE WE GO. LOOKS COZY, YEAH?
BUT... HOW...
...WHAT DO WE DO NOW?

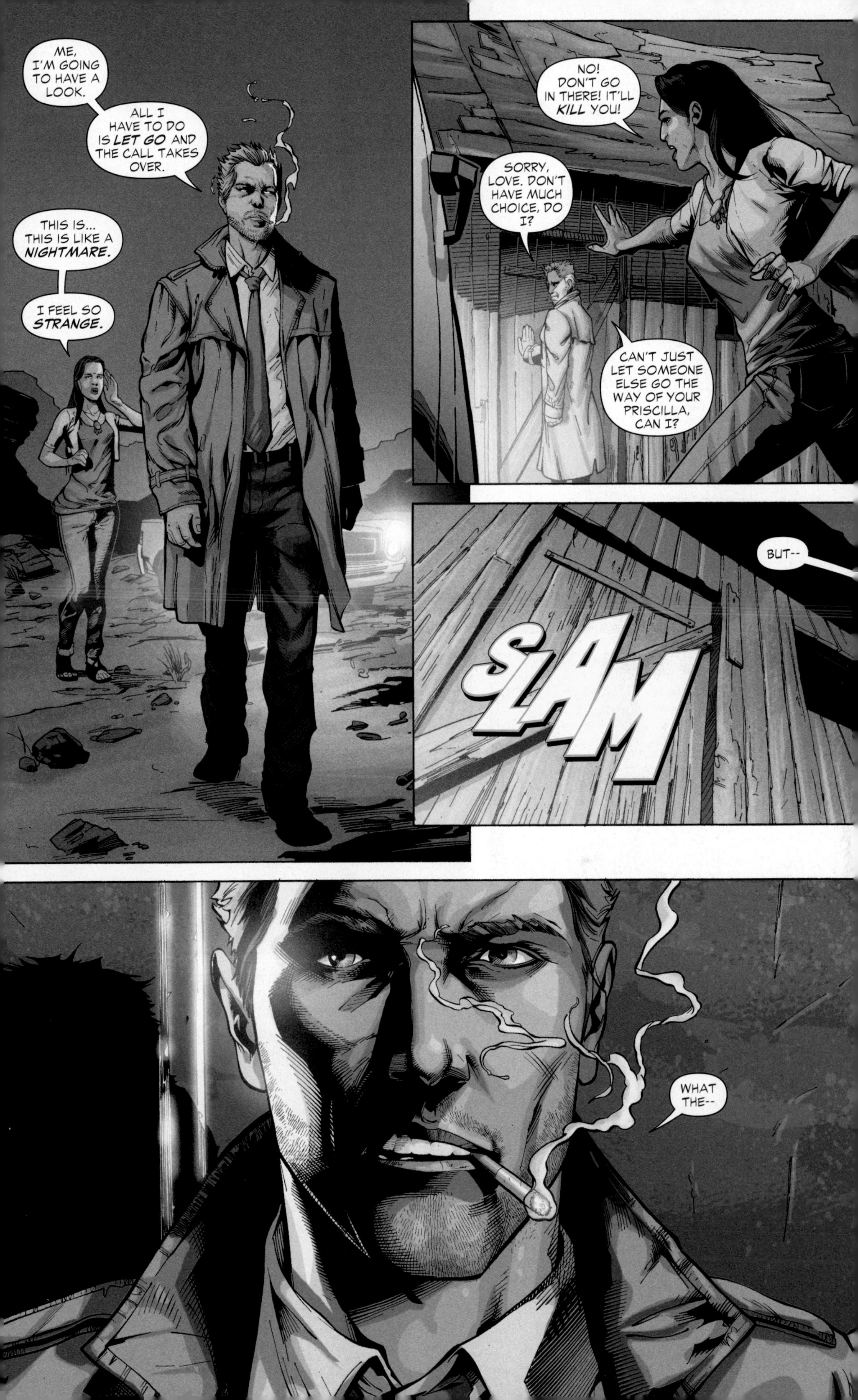

ME, I'M GOING TO HAVE A LOOK.
ALL I HAVE TO DO IS LET GO AND THE CALL TAKES OVER.
THIS IS... THIS IS LIKE A NIGHTMARE.
I FEEL SO STRANGE.
NO! DON'T GO IN THERE! IT'LL KILL YOU!
SORRY, LOVE. DON'T HAVE MUCH CHOICE, DO I?
CAN'T JUST LET SOMEONE ELSE GO THE WAY OF YOUR PRISCILLA, CAN I?
BUT--
SLAM
WHAT THE--

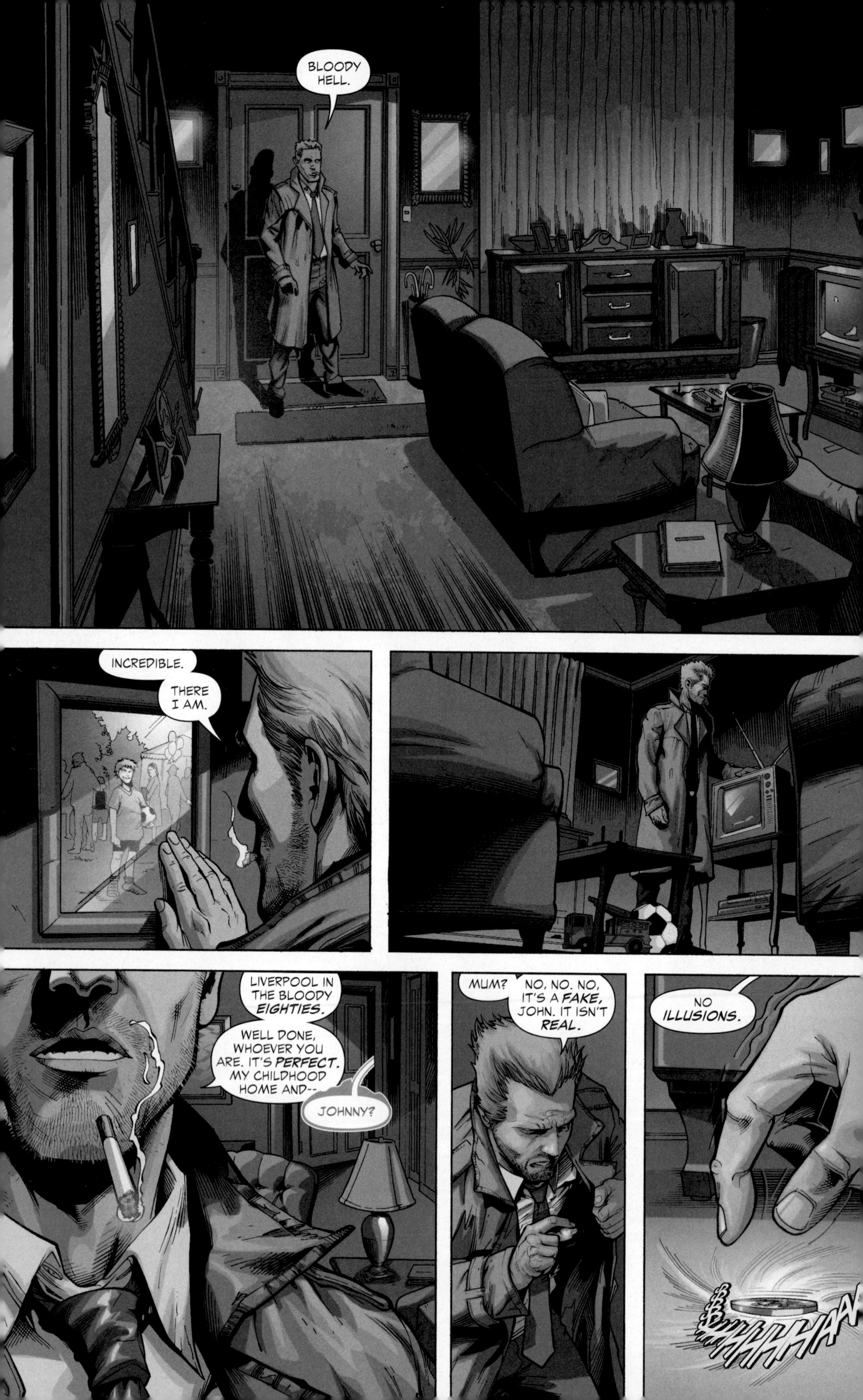
BLOODY HELL.
INCREDIBLE.
THERE I AM.
LIVERPOOL IN THE BLOODY EIGHTIES.
WELL DONE, WHOEVER YOU ARE. IT'S PERFECT. MY CHILDHOOD HOME AND--
JOHNNY?
MUM?
NO, NO. NO, IT'S A FAKE, JOHN. IT ISN'T REAL.
NO ILLUSIONS.
BBSHHHHAA

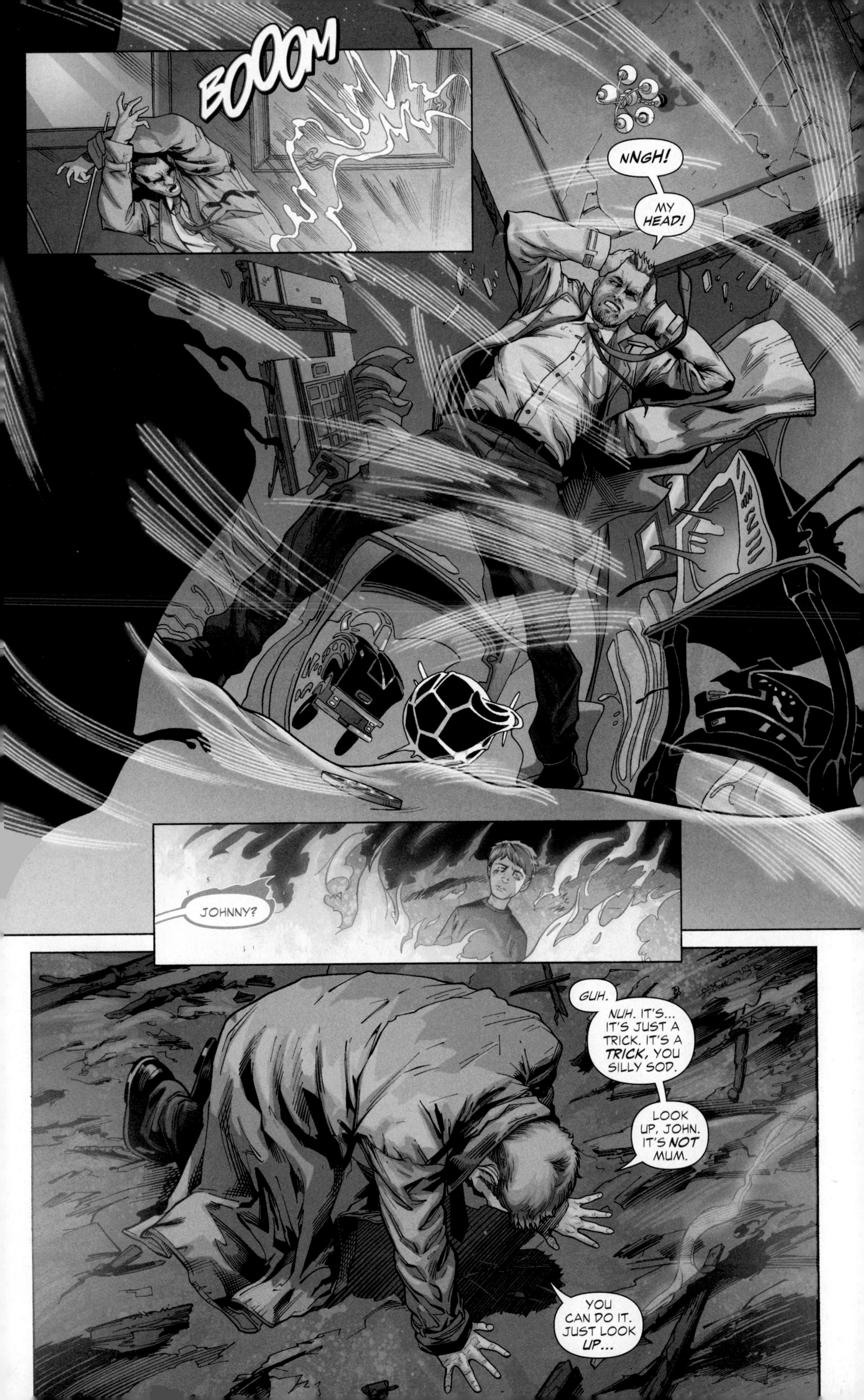
BOOOM
NNGH!
MY HEAD!
JOHNNY?
GUH.
NUH. IT'S... IT'S JUST A TRICK. IT'S A TRICK, YOU SILLY SOD.
LOOK UP, JOHN. IT'S NOT MUM.
YOU CAN DO IT. JUST LOOK UP...

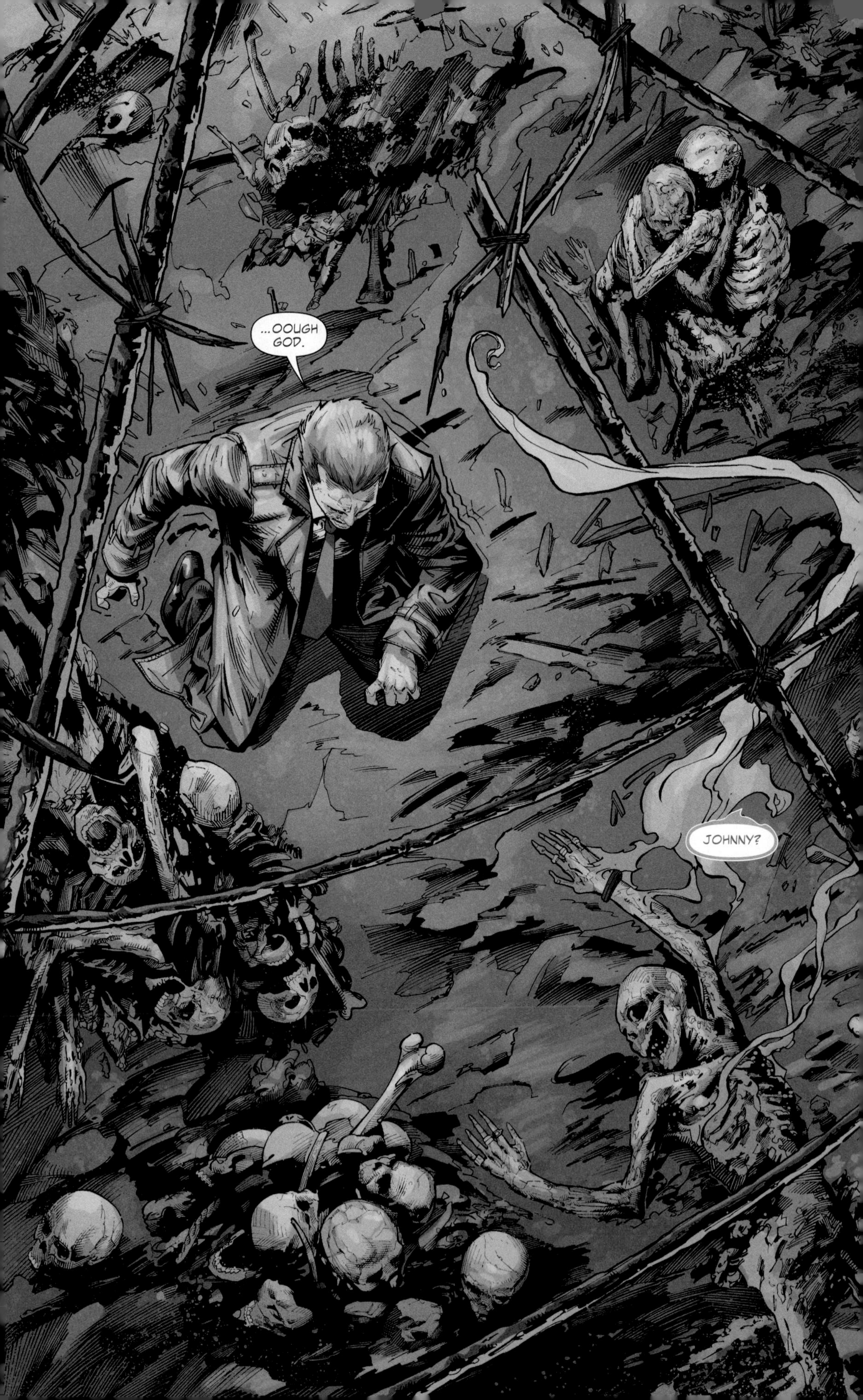
...OOUGH GOD.
JOHNNY?

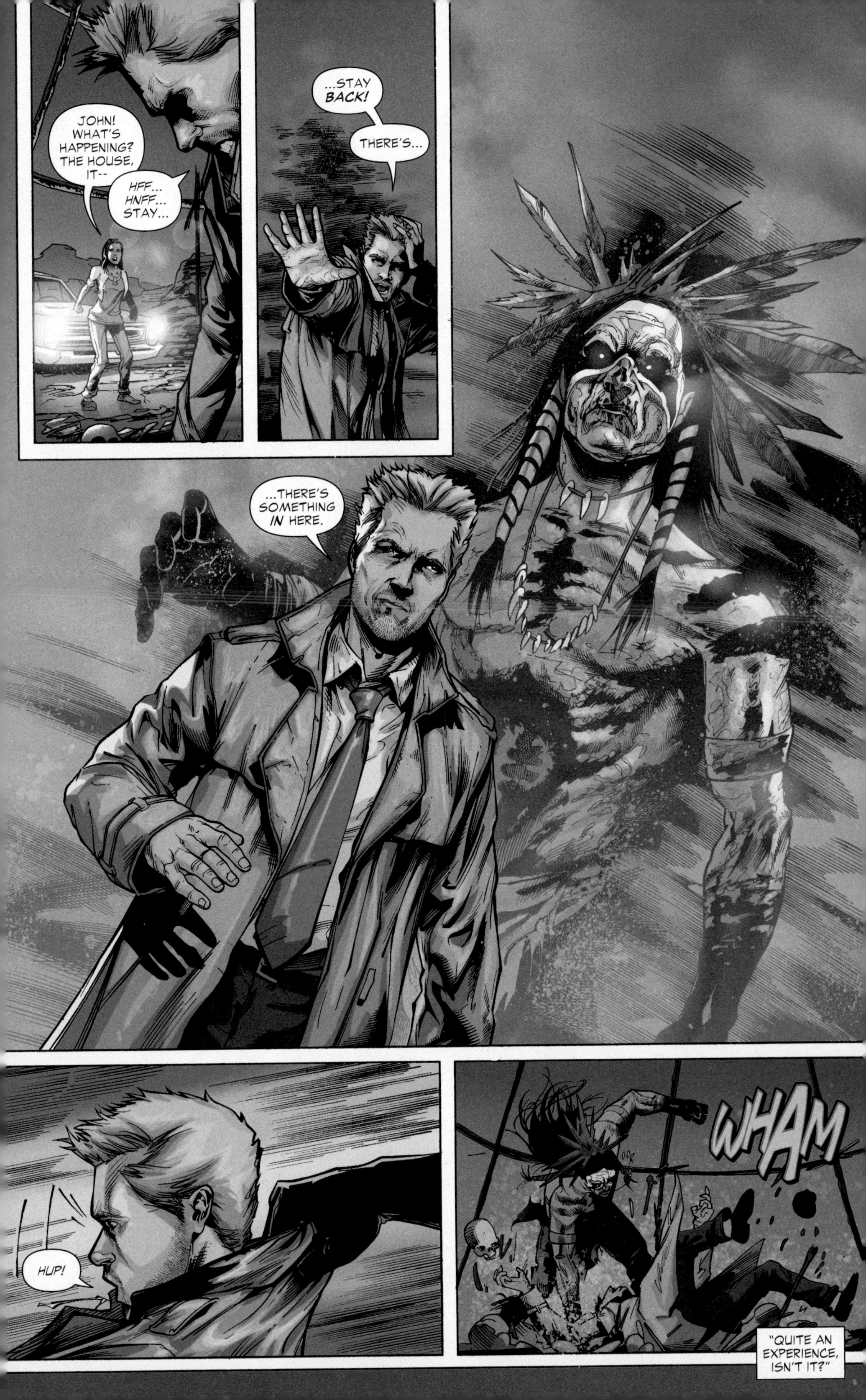
JOHN! WHAT'S HAPPENING? THE HOUSE, IT--
HFF... HNFF... STAY...
...STAY BACK!
THERE'S...
...THERE'S SOMETHING IN HERE.
HUP!
WHAM
"QUITE AN EXPERIENCE, ISN'T IT?"

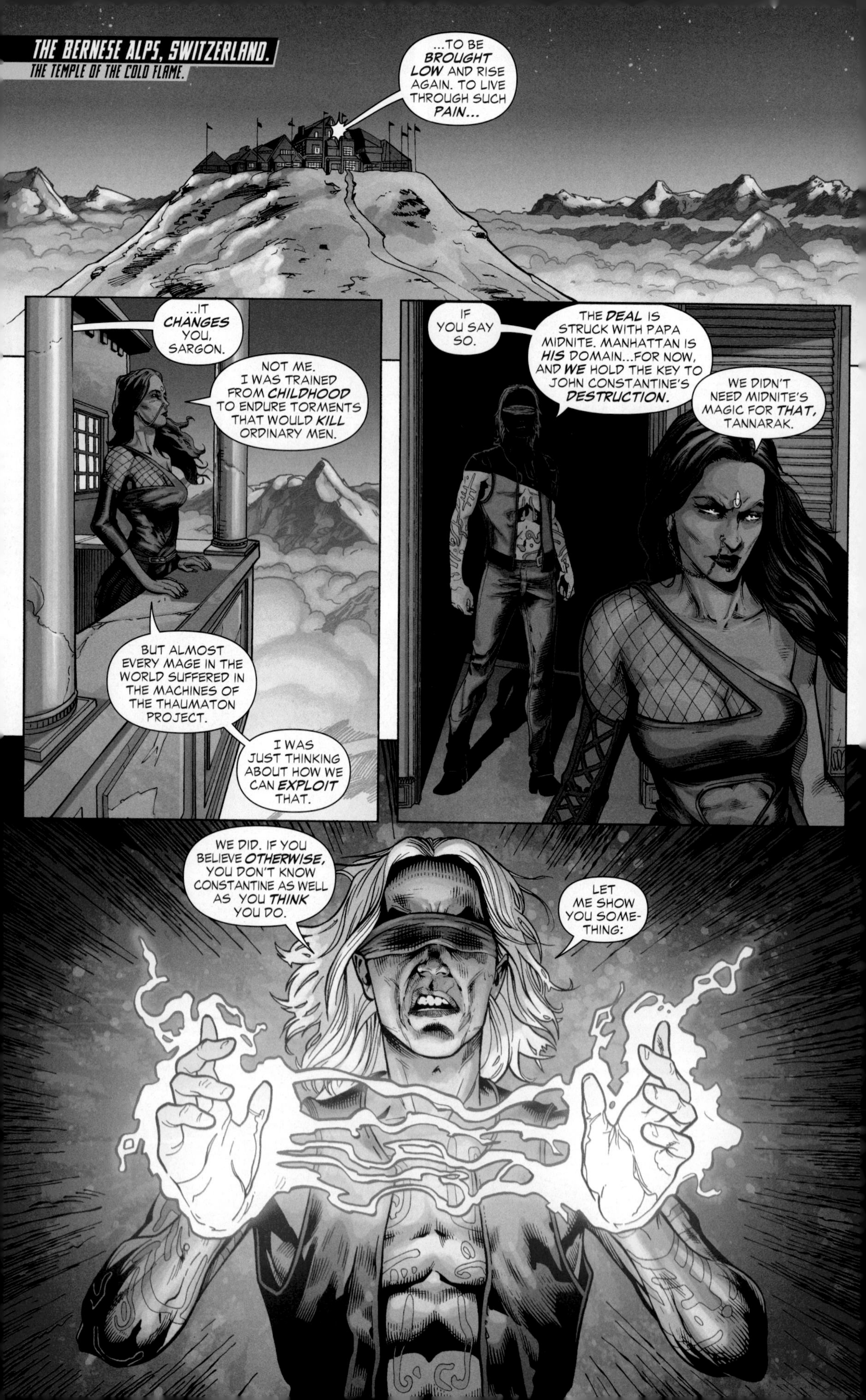
THE BERNESE ALPS, SWITZERLAND.
THE TEMPLE OF THE COLD FLAME.
...TO BE BROUGHT LOW AND RISE AGAIN. TO LIVE THROUGH SUCH PAIN...
...IT CHANGES YOU, SARGON.
NOT ME. I WAS TRAINED FROM CHILDHOOD TO ENDURE TORMENTS THAT WOULD KILL ORDINARY MEN.
BUT ALMOST EVERY MAGE IN THE WORLD SUFFERED IN THE MACHINES OF THE THAUMATON PROJECT.
I WAS JUST THINKING ABOUT HOW WE CAN EXPLOIT THAT.
IF YOU SAY SO.
THE DEAL IS STRUCK WITH PAPA MIDNITE. MANHATTAN IS HIS DOMAIN...FOR NOW, AND WE HOLD THE KEY TO JOHN CONSTANTINE'S DESTRUCTION.
WE DIDN'T NEED MIDNITE'S MAGIC FOR THAT, TANNARAK.
WE DID. IF YOU BELIEVE OTHERWISE, YOU DON'T KNOW CONSTANTINE AS WELL AS YOU THINK YOU DO.
LET ME SHOW YOU SOME-THING:

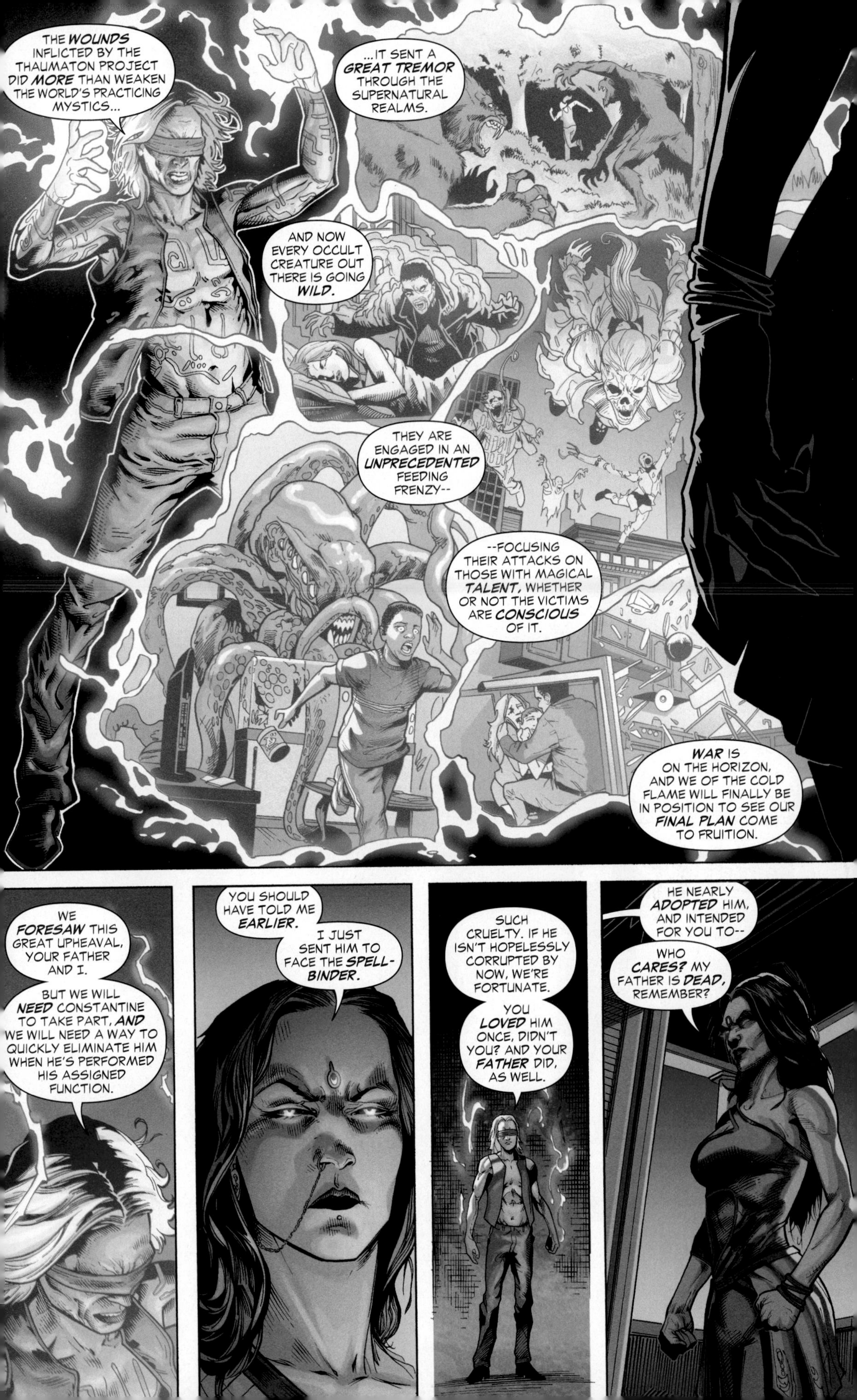
THE WOUNDS INFLICTED BY THE THAUMATON PROJECT DID MORE THAN WEAKEN THE WORLD'S PRACTICING MYSTICS...
...IT SENT A GREAT TREMOR THROUGH THE SUPERNATURAL REALMS.
AND NOW EVERY OCCULT CREATURE OUT THERE IS GOING WILD.
THEY ARE ENGAGED IN AN UNPRECEDENTED FEEDING FRENZY--
--FOCUSING THEIR ATTACKS ON THOSE WITH MAGICAL TALENT, WHETHER OR NOT THE VICTIMS ARE CONSCIOUS OF IT.
WAR IS ON THE HORIZON, AND WE OF THE COLD FLAME WILL FINALLY BE IN POSITION TO SEE OUR FINAL PLAN COME TO FRUITION.
WE FORESAW THIS GREAT UPHEAVAL, YOUR FATHER AND I.
BUT WE WILL NEED CONSTANTINE TO TAKE PART, AND WE WILL NEED A WAY TO QUICKLY ELIMINATE HIM WHEN HE'S PERFORMED HIS ASSIGNED FUNCTION.
YOU SHOULD HAVE TOLD ME EARLIER.
I JUST SENT HIM TO FACE THE SPELL-BINDER.
SUCH CRUELTY. IF HE ISN'T HOPELESSLY CORRUPTED BY NOW, WE'RE FORTUNATE.
YOU LOVED HIM ONCE, DIDN'T YOU? AND YOUR FATHER DID, AS WELL.
HE NEARLY ADOPTED HIM, AND INTENDED FOR YOU TO--
WHO CARES? MY FATHER IS DEAD, REMEMBER?

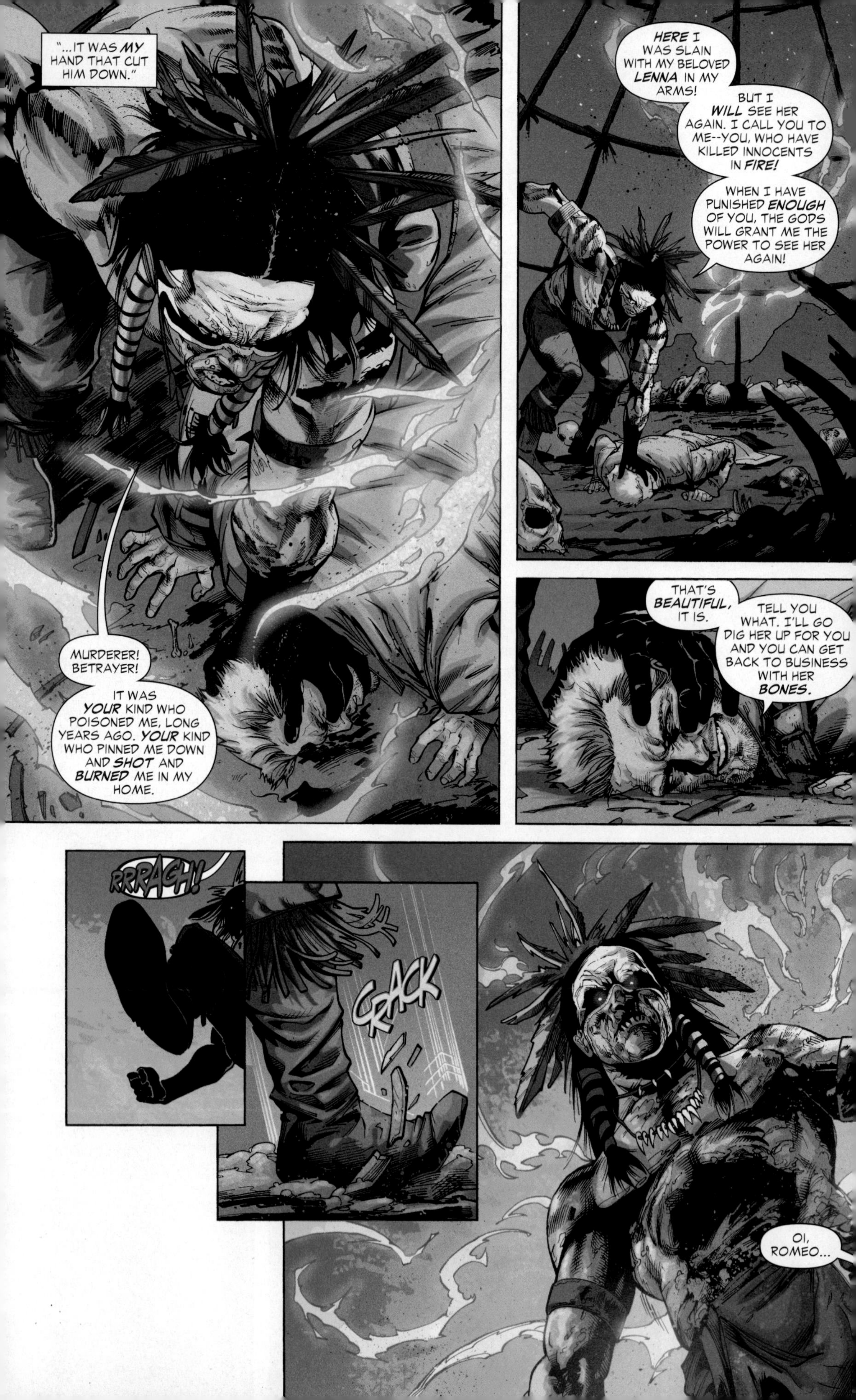
"...IT WAS MY HAND THAT CUT HIM DOWN."
MURDERER! BETRAYER!
IT WAS YOUR KIND WHO POISONED ME, LONG YEARS AGO. YOUR KIND WHO PINNED ME DOWN AND SHOT AND BURNED ME IN MY HOME.
HERE I WAS SLAIN WITH MY BELOVED LENNA IN MY ARMS!
BUT I WILL SEE HER AGAIN. I CALL YOU TO ME--YOU, WHO HAVE KILLED INNOCENTS IN FIRE!
WHEN I HAVE PUNISHED ENOUGH OF YOU, THE GODS WILL GRANT ME THE POWER TO SEE HER AGAIN!
THAT'S BEAUTIFUL, IT IS.
TELL YOU WHAT. I'LL GO DIG HER UP FOR YOU AND YOU CAN GET BACK TO BUSINESS WITH HER BONES.
RRRAGH!
CRACK
OI, ROMEO...

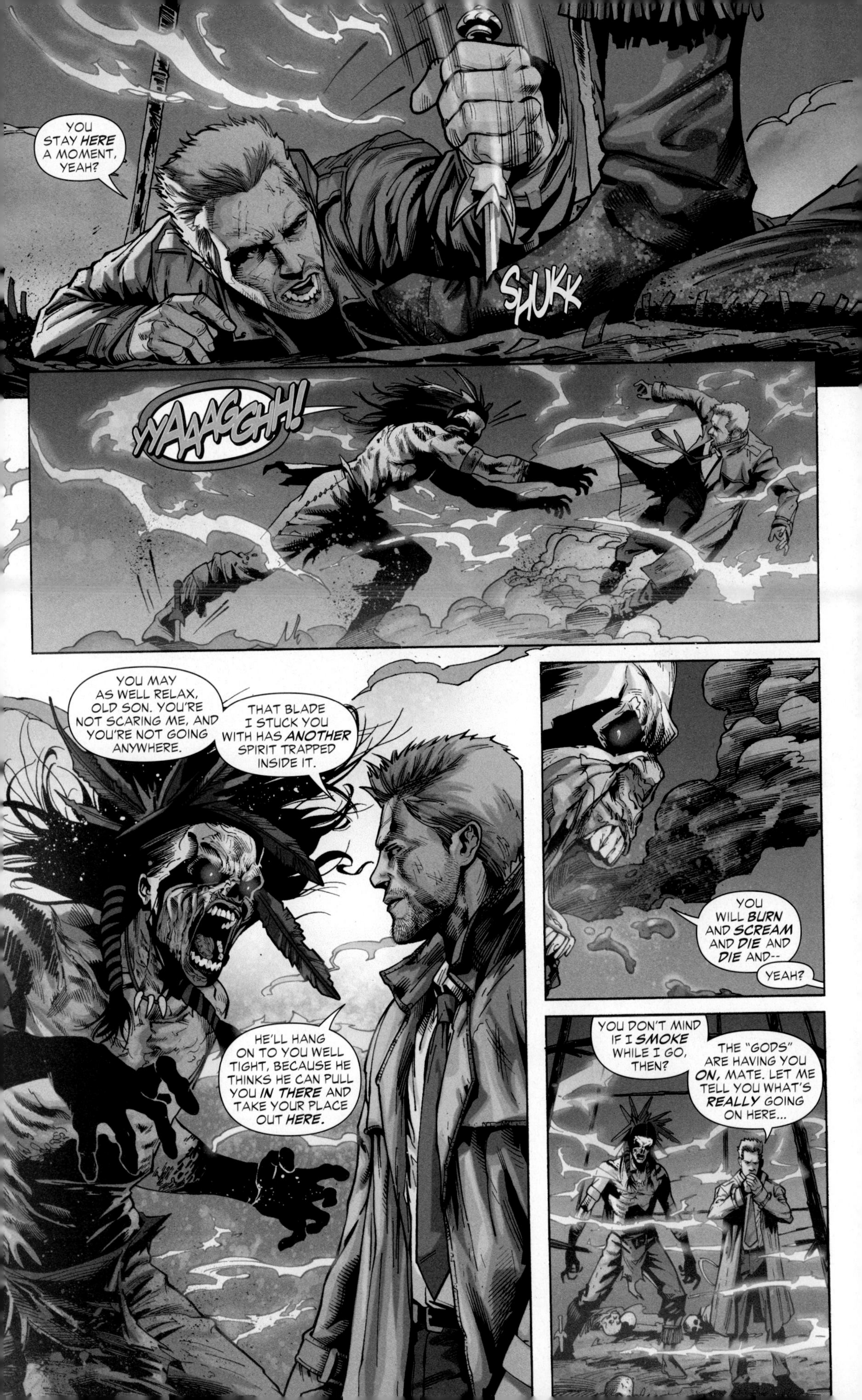
YOU STAY HERE A MOMENT, YEAH?
SHUKK
YYAAAGGHH!
YOU MAY AS WELL RELAX, OLD SON. YOU'RE NOT SCARING ME, AND YOU'RE NOT GOING ANYWHERE.
THAT BLADE I STUCK YOU WITH HAS ANOTHER SPIRIT TRAPPED INSIDE IT.
HE'LL HANG ON TO YOU WELL TIGHT, BECAUSE HE THINKS HE CAN PULL YOU IN THERE AND TAKE YOUR PLACE OUT HERE.
YOU WILL BURN AND SCREAM AND DIE AND DIE AND--
YEAH?
YOU DON'T MIND IF I SMOKE WHILE I GO, THEN?
THE "GODS" ARE HAVING YOU ON, MATE. LET ME TELL YOU WHAT'S REALLY GOING ON HERE...

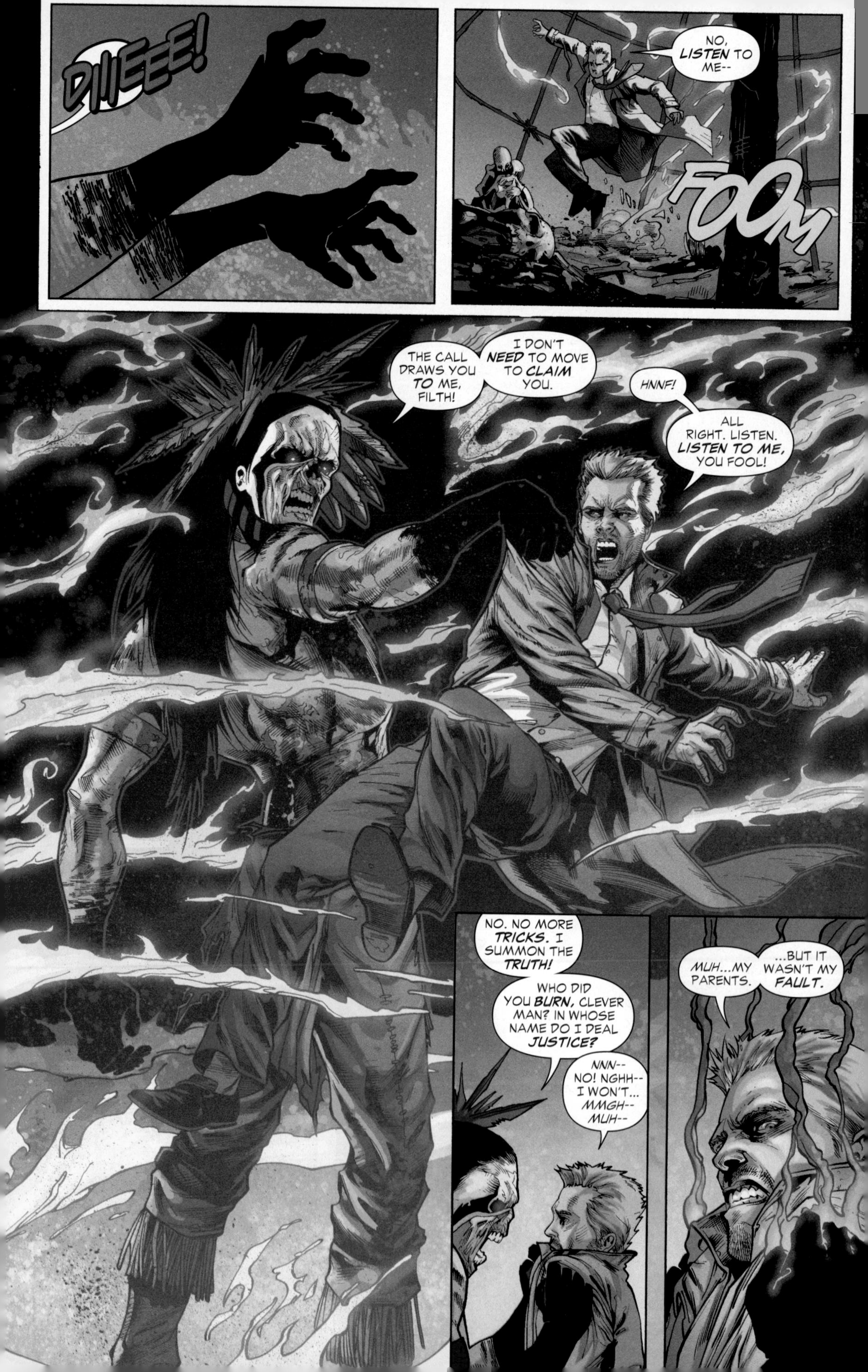
DIIIEEE!
NO, LISTEN TO ME--
FOOM
THE CALL DRAWS YOU TO ME, FILTH!
I DON'T NEED TO MOVE TO CLAIM YOU.
HNNF!
ALL RIGHT. LISTEN. LISTEN TO ME, YOU FOOL!
NO. NO MORE TRICKS. I SUMMON THE TRUTH!
WHO DID YOU BURN, CLEVER MAN? IN WHOSE NAME DO I DEAL JUSTICE?
NNN-- NO! NGHH-- I WON'T... MMGH-- MUH--
MUH...MY PARENTS.
...BUT IT WASN'T MY FAULT.

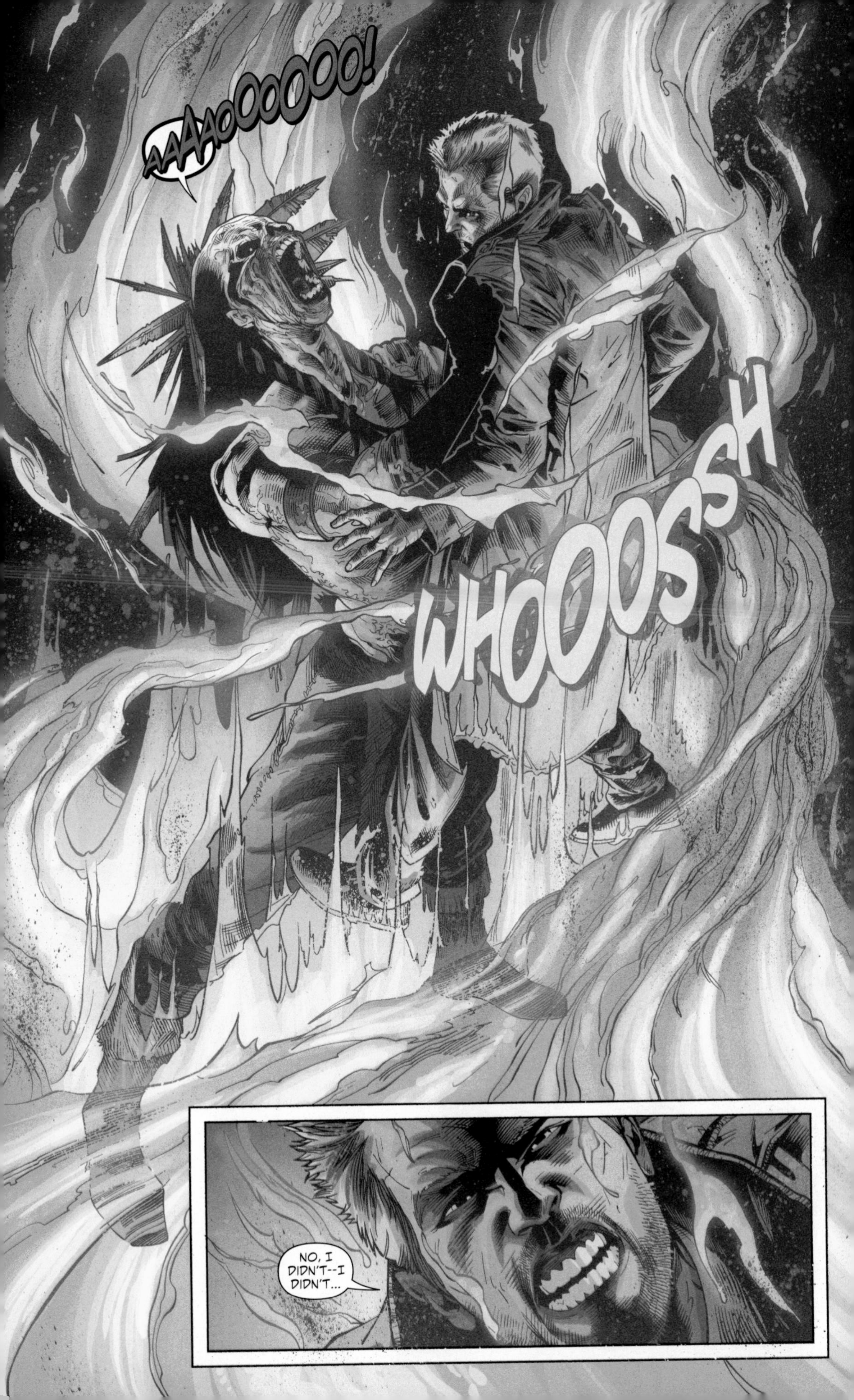
AAAAOOOOOO!
WHOOOSSH
NO, I DIDN'T--I DIDN'T...

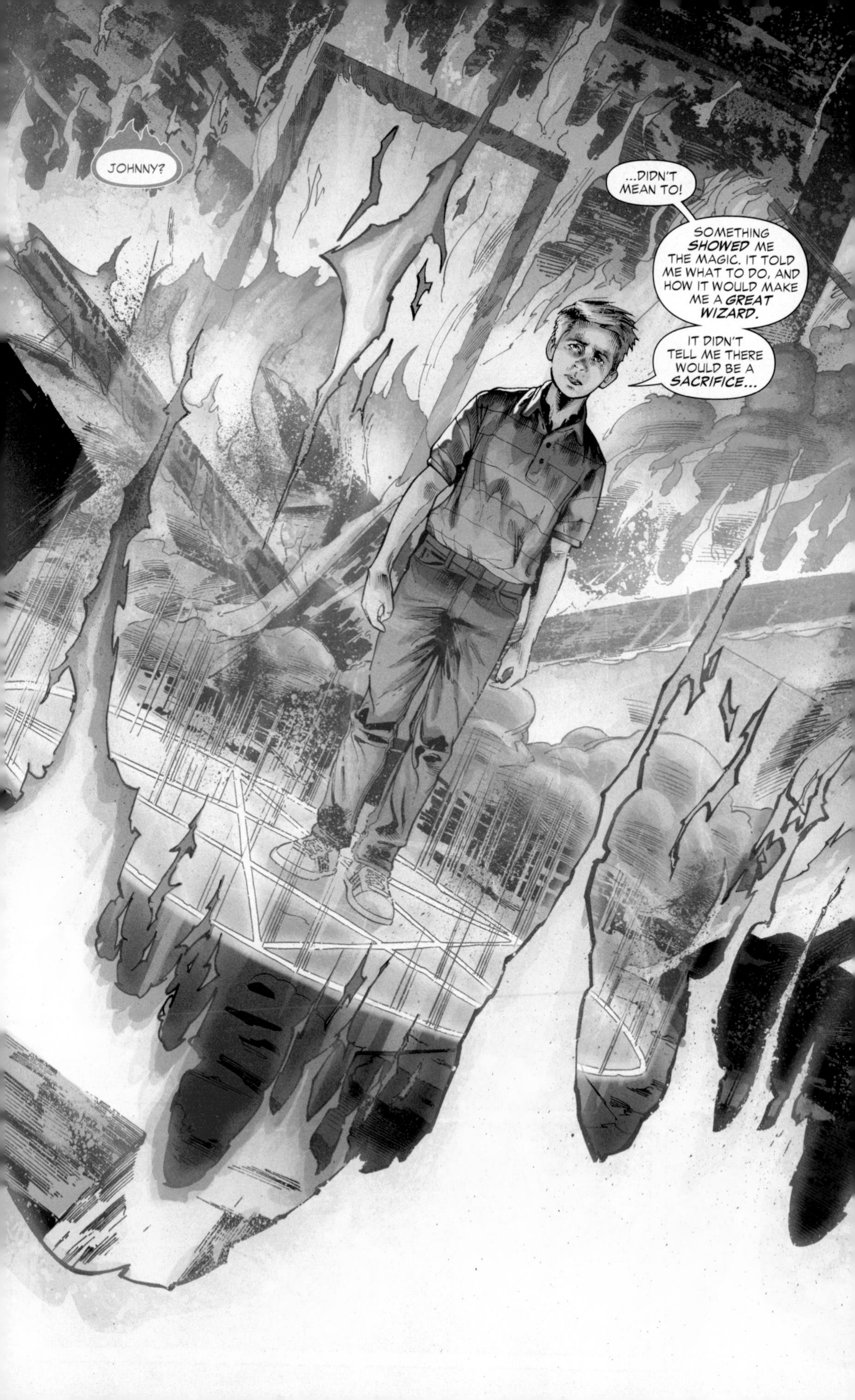
JOHNNY?
...DIDN'T MEAN TO!
SOMETHING SHOWED ME THE MAGIC. IT TOLD ME WHAT TO DO, AND HOW IT WOULD MAKE ME A GREAT WIZARD.
IT DIDN'T TELL ME THERE WOULD BE A SACRIFICE...

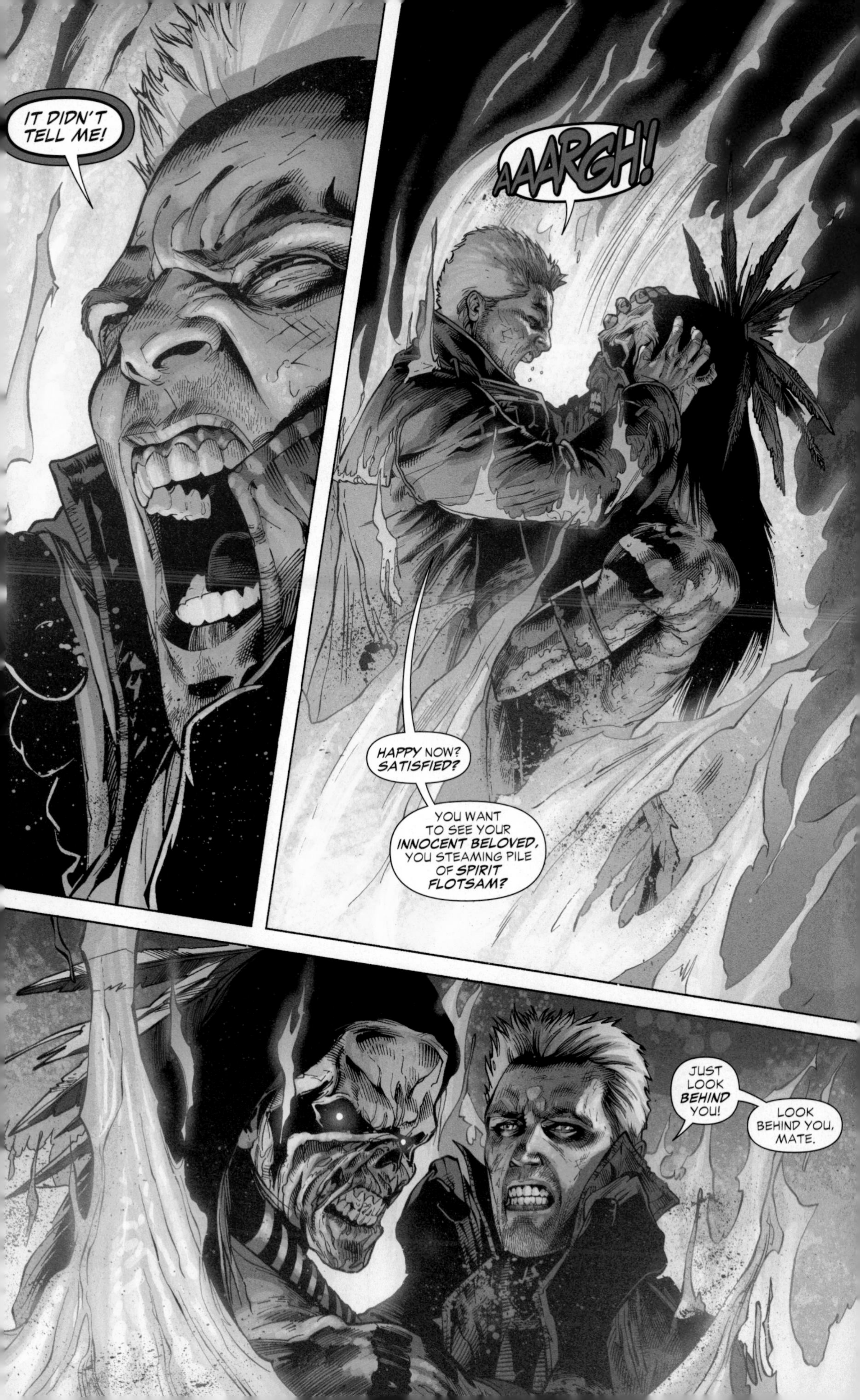
IT DIDN'T TELL ME!
AAARGH!
HAPPY NOW? SATISFIED?
YOU WANT TO SEE YOUR INNOCENT BELOVED, YOU STEAMING PILE OF SPIRIT FLOTSAM?
JUST LOOK BEHIND YOU!
LOOK BEHIND YOU, MATE.

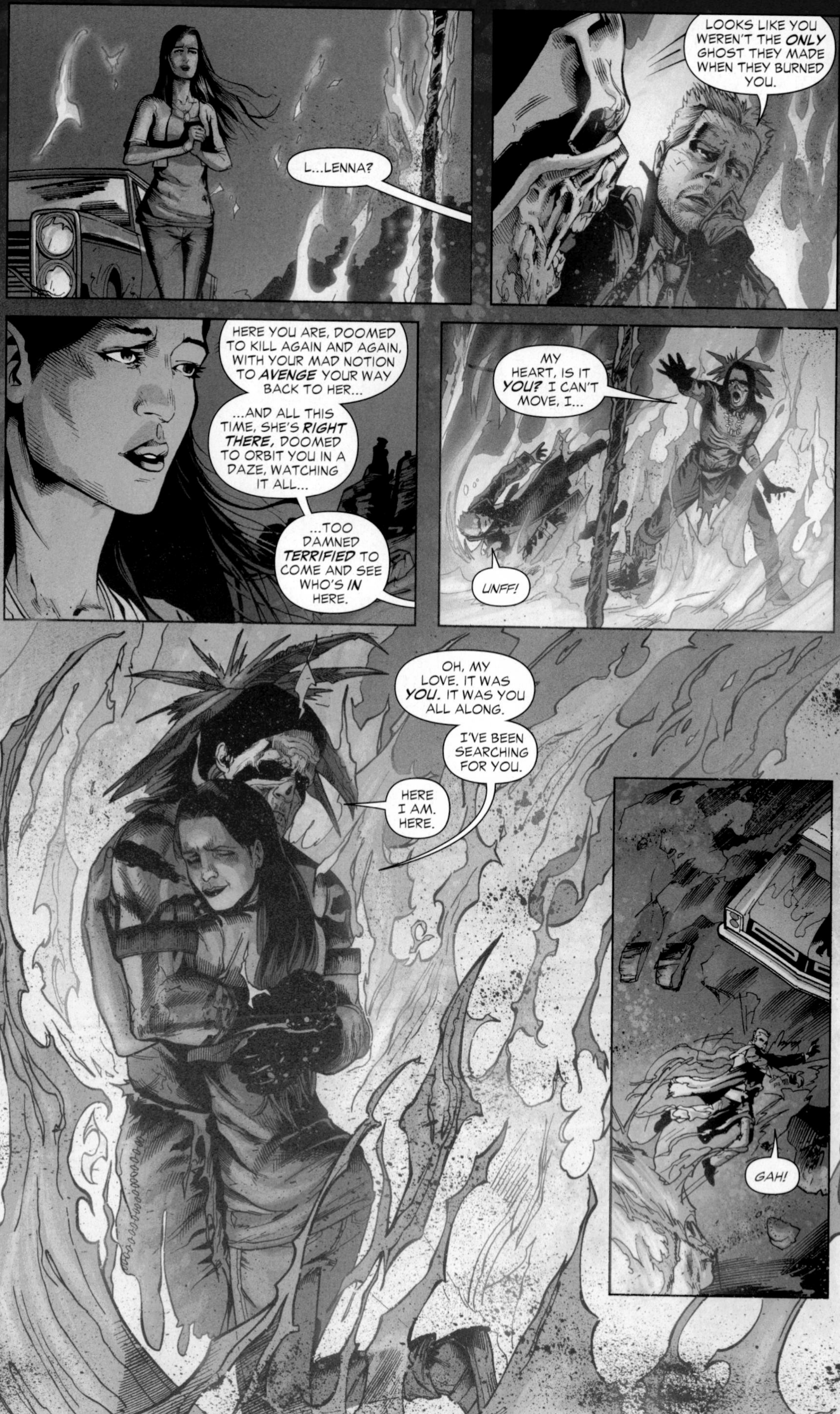

L...LENNA?
LOOKS LIKE YOU WEREN'T THE ONLY GHOST THEY MADE WHEN THEY BURNED YOU.
HERE YOU ARE, DOOMED TO KILL AGAIN AND AGAIN, WITH YOUR MAD NOTION TO AVENGE YOUR WAY BACK TO HER...
...AND ALL THIS TIME, SHE'S RIGHT THERE, DOOMED TO ORBIT YOU IN A DAZE, WATCHING IT ALL...
...TOO DAMNED TERRIFIED TO COME AND SEE WHO'S IN HERE.
MY HEART, IS IT YOU? I CAN'T MOVE, I...
UNFF!
OH, MY LOVE. IT WAS YOU. IT WAS YOU ALL ALONG.
I'VE BEEN SEARCHING FOR YOU.
HERE I AM. HERE.
GAH!

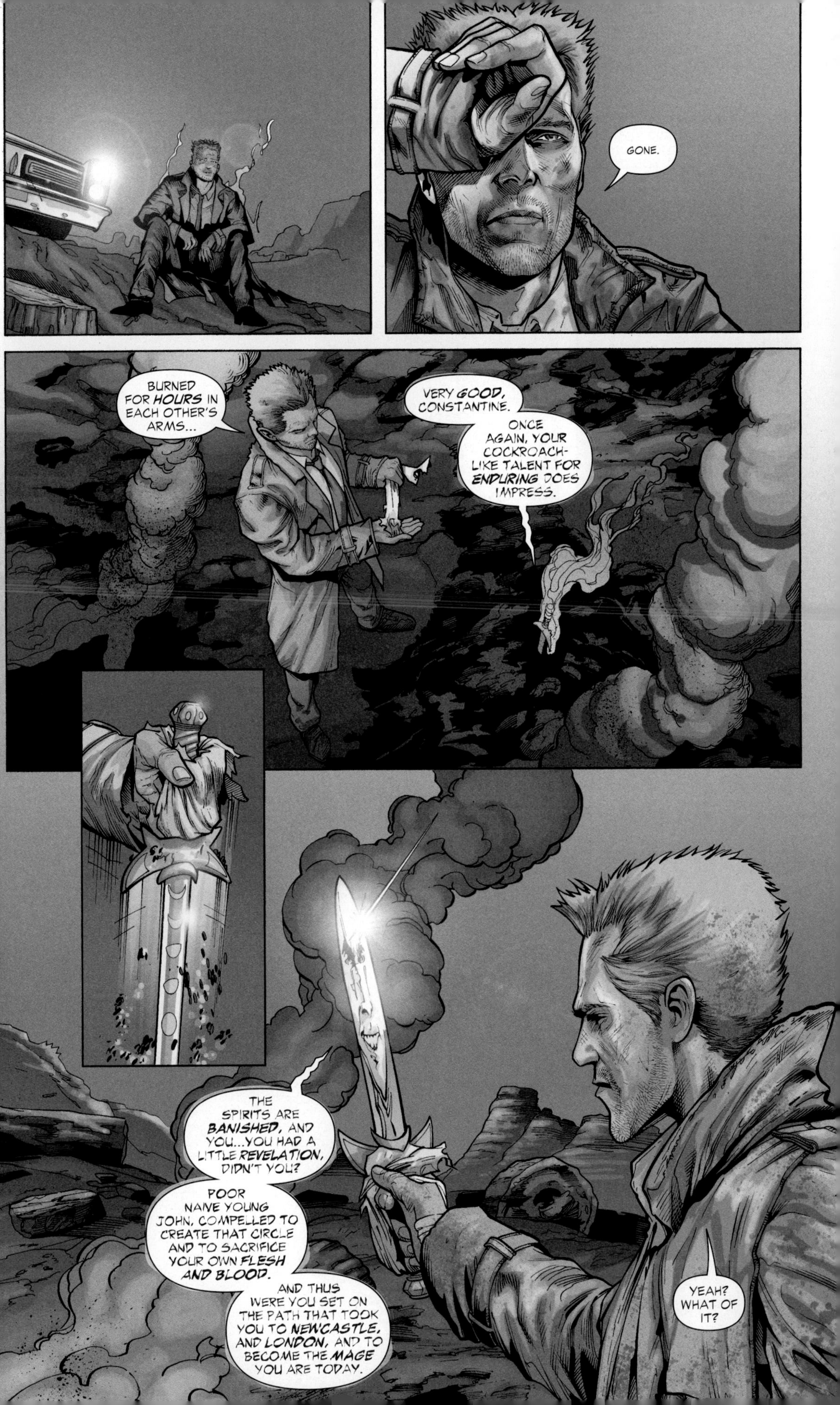
GONE.
BURNED FOR HOURS IN EACH OTHER'S ARMS...
VERY GOOD, CONSTANTINE.
ONCE AGAIN, YOUR COCKROACH-LIKE TALENT FOR ENDURING DOES IMPRESS.
THE SPIRITS ARE BANISHED, AND YOU...YOU HAD A LITTLE REVELATION, DIDN'T YOU?
POOR NAIVE YOUNG JOHN, COMPELLED TO CREATE THAT CIRCLE AND TO SACRIFICE YOUR OWN FLESH AND BLOOD.
AND THUS WERE YOU SET ON THE PATH THAT TOOK YOU TO NEWCASTLE, AND LONDON, AND TO BECOME THE MAGE YOU ARE TODAY.
YEAH? WHAT OF IT?

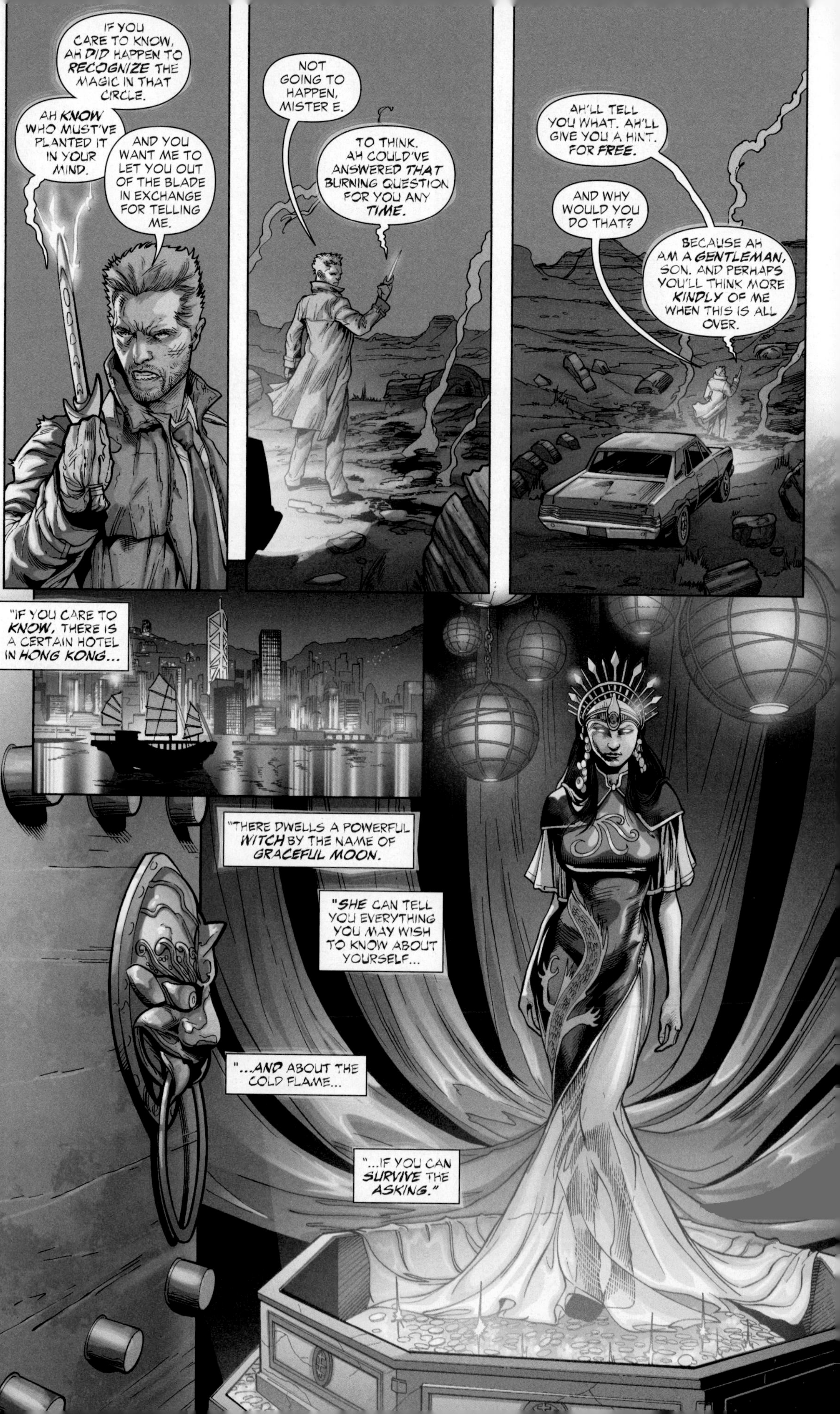
IF YOU CARE TO KNOW, AH DID HAPPEN TO RECOGNIZE THE MAGIC IN THAT CIRCLE.
AH KNOW WHO MUST'VE PLANTED IT IN YOUR MIND.
AND YOU WANT ME TO LET YOU OUT OF THE BLADE IN EXCHANGE FOR TELLING ME.
NOT GOING TO HAPPEN, MISTER E.
TO THINK. AH COULD'VE ANSWERED THAT BURNING QUESTION FOR YOU ANY TIME.
AH'LL TELL YOU WHAT. AH'LL GIVE YOU A HINT. FOR FREE.
AND WHY WOULD YOU DO THAT?
BECAUSE AH AM A GENTLEMAN, SON. AND PERHAPS YOU'LL THINK MORE KINDLY OF ME WHEN THIS IS ALL OVER.
"IF YOU CARE TO KNOW, THERE IS A CERTAIN HOTEL IN HONG KONG...
"THERE DWELLS A POWERFUL WITCH BY THE NAME OF GRACEFUL MOON.
"SHE CAN TELL YOU EVERYTHING YOU MAY WISH TO KNOW ABOUT YOURSELF...
"...AND ABOUT THE COLD FLAME...
"...IF YOU CAN SURVIVE THE ASKING."

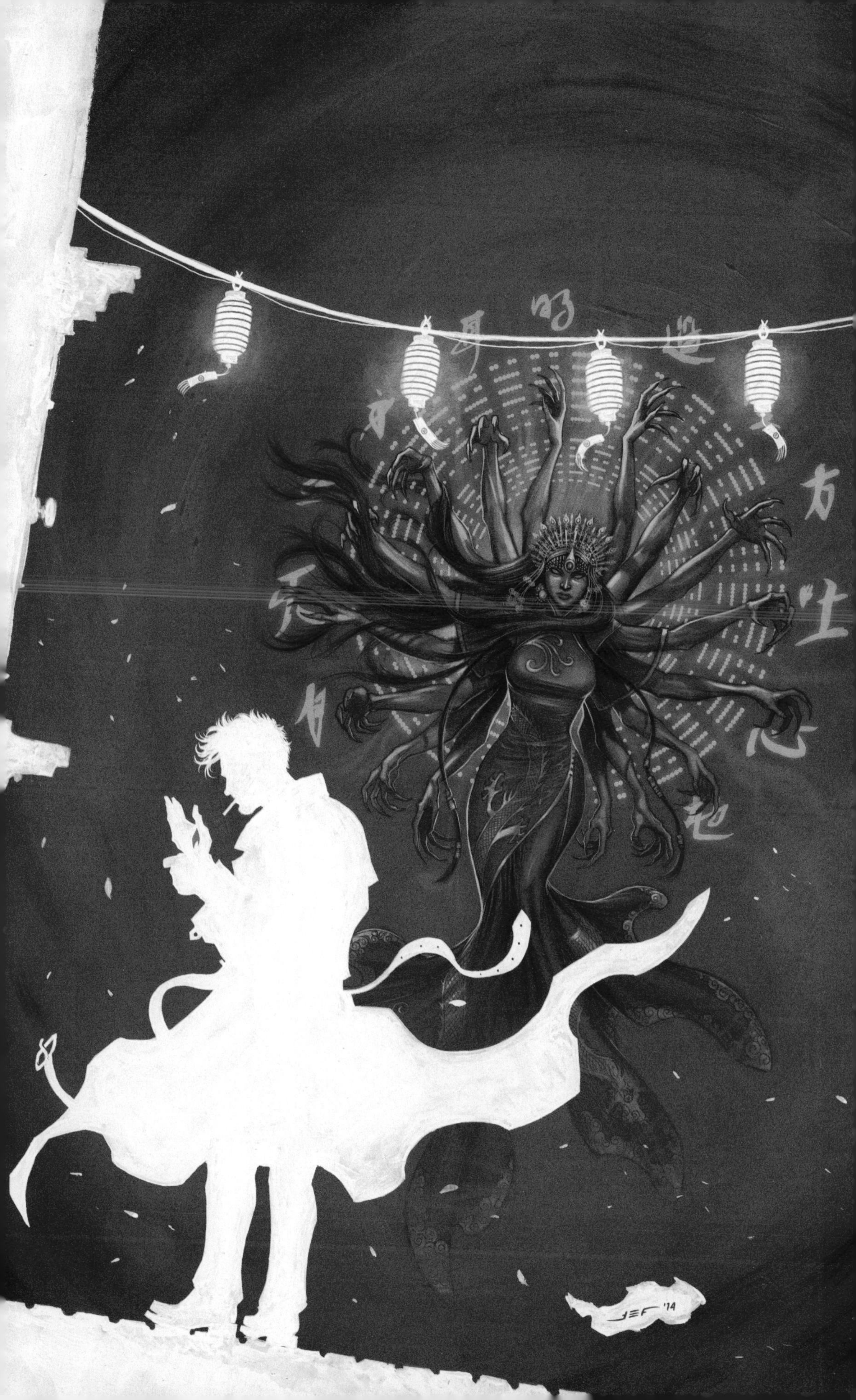
JEF '14

FORTUNE'S FRIEND

RAY FAWKES
writer

ACO
artist

TANYA and RICHARD HORIE
colorists

TAYLOR ESPOSITO
letterer

cover art by
JUAN FERREYRA

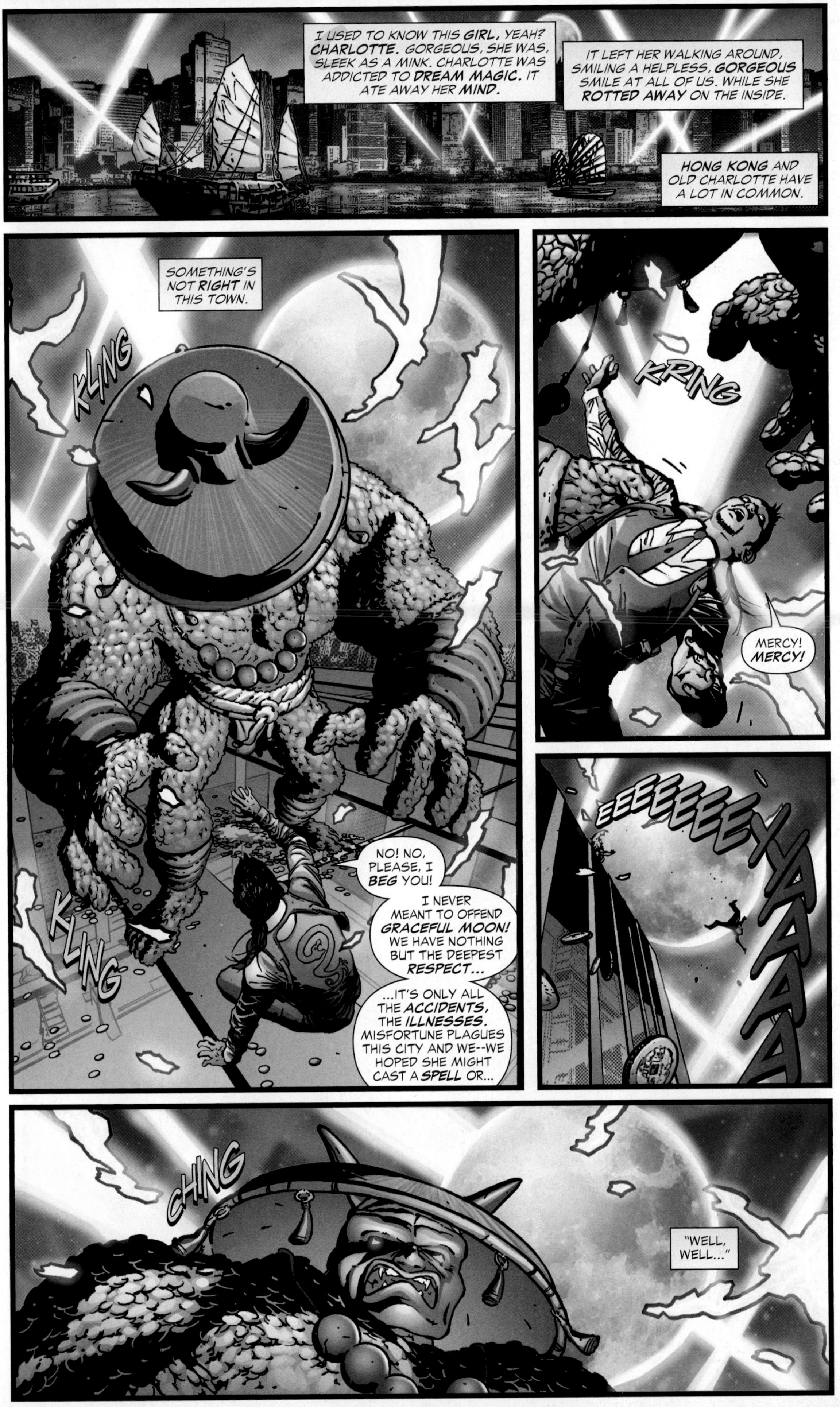

I USED TO KNOW THIS GIRL, YEAH? CHARLOTTE. GORGEOUS, SHE WAS, SLEEK AS A MINK. CHARLOTTE WAS ADDICTED TO DREAM MAGIC. IT ATE AWAY HER MIND.
IT LEFT HER WALKING AROUND, SMILING A HELPLESS, GORGEOUS SMILE AT ALL OF US. WHILE SHE ROTTED AWAY ON THE INSIDE.
HONG KONG AND OLD CHARLOTTE HAVE A LOT IN COMMON.
SOMETHING'S NOT RIGHT IN THIS TOWN.
KLING
KLING
NO! NO, PLEASE, I BEG YOU!
I NEVER MEANT TO OFFEND GRACEFUL MOON! WE HAVE NOTHING BUT THE DEEPEST RESPECT...
...IT'S ONLY ALL THE ACCIDENTS, THE ILLNESSES. MISFORTUNE PLAGUES THIS CITY AND WE--WE HOPED SHE MIGHT CAST A SPELL OR...
KRING
MERCY! MERCY!
EEEEEEEYAAAAAA
CHING
"WELL, WELL..."

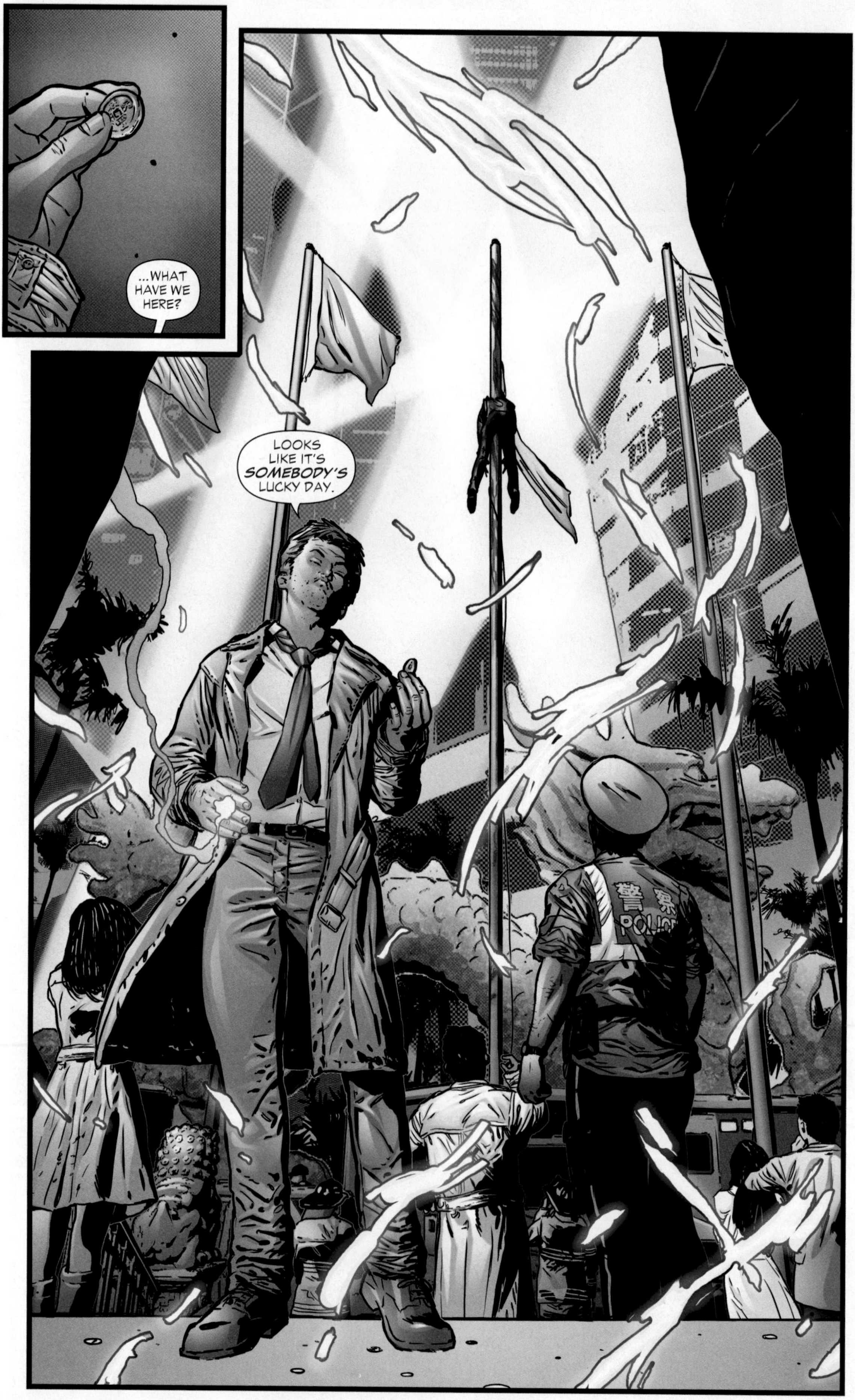
...WHAT HAVE WE HERE?
LOOKS LIKE IT'S *SOMEBODY'S* LUCKY DAY.
警察
POLICE

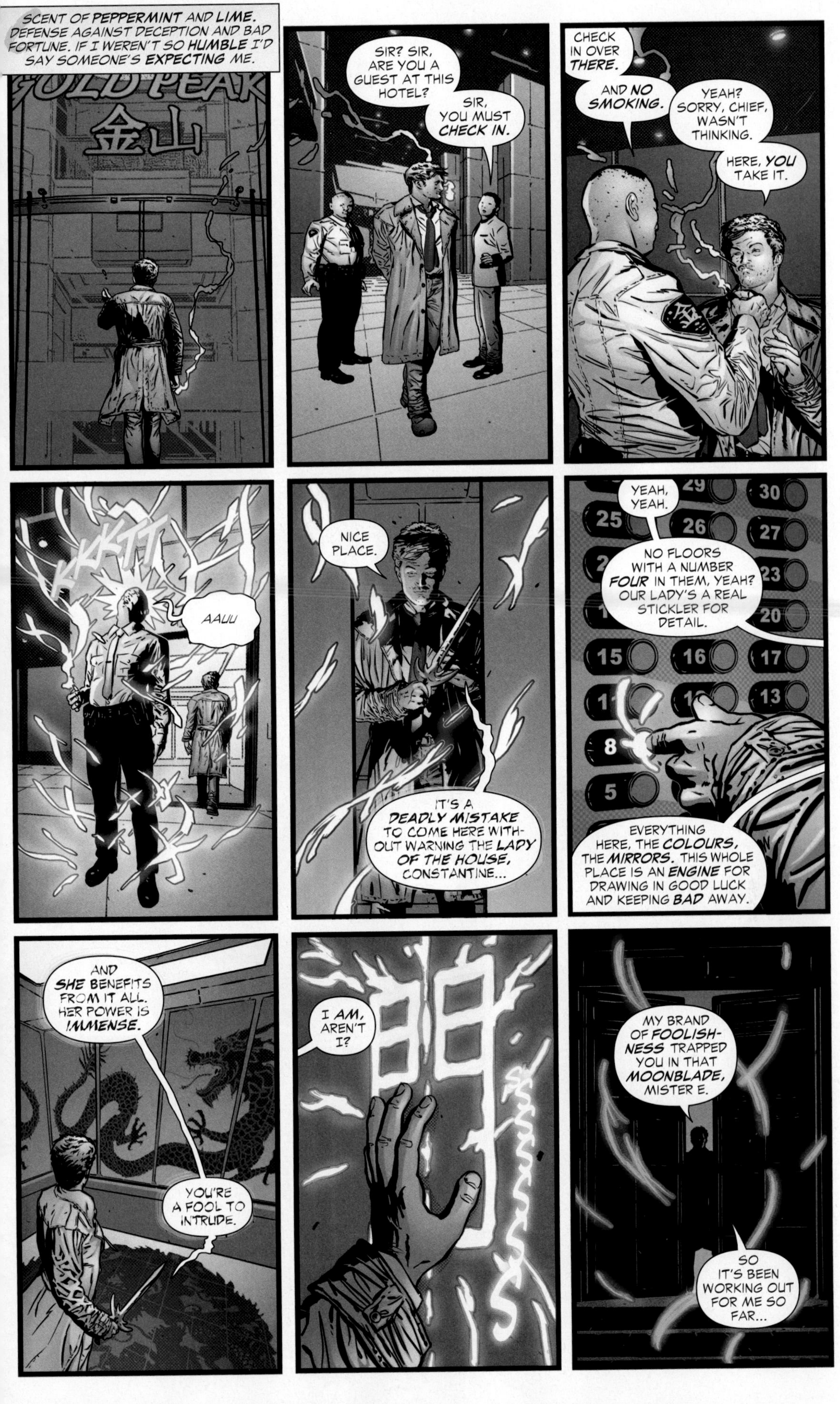

SCENT OF PEPPERMINT AND LIME. DEFENSE AGAINST DECEPTION AND BAD FORTUNE. IF I WEREN'T SO HUMBLE I'D SAY SOMEONE'S EXPECTING ME.
GOLD PEAK
金山
SIR? SIR, ARE YOU A GUEST AT THIS HOTEL?
SIR, YOU MUST CHECK IN.
CHECK IN OVER THERE.
AND NO SMOKING.
YEAH? SORRY, CHIEF, WASN'T THINKING.
HERE, YOU TAKE IT.
KKKTT
AAUU
NICE PLACE.
IT'S A DEADLY MISTAKE TO COME HERE WITHOUT WARNING THE LADY OF THE HOUSE, CONSTANTINE...
YEAH, YEAH.
NO FLOORS WITH A NUMBER FOUR IN THEM, YEAH? OUR LADY'S A REAL STICKLER FOR DETAIL.
EVERYTHING HERE, THE COLOURS, THE MIRRORS. THIS WHOLE PLACE IS AN ENGINE FOR DRAWING IN GOOD LUCK AND KEEPING BAD AWAY.
AND SHE BENEFITS FROM IT ALL. HER POWER IS IMMENSE.
YOU'RE A FOOL TO INTRUDE.
I AM, AREN'T I?
SSSSSSSSS
MY BRAND OF FOOLISHNESS TRAPPED YOU IN THAT MOONBLADE, MISTER E.
SO IT'S BEEN WORKING OUT FOR ME SO FAR...

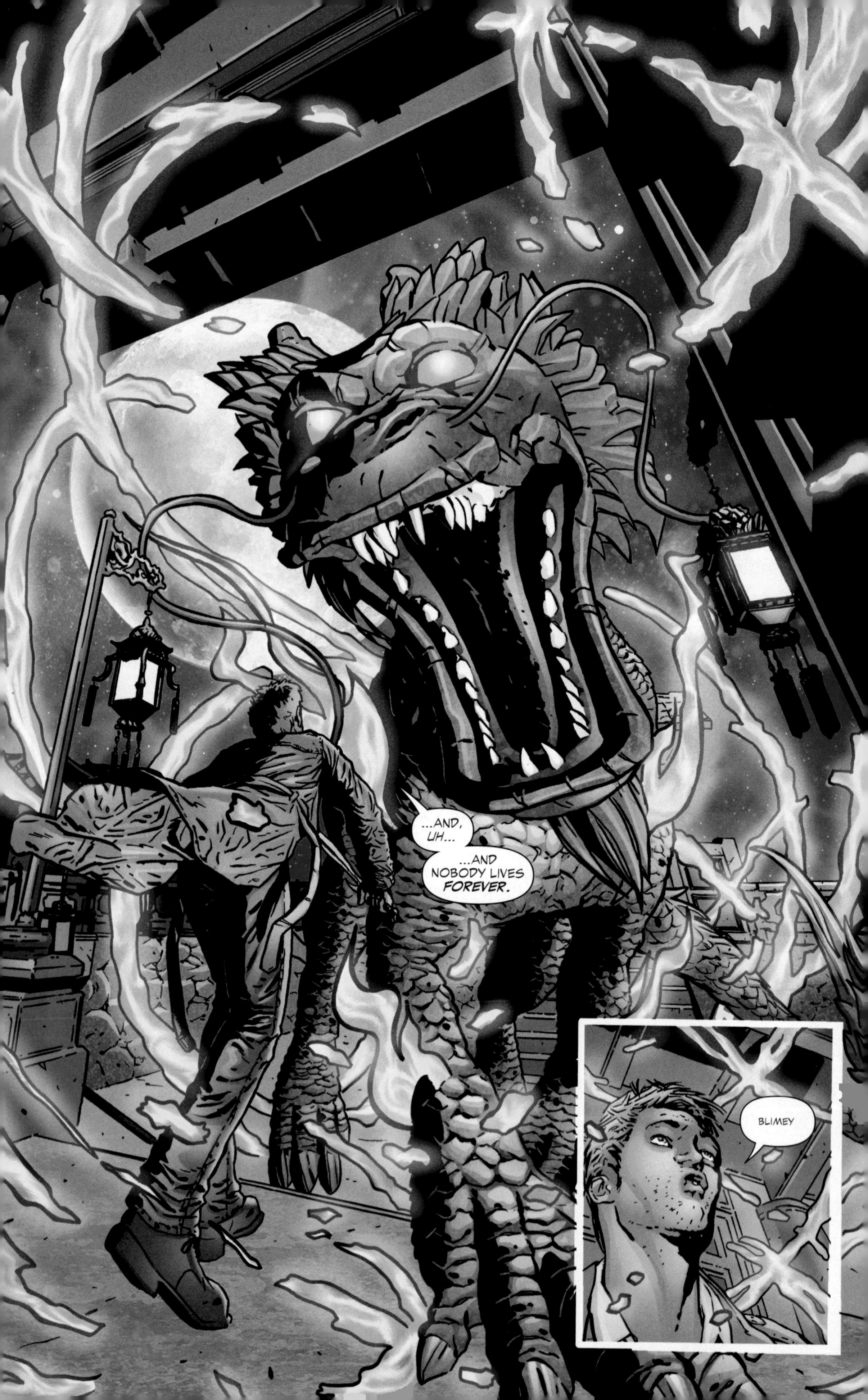
...AND, UH...
...AND NOBODY LIVES FOREVER.
BLIMEY

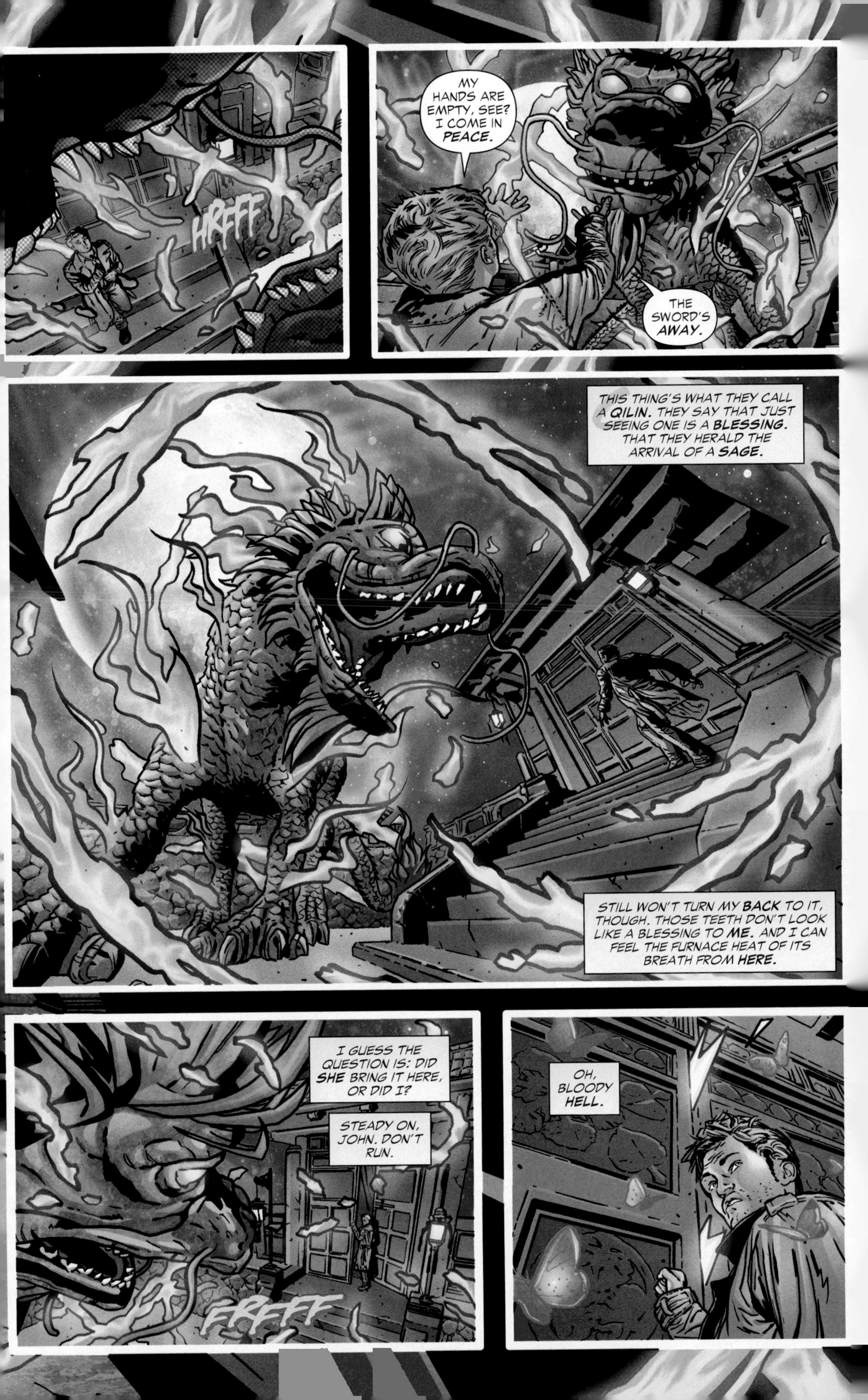
HRFFF
MY HANDS ARE EMPTY, SEE? I COME IN PEACE.
THE SWORD'S AWAY.
THIS THING'S WHAT THEY CALL A QILIN. THEY SAY THAT JUST SEEING ONE IS A BLESSING. THAT THEY HERALD THE ARRIVAL OF A SAGE.
STILL WON'T TURN MY BACK TO IT, THOUGH. THOSE TEETH DON'T LOOK LIKE A BLESSING TO ME. AND I CAN FEEL THE FURNACE HEAT OF ITS BREATH FROM HERE.
I GUESS THE QUESTION IS: DID SHE BRING IT HERE, OR DID I?
STEADY ON, JOHN. DON'T RUN.
FRFFF
OH, BLOODY HELL.

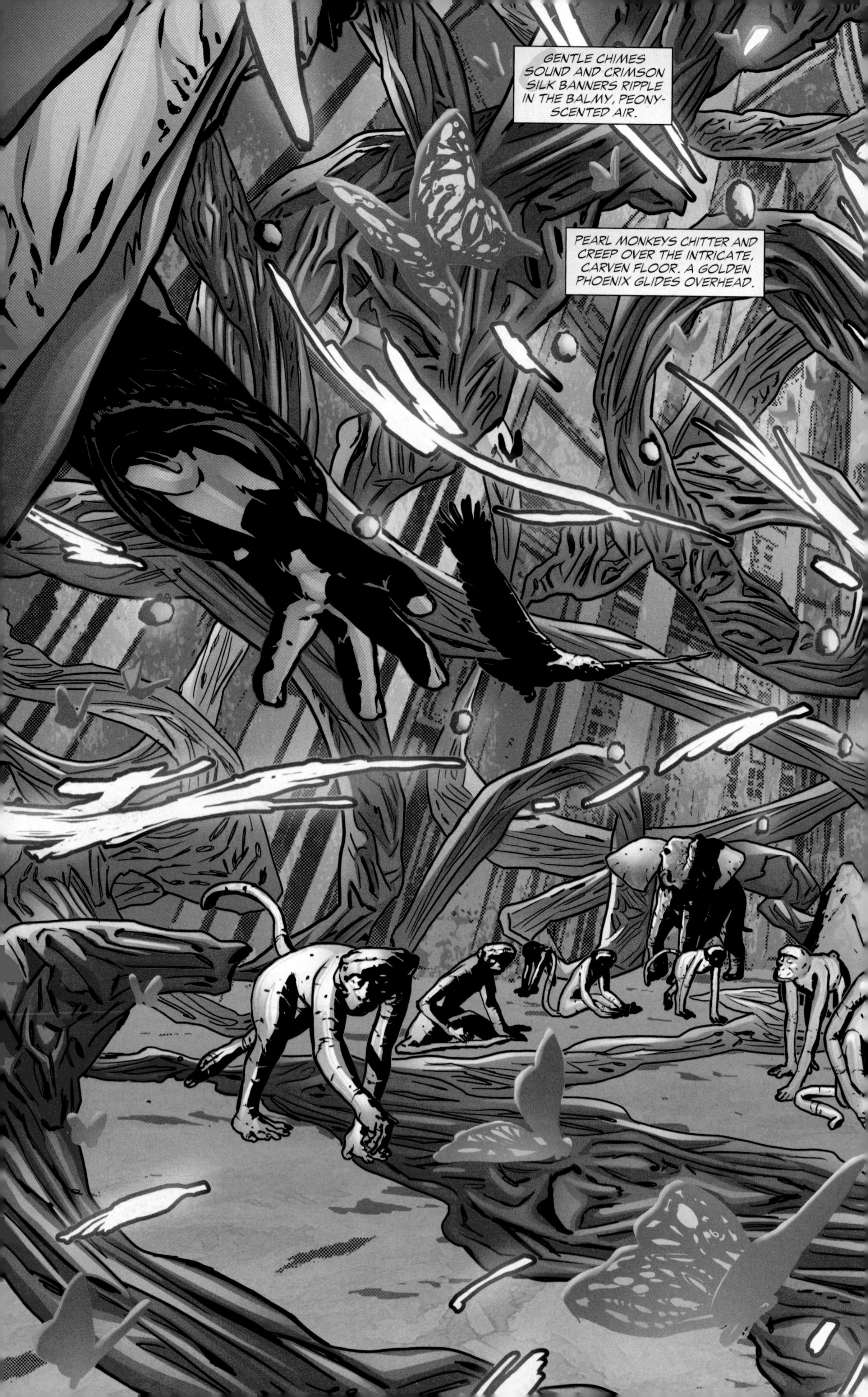
GENTLE CHIMES SOUND AND CRIMSON SILK BANNERS RIPPLE IN THE BALMY, PEONY-SCENTED AIR.
PEARL MONKEYS CHITTER AND CREEP OVER THE INTRICATE, CARVEN FLOOR. A GOLDEN PHOENIX GLIDES OVERHEAD.

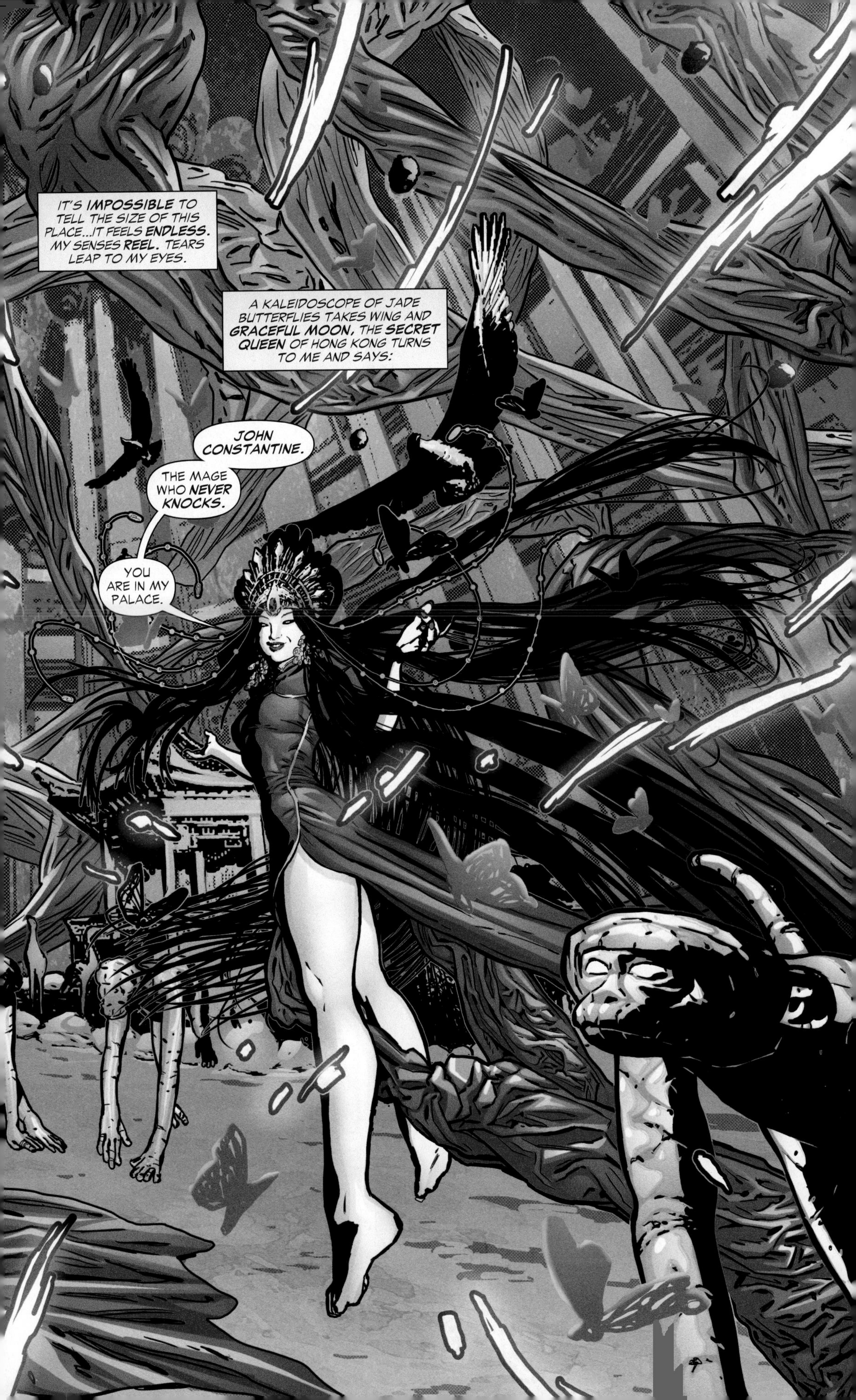
IT'S IMPOSSIBLE TO TELL THE SIZE OF THIS PLACE...IT FEELS ENDLESS. MY SENSES REEL. TEARS LEAP TO MY EYES.
A KALEIDOSCOPE OF JADE BUTTERFLIES TAKES WING AND GRACEFUL MOON, THE SECRET QUEEN OF HONG KONG TURNS TO ME AND SAYS:
JOHN CONSTANTINE.
THE MAGE WHO NEVER KNOCKS.
YOU ARE IN MY PALACE.

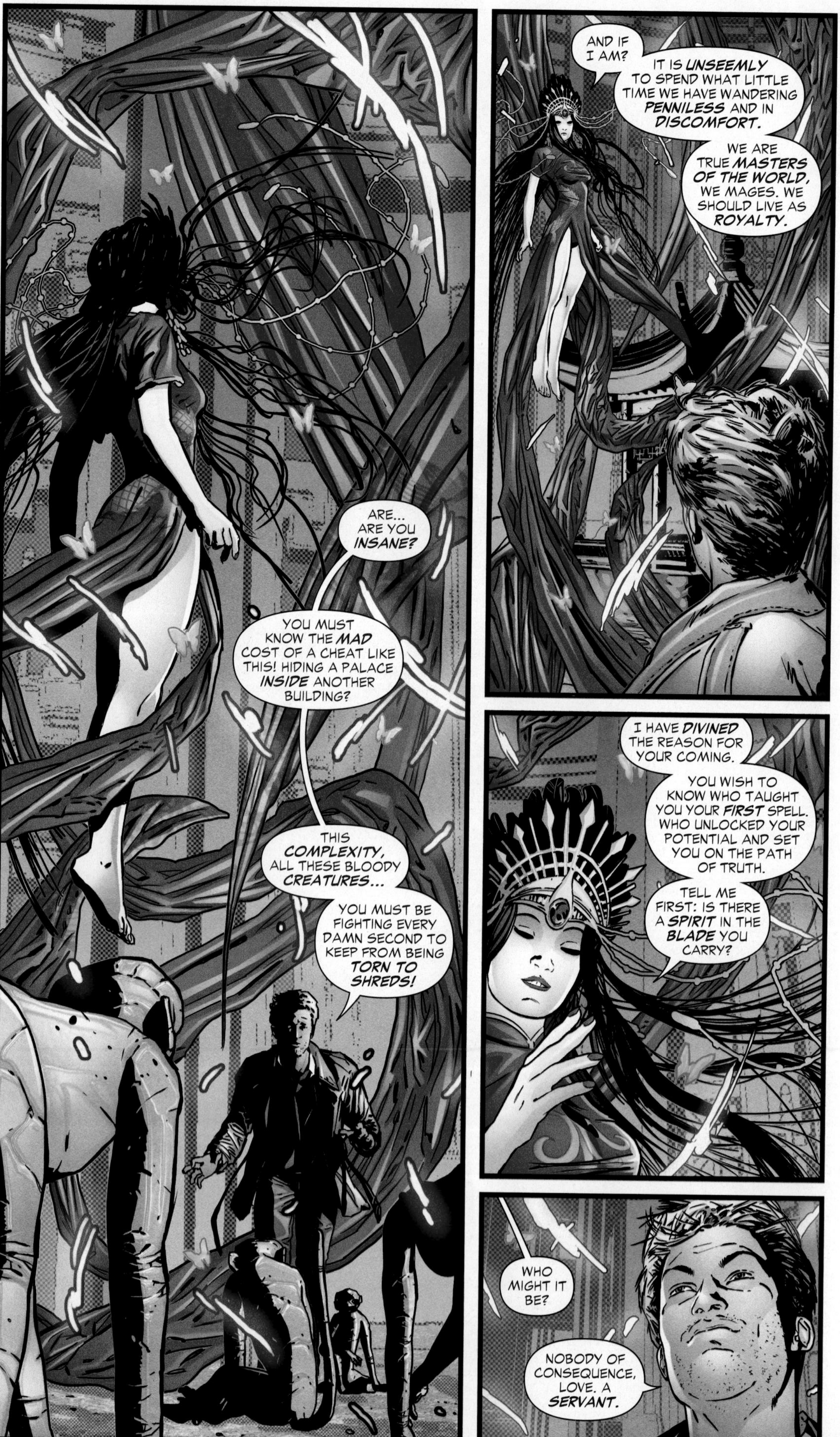
ARE... ARE YOU INSANE?
YOU MUST KNOW THE MAD COST OF A CHEAT LIKE THIS! HIDING A PALACE INSIDE ANOTHER BUILDING?
THIS COMPLEXITY, ALL THESE BLOODY CREATURES...
YOU MUST BE FIGHTING EVERY DAMN SECOND TO KEEP FROM BEING TORN TO SHREDS!
AND IF I AM?
IT IS UNSEEMLY TO SPEND WHAT LITTLE TIME WE HAVE WANDERING PENNILESS AND IN DISCOMFORT.
WE ARE TRUE MASTERS OF THE WORLD, WE MAGES. WE SHOULD LIVE AS ROYALTY.
I HAVE DIVINED THE REASON FOR YOUR COMING.
YOU WISH TO KNOW WHO TAUGHT YOU YOUR FIRST SPELL. WHO UNLOCKED YOUR POTENTIAL AND SET YOU ON THE PATH OF TRUTH.
TELL ME FIRST: IS THERE A SPIRIT IN THE BLADE YOU CARRY?
WHO MIGHT IT BE?
NOBODY OF CONSEQUENCE, LOVE. A SERVANT.

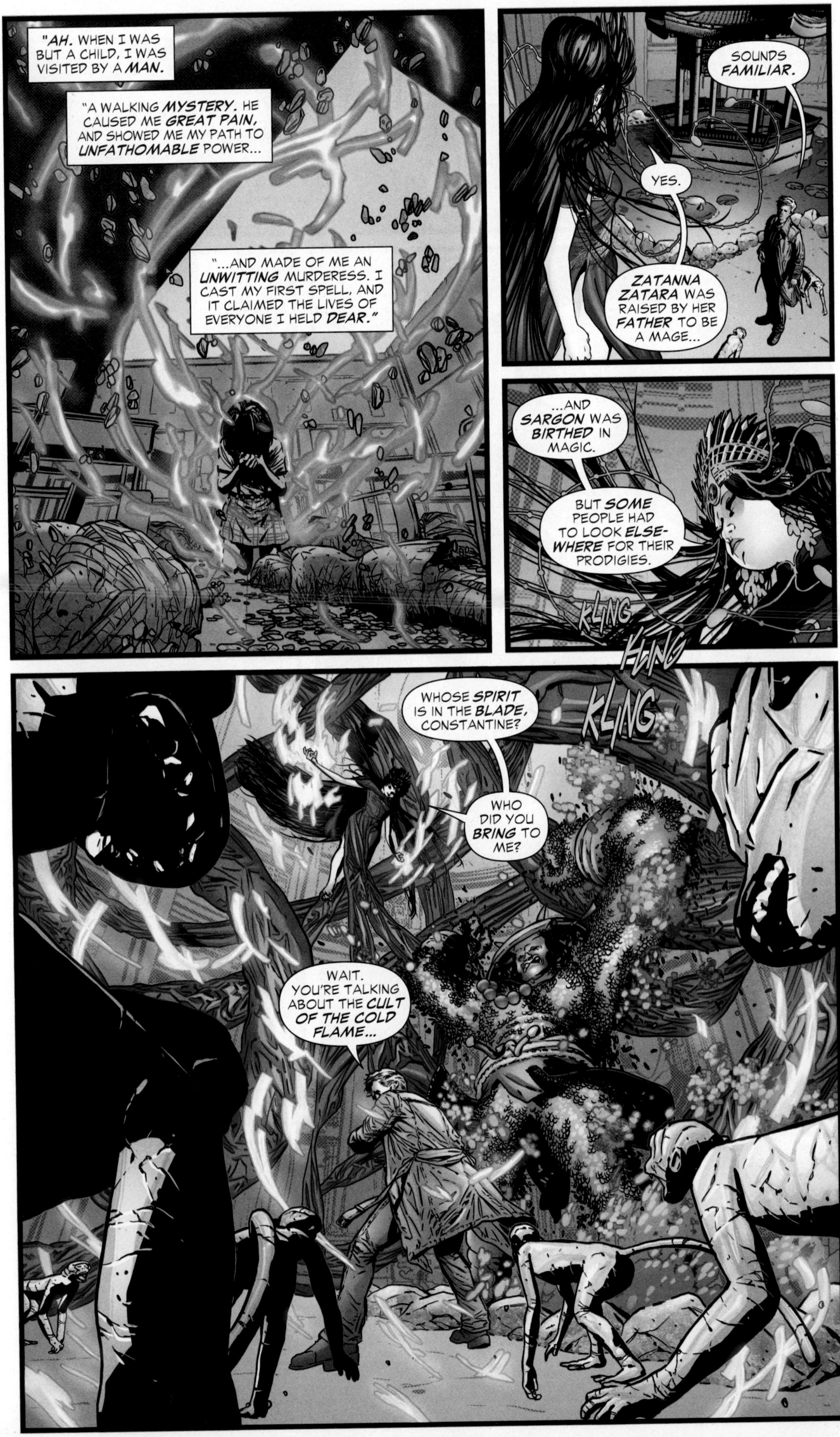
"AH. WHEN I WAS BUT A CHILD, I WAS VISITED BY A MAN.
"A WALKING MYSTERY. HE CAUSED ME GREAT PAIN, AND SHOWED ME MY PATH TO UNFATHOMABLE POWER...
"...AND MADE OF ME AN UNWITTING MURDERESS. I CAST MY FIRST SPELL, AND IT CLAIMED THE LIVES OF EVERYONE I HELD DEAR."
SOUNDS FAMILIAR.
YES.
ZATANNA ZATARA WAS RAISED BY HER FATHER TO BE A MAGE...
...AND SARGON WAS BIRTHED IN MAGIC.
BUT SOME PEOPLE HAD TO LOOK ELSE-WHERE FOR THEIR PRODIGIES.
KLING
KLING
KLING
WHOSE SPIRIT IS IN THE BLADE, CONSTANTINE?
WHO DID YOU BRING TO ME?
WAIT. YOU'RE TALKING ABOUT THE CULT OF THE COLD FLAME...

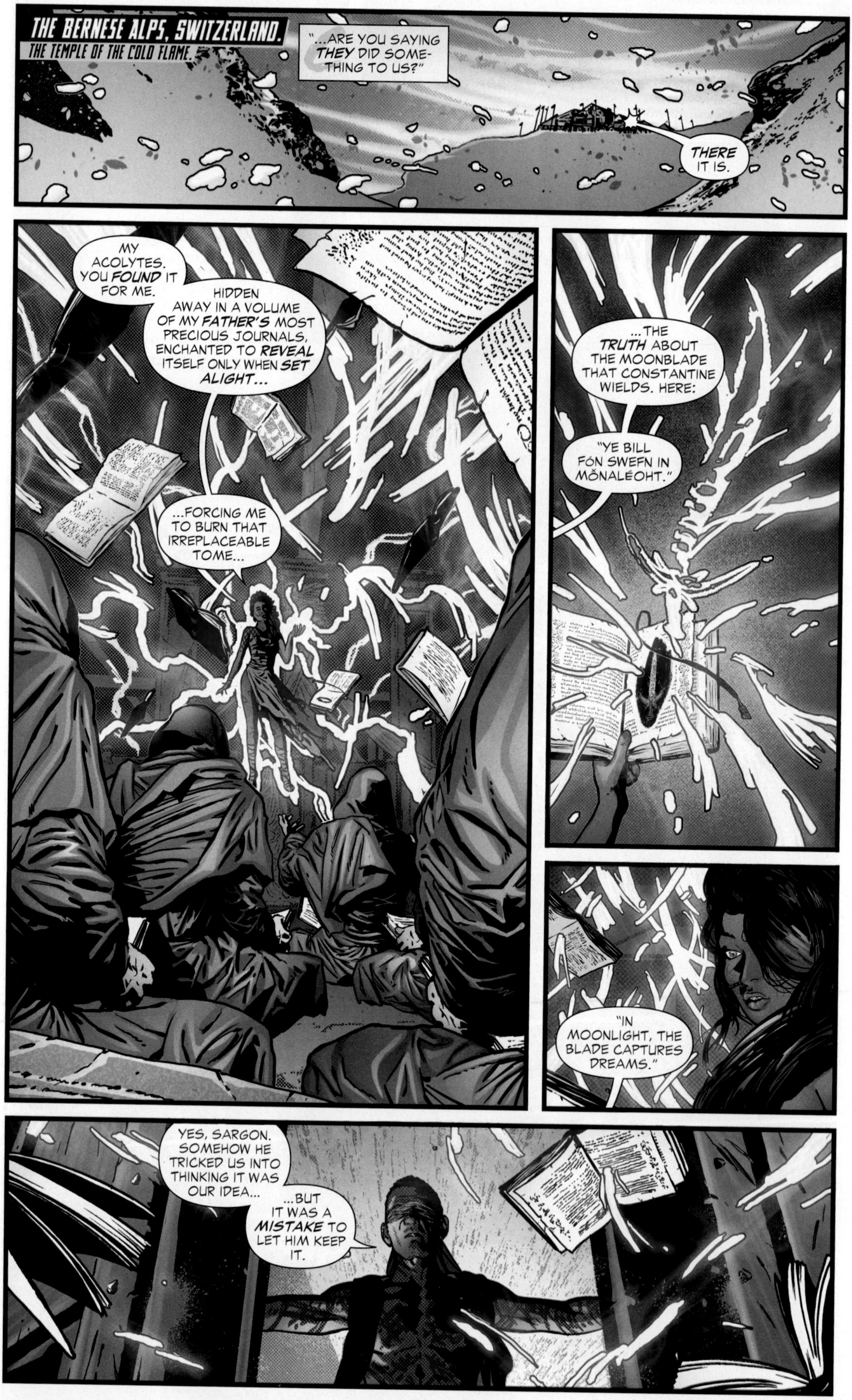
THE BERNESE ALPS, SWITZERLAND.
THE TEMPLE OF THE COLD FLAME.
"...ARE YOU SAYING THEY DID SOMETHING TO US?"
THERE IT IS.
MY ACOLYTES. YOU FOUND IT FOR ME.
HIDDEN AWAY IN A VOLUME OF MY FATHER'S MOST PRECIOUS JOURNALS, ENCHANTED TO REVEAL ITSELF ONLY WHEN SET ALIGHT...
...FORCING ME TO BURN THAT IRREPLACEABLE TOME...
...THE TRUTH ABOUT THE MOONBLADE THAT CONSTANTINE WIELDS. HERE:
"YE BILL FÓN SWEFN IN MǑNALÉOHT."
"IN MOONLIGHT, THE BLADE CAPTURES DREAMS."
YES, SARGON. SOMEHOW HE TRICKED US INTO THINKING IT WAS OUR IDEA...
...BUT IT WAS A MISTAKE TO LET HIM KEEP IT.

I'M NOT COMFORTABLE WITH *UNKNOWNS,* TANNARAK.

CONSTANTINE IS CLEARLY WORKING *AGAINST* US DESPITE THE OATHS HE'S SWORN. WHO KNOWS WHAT HE CARRIES IN THAT BLADE?

YOU SHOULD USE THE *DEATH HEX* PAPA MIDNITE PROVIDED AND DESTROY HIM *NOW.*

LESS CONTAINMENT NOT!

MY SERVANTS... YOU *KILLED* THEM!

WHY?

WE HAVE THE STRENGTH TO HANDLE CONSTANTINE. *WE* COMMAND THE GREATEST POOL OF MAGIC IN *HISTORY...*

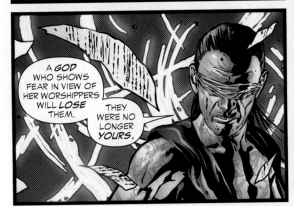

A *GOD* WHO SHOWS FEAR IN VIEW OF HER WORSHIPPERS WILL *LOSE* THEM.

THEY WERE NO LONGER *YOURS.*

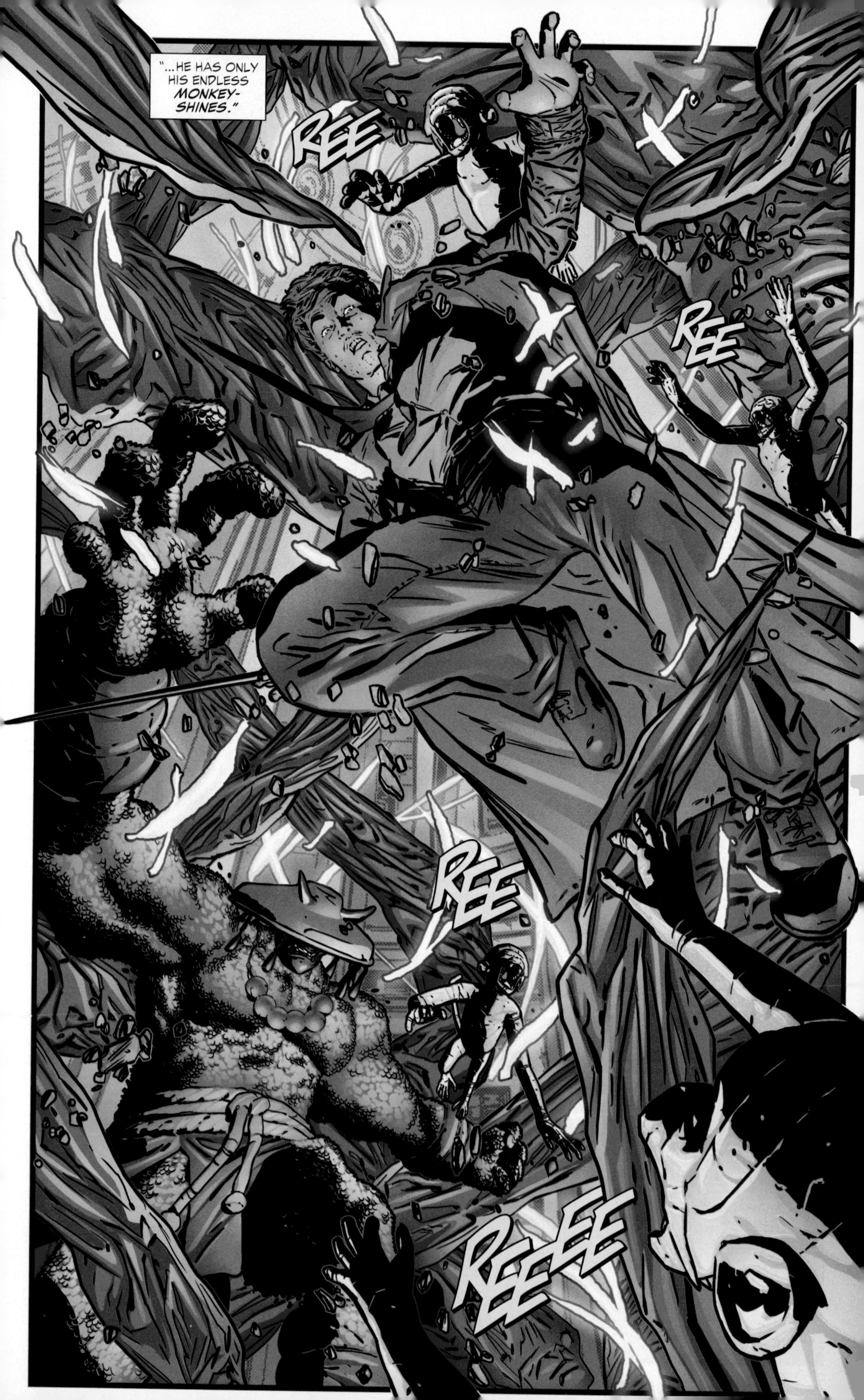
"...HE HAS ONLY HIS ENDLESS MONKEY-SHINES."
REE
REE
REE
REEEEE

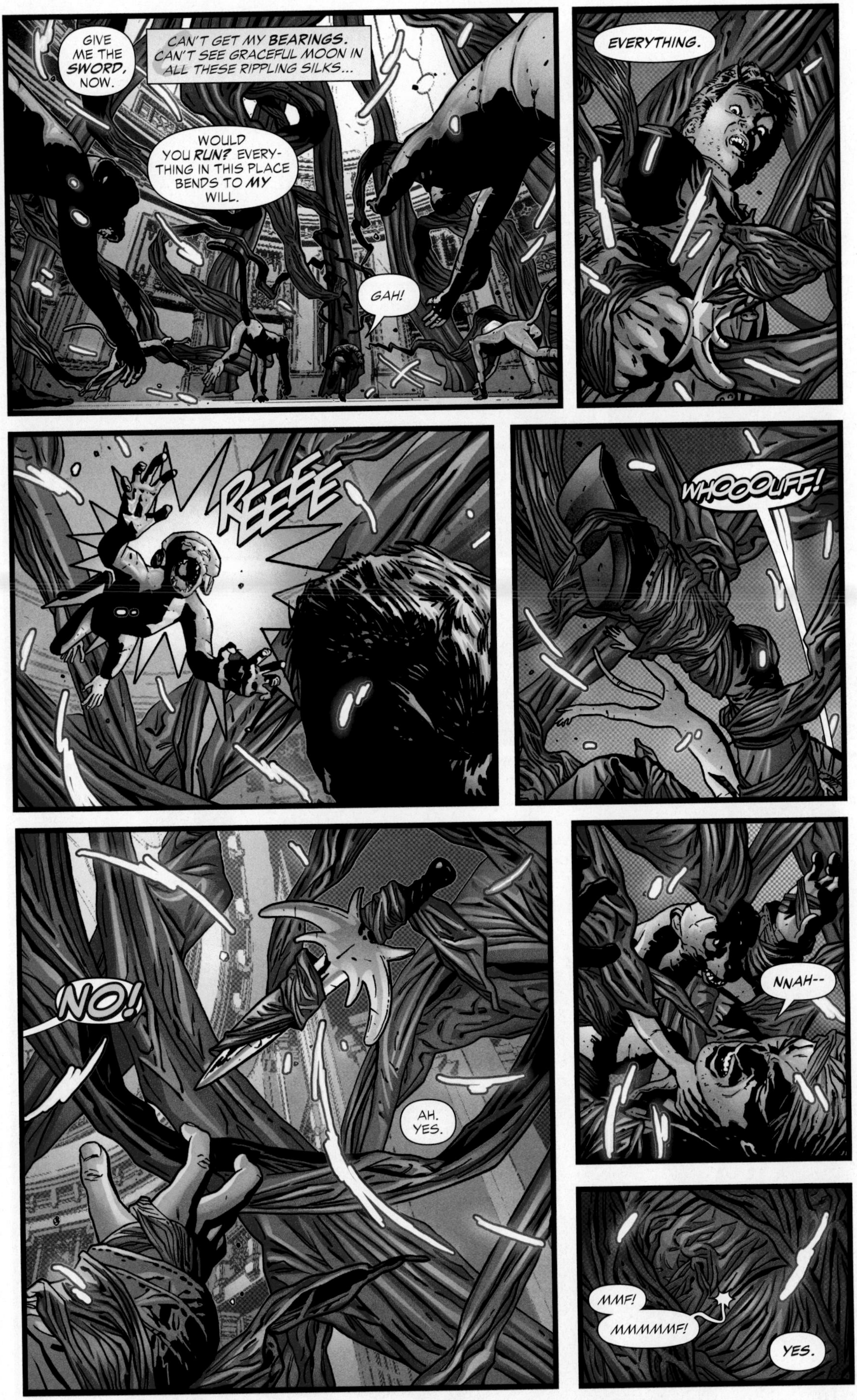
GIVE ME THE SWORD, NOW.
CAN'T GET MY BEARINGS. CAN'T SEE GRACEFUL MOON IN ALL THESE RIPPLING SILKS...
WOULD YOU RUN? EVERYTHING IN THIS PLACE BENDS TO MY WILL.
GAH!
EVERYTHING.
REEEEE
WHOOOOUFF!
NO!
AH. YES.
NNAH--
MMF!
MMMMMF!
YES.

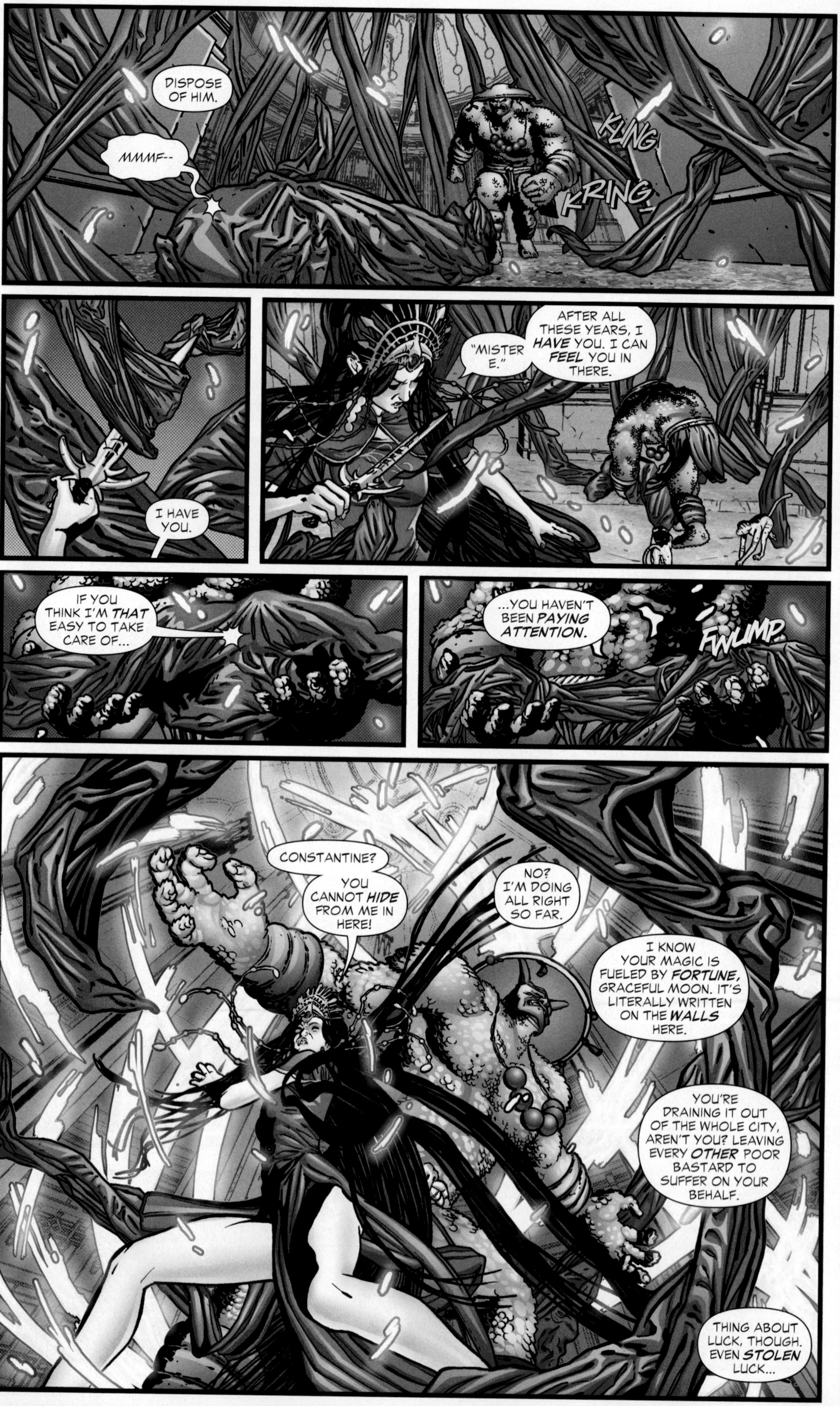
DISPOSE OF HIM.
MMMF--
KLING
KRING
I HAVE YOU.
"MISTER E."
AFTER ALL THESE YEARS, I HAVE YOU. I CAN FEEL YOU IN THERE.
IF YOU THINK I'M THAT EASY TO TAKE CARE OF...
...YOU HAVEN'T BEEN PAYING ATTENTION.
FWUMP
CONSTANTINE?
YOU CANNOT HIDE FROM ME IN HERE!
NO? I'M DOING ALL RIGHT SO FAR.
I KNOW YOUR MAGIC IS FUELED BY FORTUNE, GRACEFUL MOON. IT'S LITERALLY WRITTEN ON THE WALLS HERE.
YOU'RE DRAINING IT OUT OF THE WHOLE CITY, AREN'T YOU? LEAVING EVERY OTHER POOR BASTARD TO SUFFER ON YOUR BEHALF.
THING ABOUT LUCK, THOUGH. EVEN STOLEN LUCK...

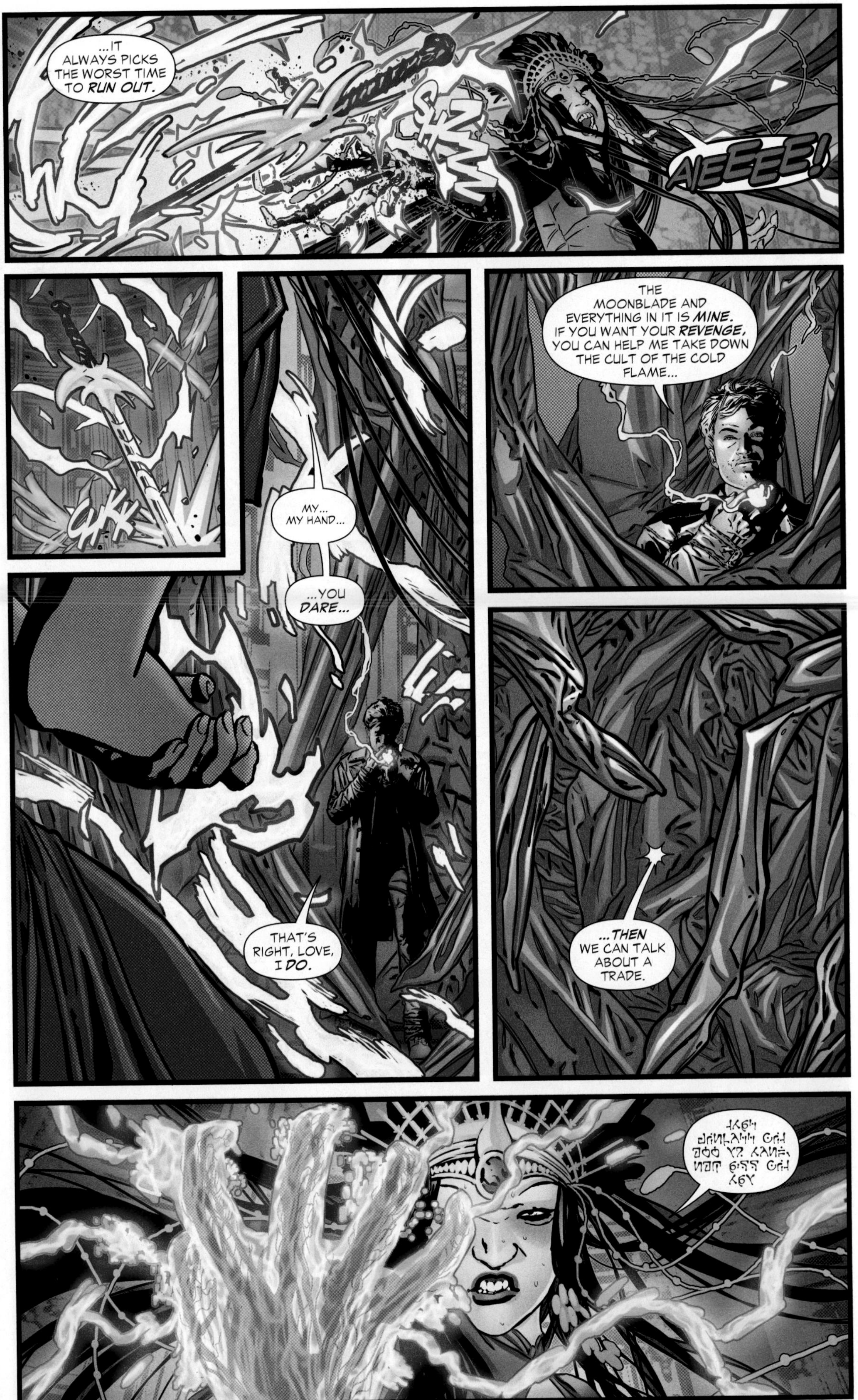
...IT ALWAYS PICKS THE WORST TIME TO RUN OUT.
AIEEEEE!
MY... MY HAND...
...YOU DARE...
THAT'S RIGHT, LOVE, I DO.
THE MOONBLADE AND EVERYTHING IN IT IS MINE. IF YOU WANT YOUR REVENGE, YOU CAN HELP ME TAKE DOWN THE CULT OF THE COLD FLAME...
...THEN WE CAN TALK ABOUT A TRADE.

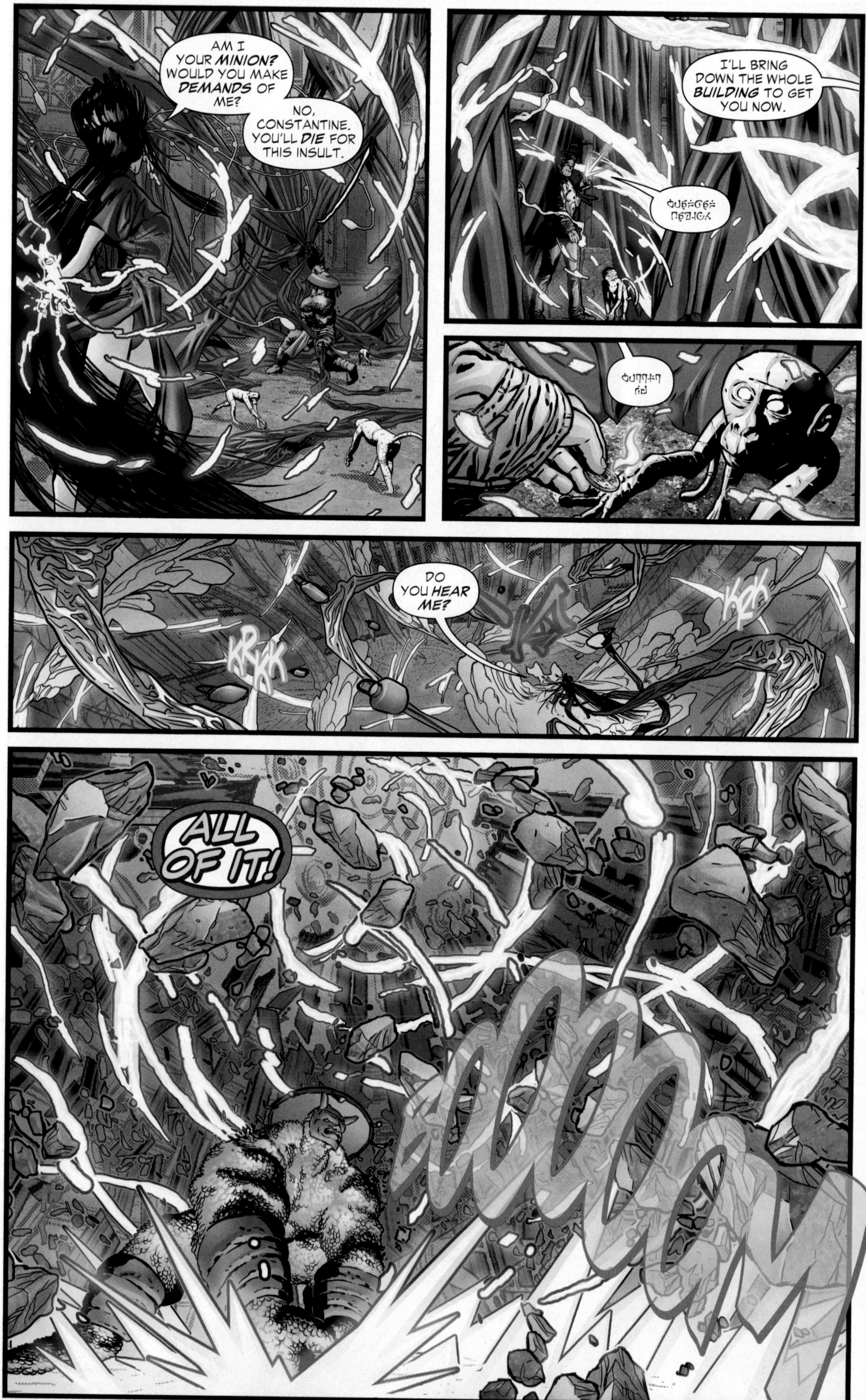
AM I YOUR MINION? WOULD YOU MAKE DEMANDS OF ME?
NO, CONSTANTINE. YOU'LL DIE FOR THIS INSULT.
I'LL BRING DOWN THE WHOLE BUILDING TO GET YOU NOW.
DO YOU HEAR ME?
KRKK
KRK
ALL OF IT!

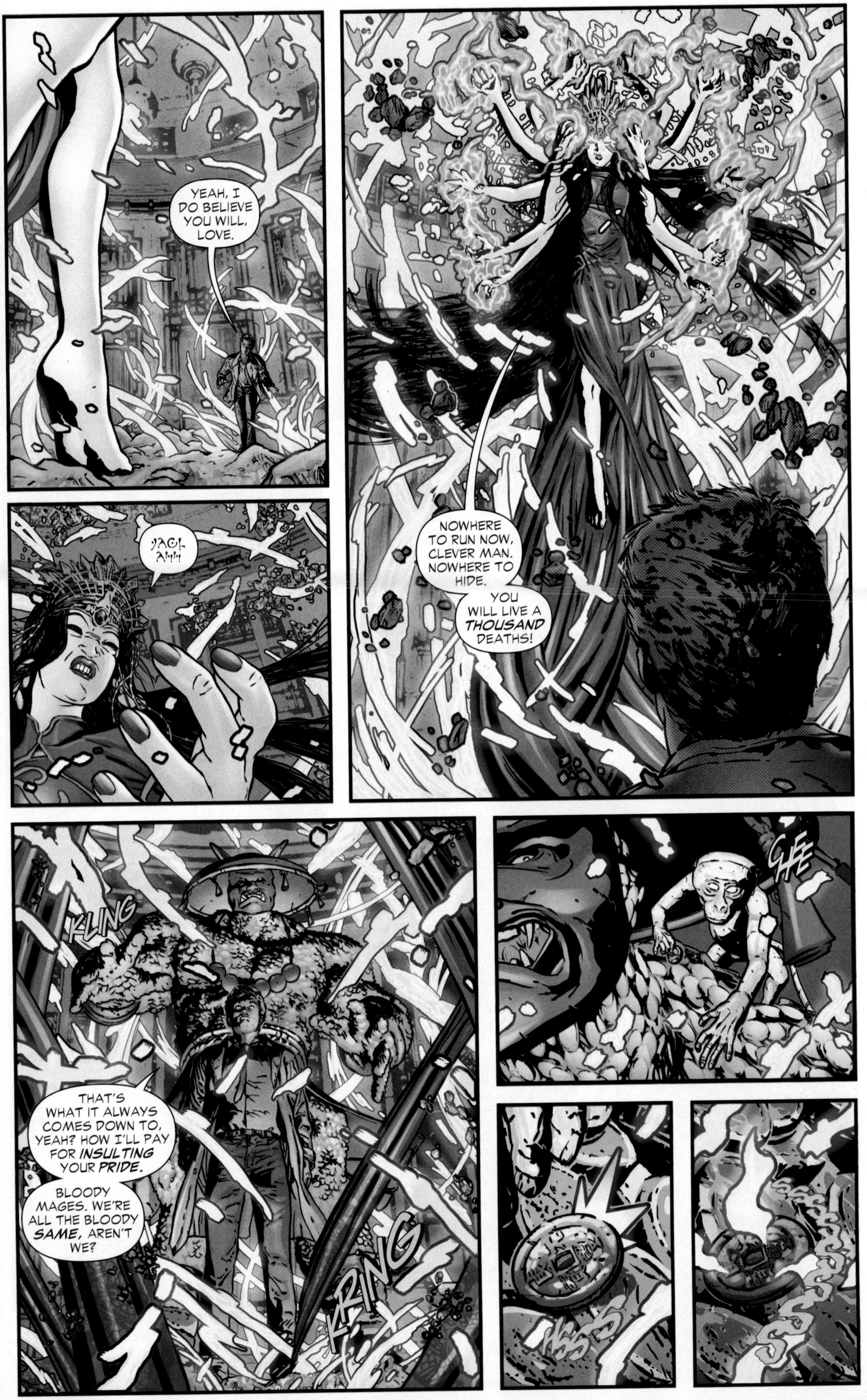
YEAH, I DO BELIEVE YOU WILL, LOVE.
NOWHERE TO RUN NOW, CLEVER MAN. NOWHERE TO HIDE.
YOU WILL LIVE A *THOUSAND* DEATHS!
KLING
THAT'S WHAT IT ALWAYS COMES DOWN TO, YEAH? HOW I'LL PAY FOR *INSULTING* YOUR *PRIDE*.
BLOODY MAGES. WE'RE ALL THE BLOODY *SAME*, AREN'T WE?
KRING
CHEE
HSSSS

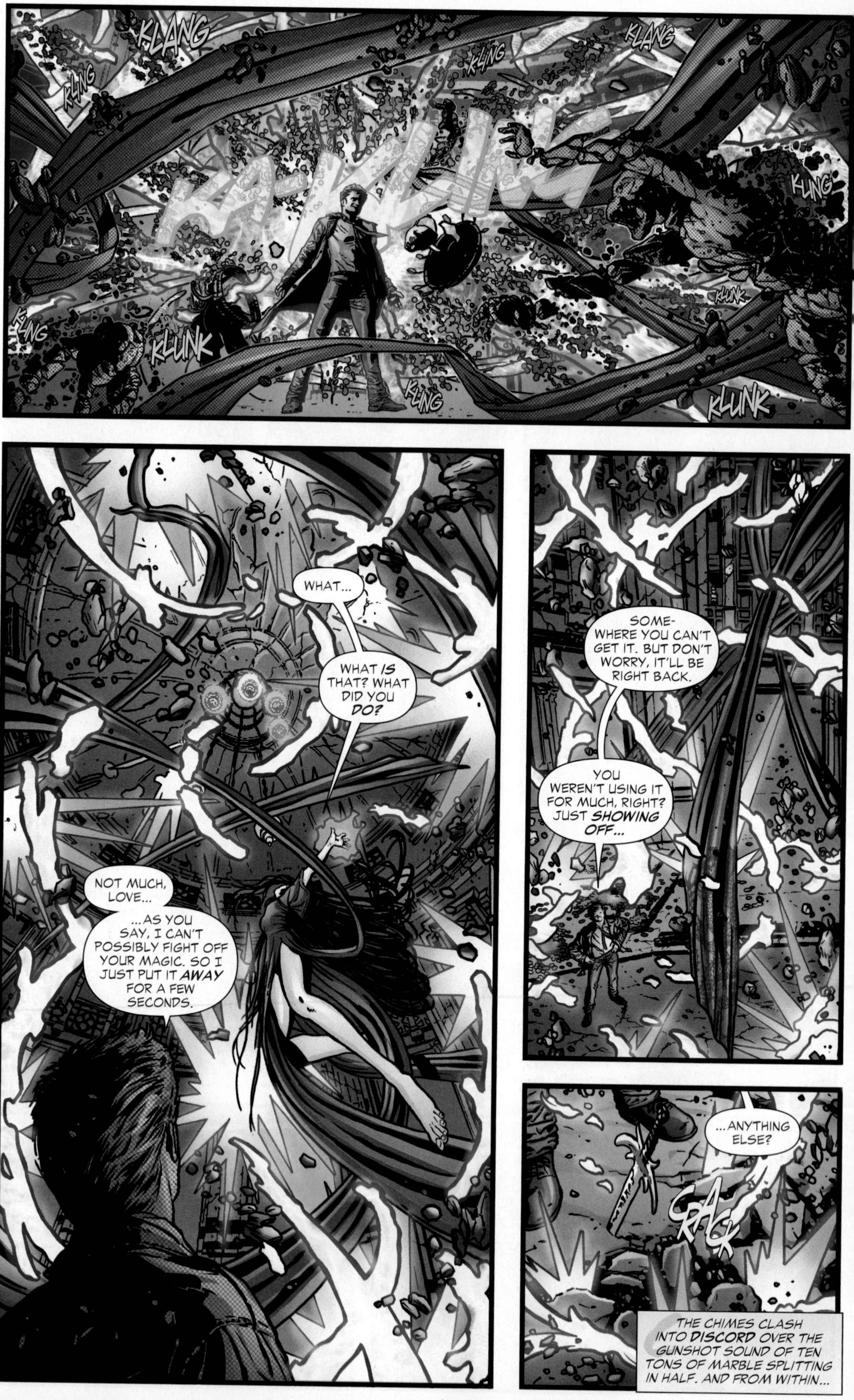
KLANG
KLING
KLING
KLANG
KA-KLING
KLING
KLING
KLUNK
KLUNK
KLING
KLUNK
WHAT...
WHAT IS THAT? WHAT DID YOU DO?
NOT MUCH, LOVE...
...AS YOU SAY, I CAN'T POSSIBLY FIGHT OFF YOUR MAGIC. SO I JUST PUT IT AWAY FOR A FEW SECONDS.
SOME-WHERE YOU CAN'T GET IT. BUT DON'T WORRY, IT'LL BE RIGHT BACK.
YOU WEREN'T USING IT FOR MUCH, RIGHT? JUST SHOWING OFF...
...ANYTHING ELSE?
CRACK
THE CHIMES CLASH INTO DISCORD OVER THE GUNSHOT SOUND OF TEN TONS OF MARBLE SPLITTING IN HALF. AND FROM WITHIN...

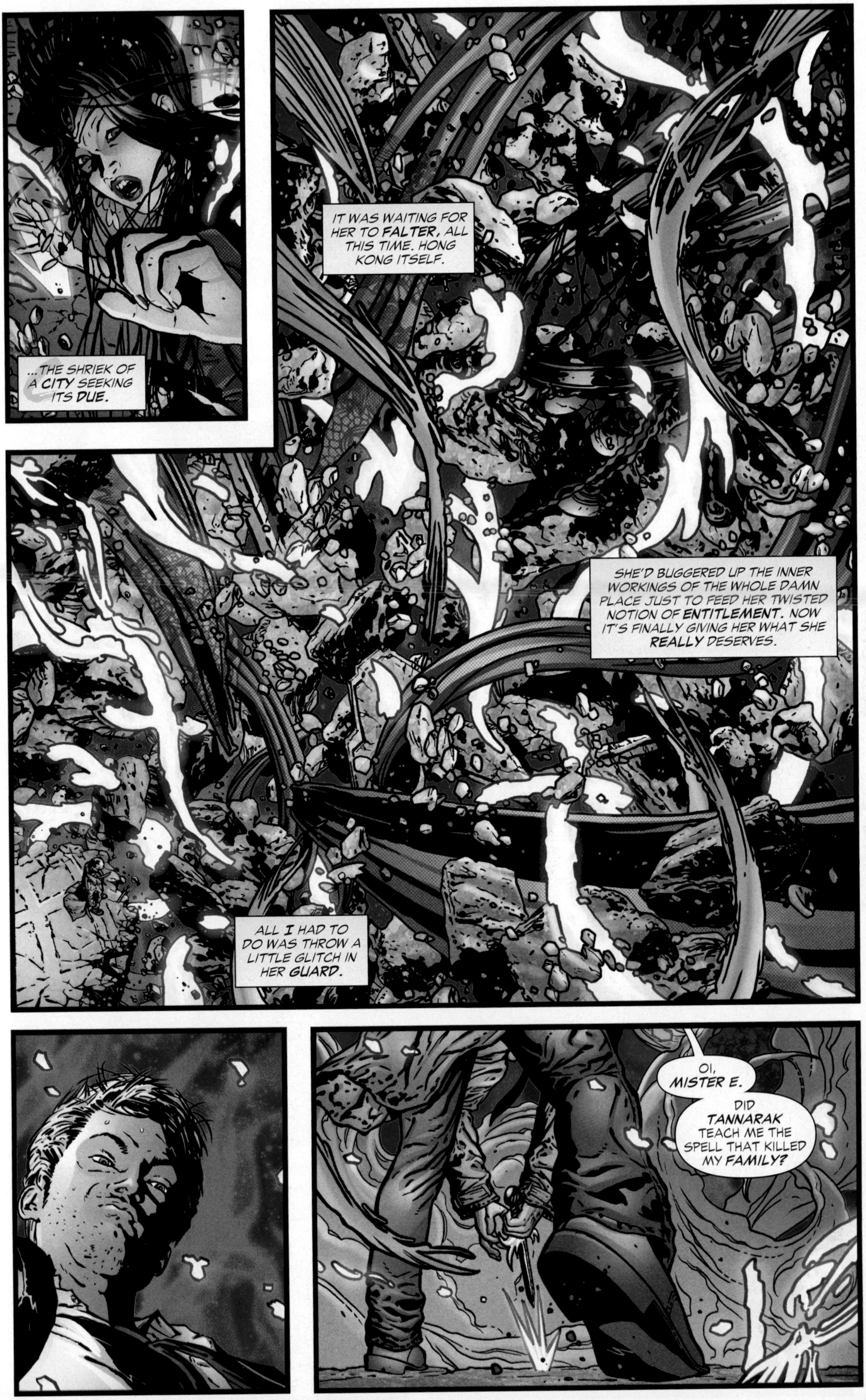
...THE SHRIEK OF A CITY SEEKING ITS DUE.
IT WAS WAITING FOR HER TO FALTER, ALL THIS TIME. HONG KONG ITSELF.
SHE'D BUGGERED UP THE INNER WORKINGS OF THE WHOLE DAMN PLACE JUST TO FEED HER TWISTED NOTION OF ENTITLEMENT. NOW IT'S FINALLY GIVING HER WHAT SHE REALLY DESERVES.
ALL I HAD TO DO WAS THROW A LITTLE GLITCH IN HER GUARD.
OI, MISTER E.
DID TANNARAK TEACH ME THE SPELL THAT KILLED MY FAMILY?

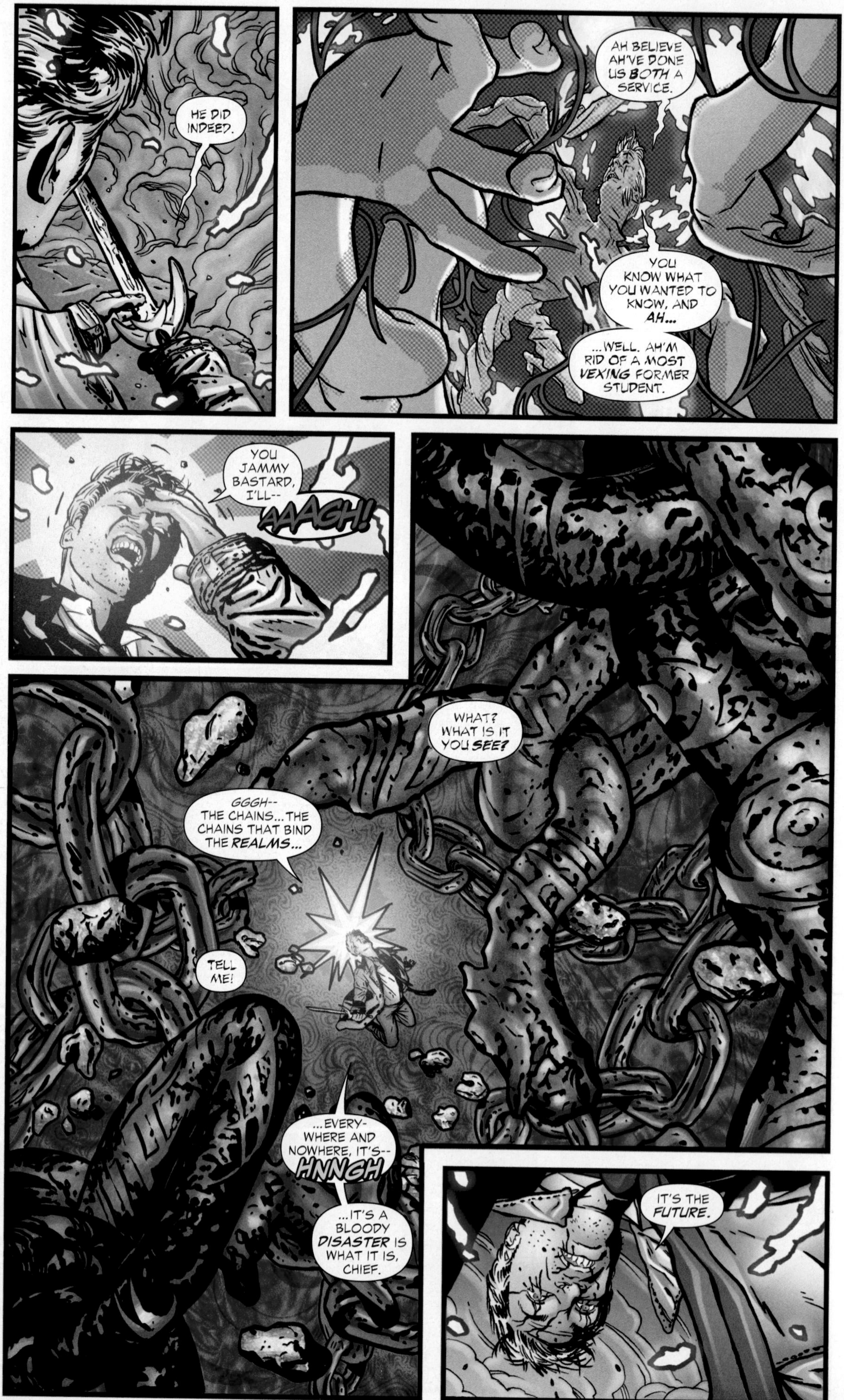
HE DID INDEED.
AH BELIEVE AH'VE DONE US BOTH A SERVICE.
YOU KNOW WHAT YOU WANTED TO KNOW, AND AH...
...WELL. AH'M RID OF A MOST VEXING FORMER STUDENT.
YOU JAMMY BASTARD, I'LL--
AAAGH!
WHAT? WHAT IS IT YOU SEE?
GGGH-- THE CHAINS... THE CHAINS THAT BIND THE REALMS...
TELL ME!
...EVERY-WHERE AND NOWHERE, IT'S--
HNNGH
...IT'S A BLOODY DISASTER IS WHAT IT IS, CHIEF.
IT'S THE FUTURE.

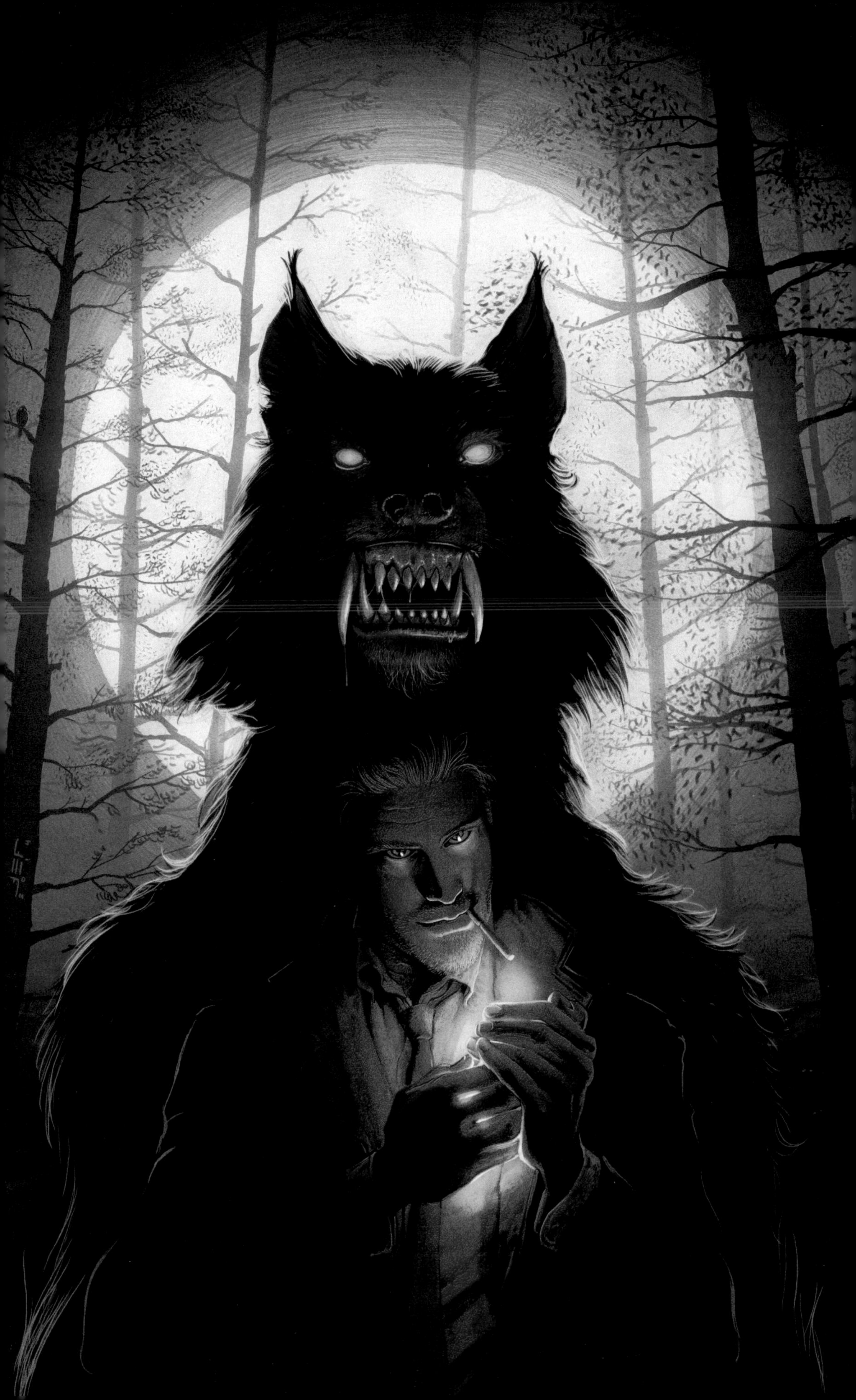

THE GESTALT

RAY FAWKES
writer

EDGAR SALAZAR
penciller

JAY LEISTEN
inker

TANYA and RICHARD HORIE
colorists

TAYLOR ESPOSITO
letterer

cover art by
JUAN FERREYRA

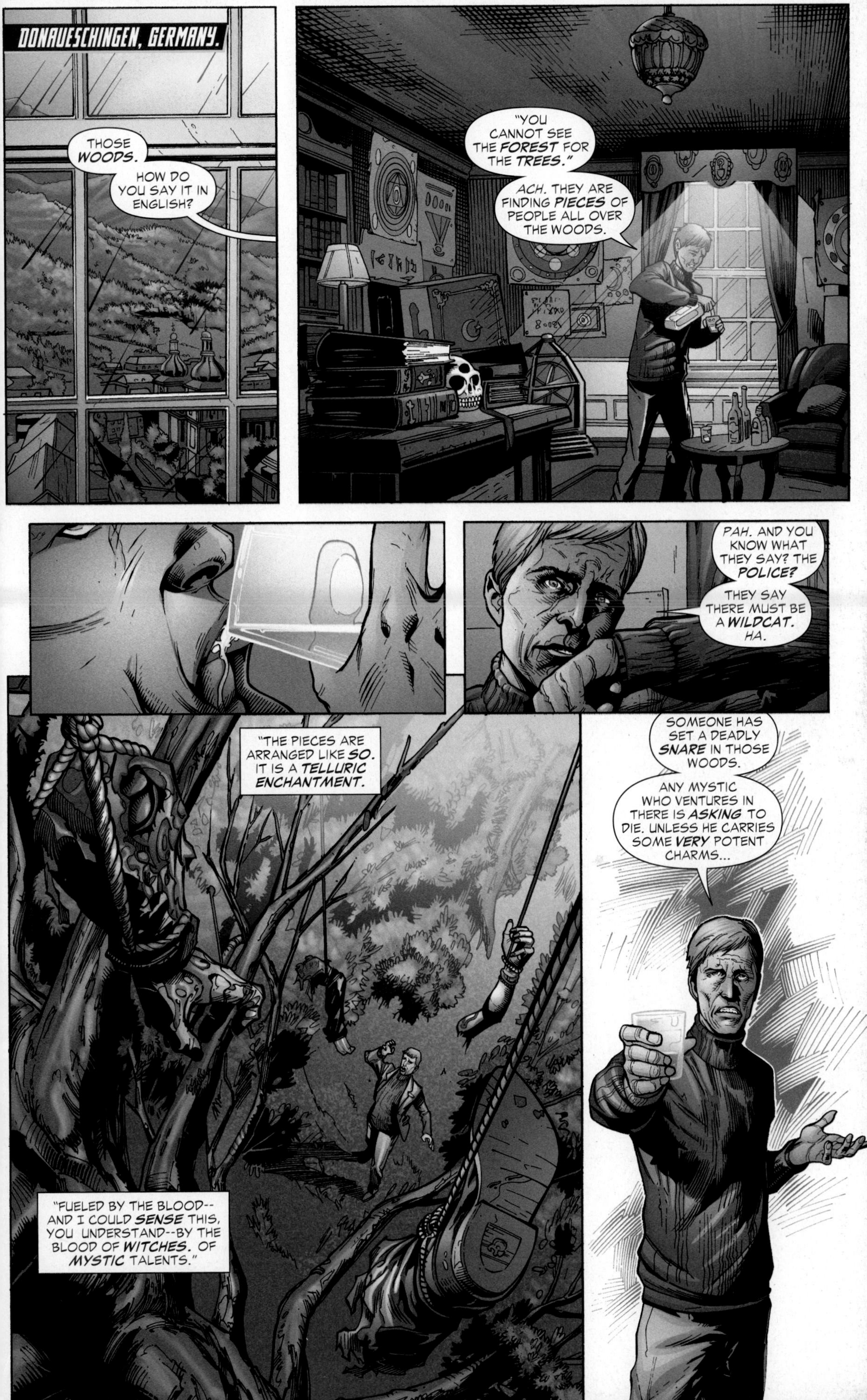
DONAUESCHINGEN, GERMANY.
THOSE WOODS.
HOW DO YOU SAY IT IN ENGLISH?
"YOU CANNOT SEE THE FOREST FOR THE TREES."
ACH. THEY ARE FINDING PIECES OF PEOPLE ALL OVER THE WOODS.
PAH. AND YOU KNOW WHAT THEY SAY? THE POLICE?
THEY SAY THERE MUST BE A WILDCAT. HA.
"THE PIECES ARE ARRANGED LIKE SO. IT IS A TELLURIC ENCHANTMENT.
"FUELED BY THE BLOOD-- AND I COULD SENSE THIS, YOU UNDERSTAND--BY THE BLOOD OF WITCHES. OF MYSTIC TALENTS."
SOMEONE HAS SET A DEADLY SNARE IN THOSE WOODS.
ANY MYSTIC WHO VENTURES IN THERE IS ASKING TO DIE. UNLESS HE CARRIES SOME VERY POTENT CHARMS...

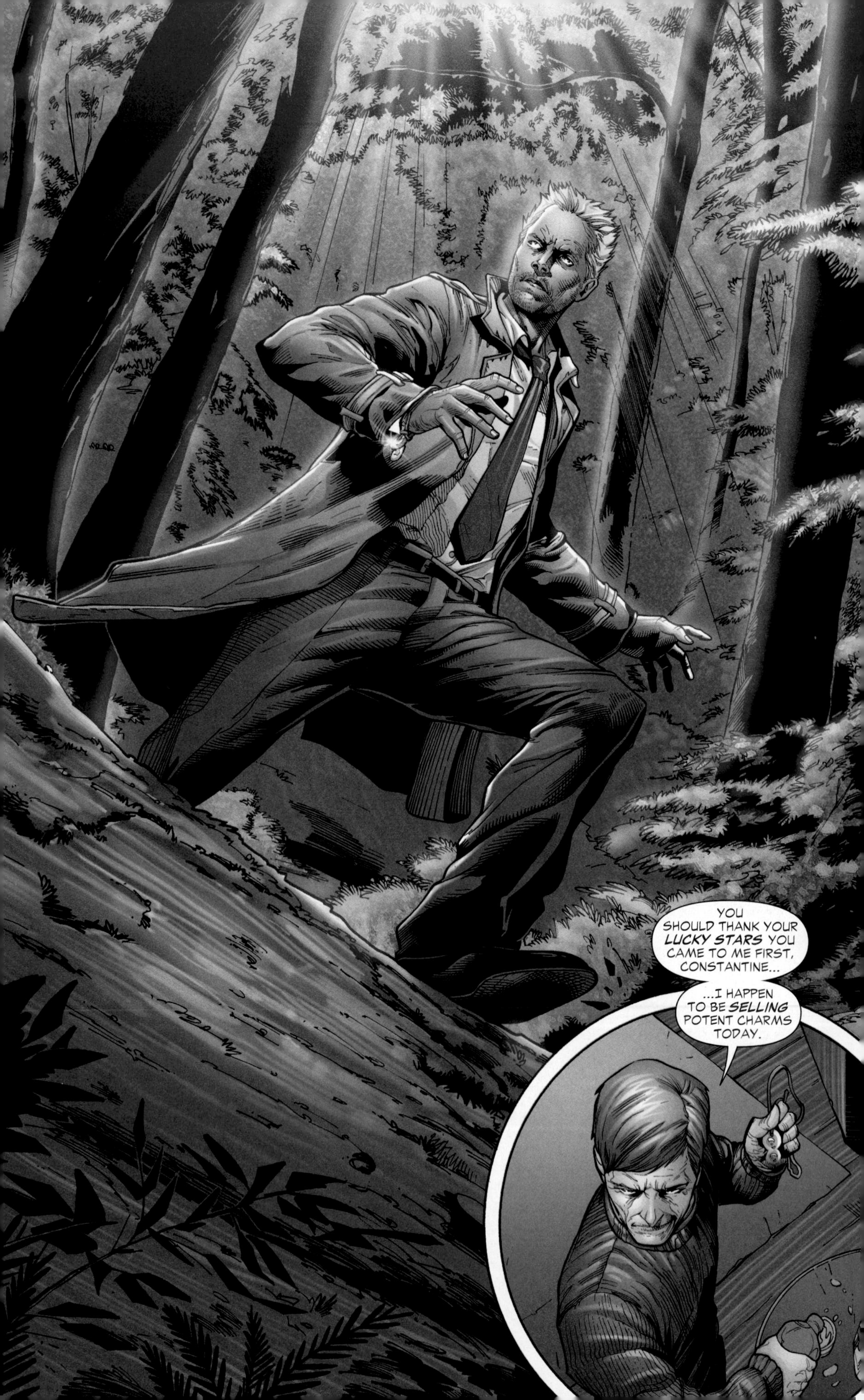
YOU SHOULD THANK YOUR LUCKY STARS YOU CAME TO ME FIRST, CONSTANTINE...
...I HAPPEN TO BE SELLING POTENT CHARMS TODAY.

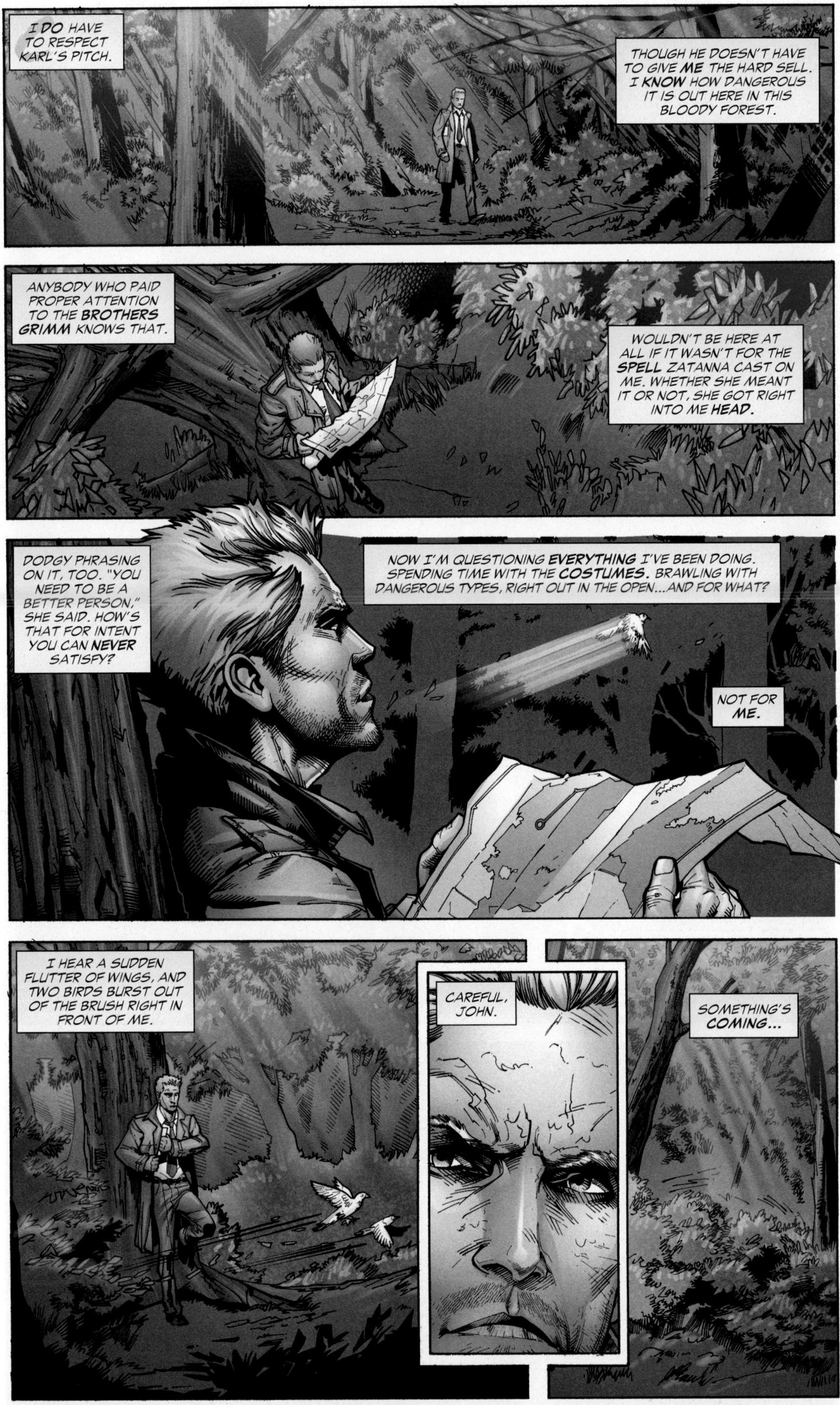
I DO HAVE TO RESPECT KARL'S PITCH.
THOUGH HE DOESN'T HAVE TO GIVE ME THE HARD SELL. I KNOW HOW DANGEROUS IT IS OUT HERE IN THIS BLOODY FOREST.
ANYBODY WHO PAID PROPER ATTENTION TO THE BROTHERS GRIMM KNOWS THAT.
WOULDN'T BE HERE AT ALL IF IT WASN'T FOR THE SPELL ZATANNA CAST ON ME. WHETHER SHE MEANT IT OR NOT, SHE GOT RIGHT INTO ME HEAD.
DODGY PHRASING ON IT, TOO. "YOU NEED TO BE A BETTER PERSON," SHE SAID. HOW'S THAT FOR INTENT YOU CAN NEVER SATISFY?
NOW I'M QUESTIONING EVERYTHING I'VE BEEN DOING. SPENDING TIME WITH THE COSTUMES. BRAWLING WITH DANGEROUS TYPES, RIGHT OUT IN THE OPEN...AND FOR WHAT?
NOT FOR ME.
I HEAR A SUDDEN FLUTTER OF WINGS, AND TWO BIRDS BURST OUT OF THE BRUSH RIGHT IN FRONT OF ME.
CAREFUL, JOHN.
SOMETHING'S COMING...

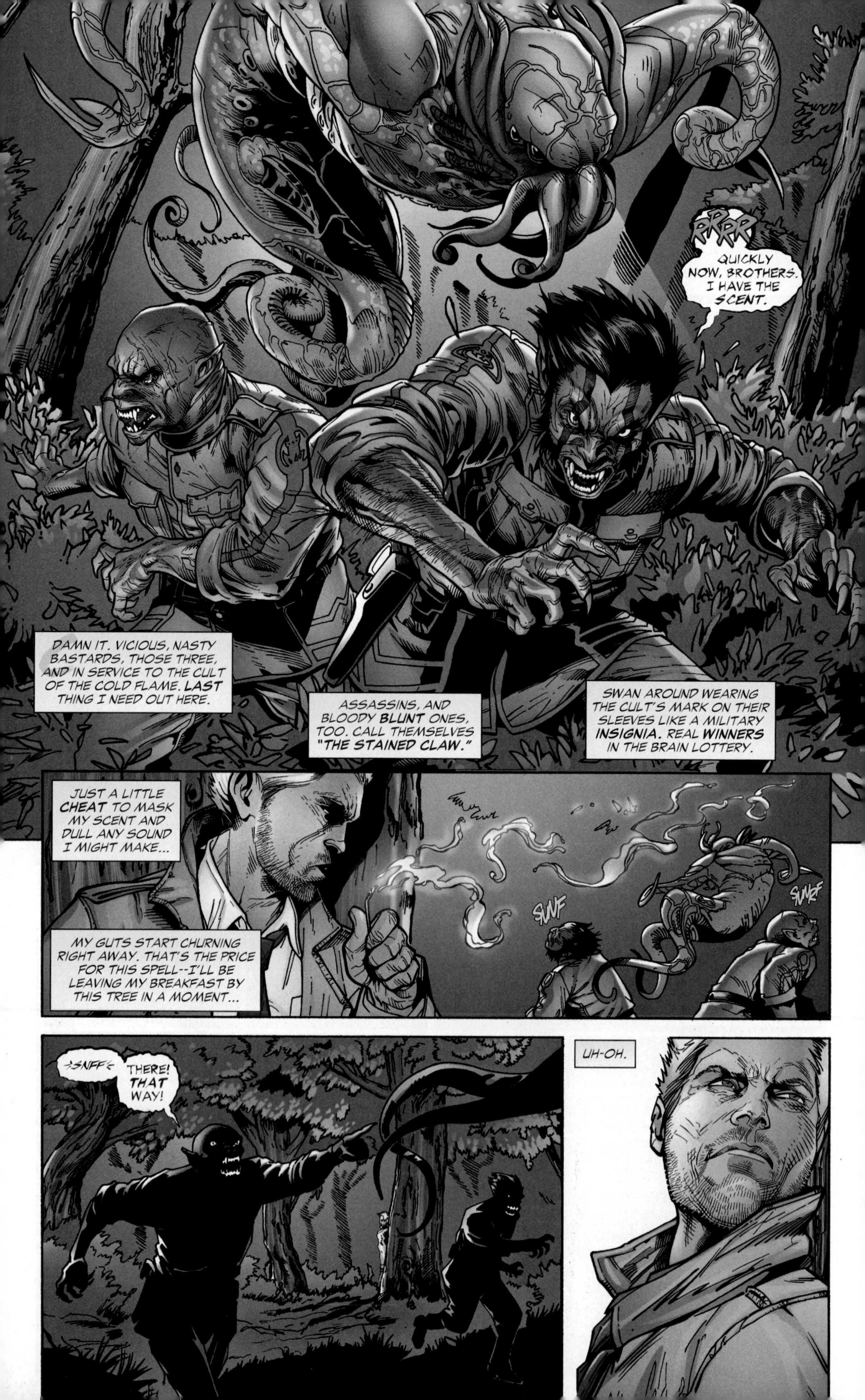
RRRR
QUICKLY NOW, BROTHERS. I HAVE THE SCENT.
DAMN IT. VICIOUS, NASTY BASTARDS, THOSE THREE, AND IN SERVICE TO THE CULT OF THE COLD FLAME. LAST THING I NEED OUT HERE.
ASSASSINS, AND BLOODY BLUNT ONES, TOO. CALL THEMSELVES "THE STAINED CLAW."
SWAN AROUND WEARING THE CULT'S MARK ON THEIR SLEEVES LIKE A MILITARY INSIGNIA. REAL WINNERS IN THE BRAIN LOTTERY.
JUST A LITTLE CHEAT TO MASK MY SCENT AND DULL ANY SOUND I MIGHT MAKE...
MY GUTS START CHURNING RIGHT AWAY. THAT'S THE PRICE FOR THIS SPELL--I'LL BE LEAVING MY BREAKFAST BY THIS TREE IN A MOMENT...
SNIF
SNARF
SNFF
THERE! THAT WAY!
UH-OH.

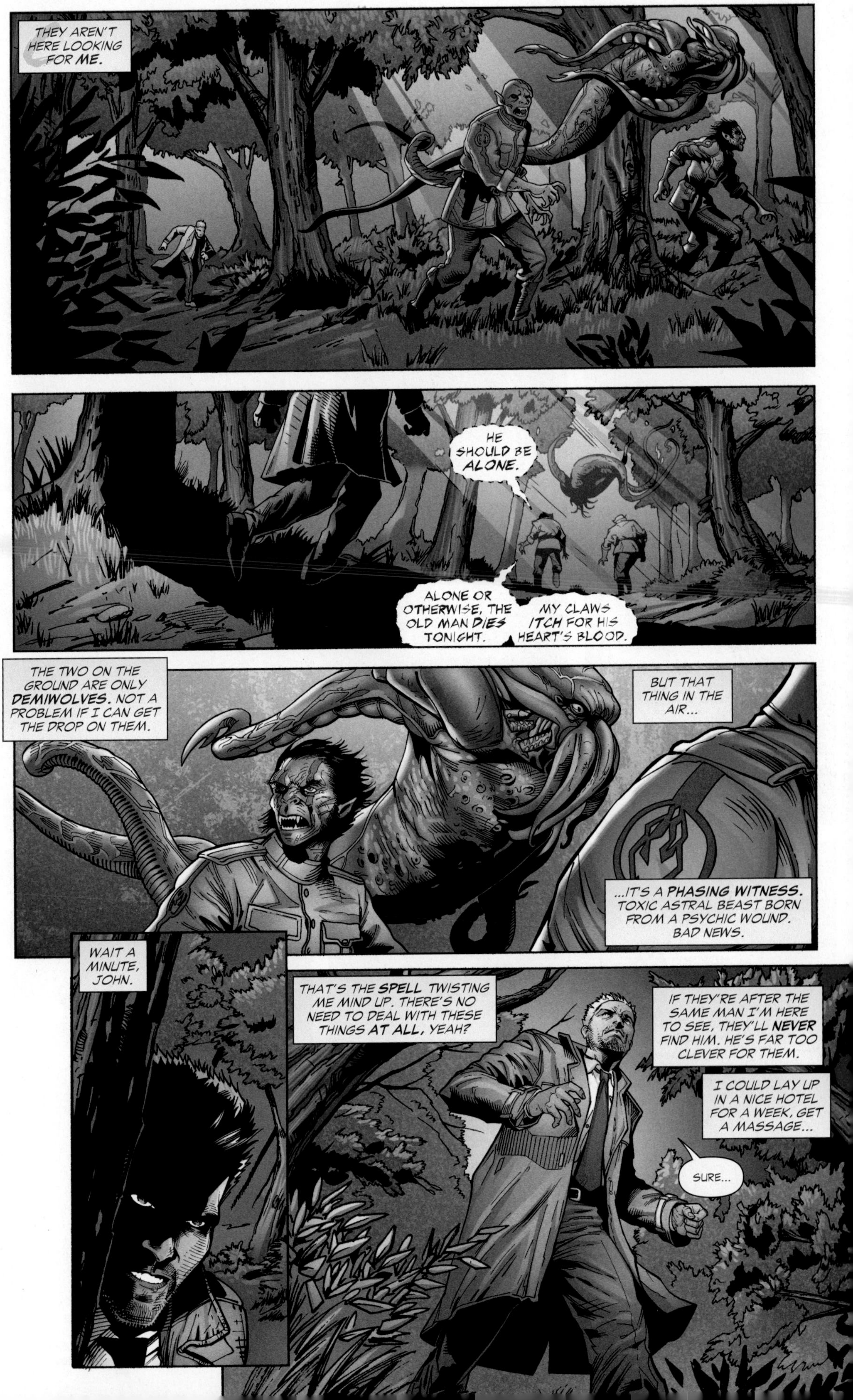

THEY AREN'T HERE LOOKING FOR ME.
HE SHOULD BE ALONE.
ALONE OR OTHERWISE, THE OLD MAN DIES TONIGHT.
MY CLAWS ITCH FOR HIS HEART'S BLOOD.
THE TWO ON THE GROUND ARE ONLY DEMIWOLVES. NOT A PROBLEM IF I CAN GET THE DROP ON THEM.
BUT THAT THING IN THE AIR...
...IT'S A PHASING WITNESS. TOXIC ASTRAL BEAST BORN FROM A PSYCHIC WOUND. BAD NEWS.
WAIT A MINUTE, JOHN.
THAT'S THE SPELL TWISTING ME MIND UP. THERE'S NO NEED TO DEAL WITH THESE THINGS AT ALL, YEAH?
IF THEY'RE AFTER THE SAME MAN I'M HERE TO SEE, THEY'LL NEVER FIND HIM. HE'S FAR TOO CLEVER FOR THEM.
I COULD LAY UP IN A NICE HOTEL FOR A WEEK, GET A MASSAGE...
SURE...

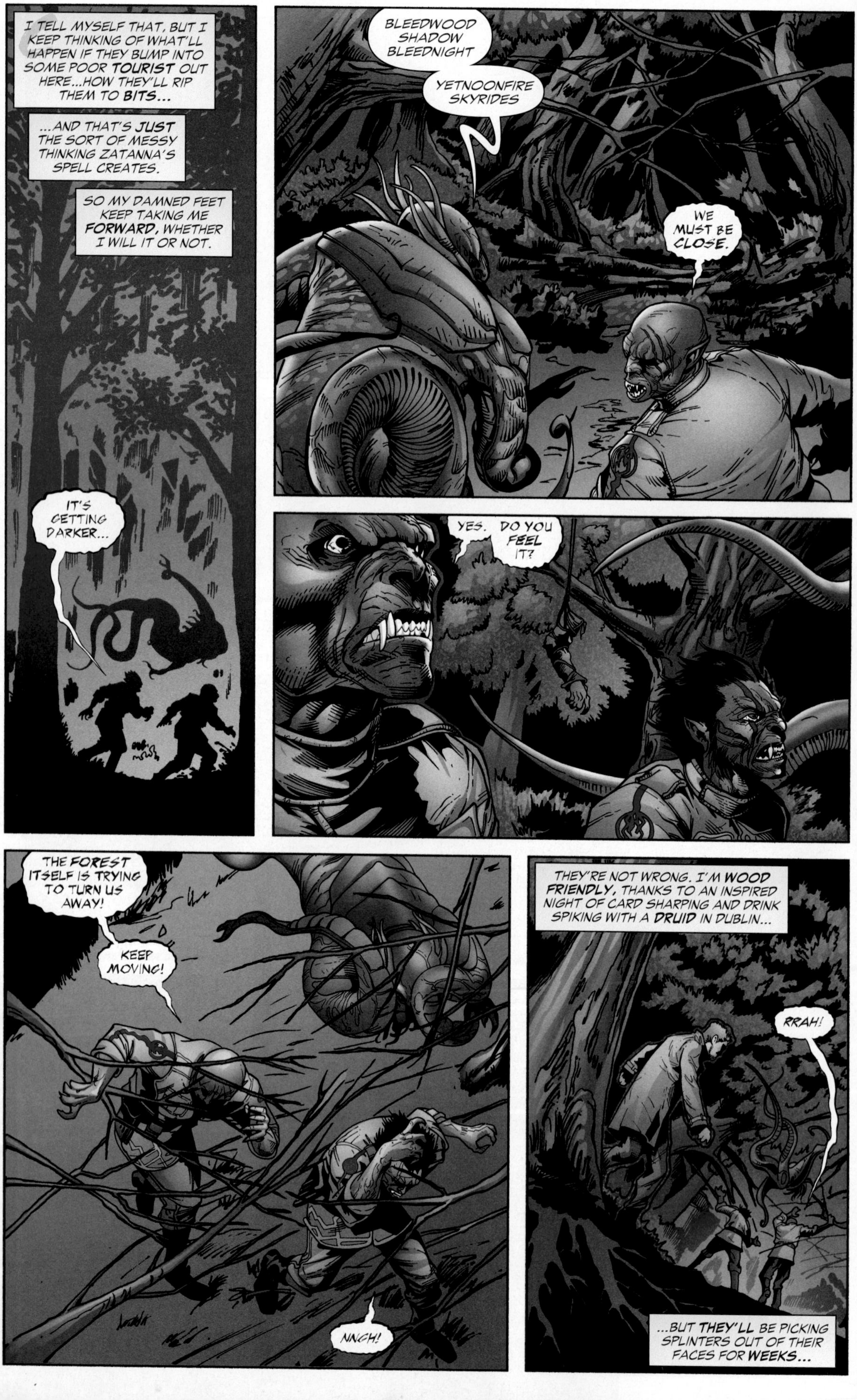
I TELL MYSELF THAT, BUT I KEEP THINKING OF WHAT'LL HAPPEN IF THEY BUMP INTO SOME POOR TOURIST OUT HERE...HOW THEY'LL RIP THEM TO BITS...
...AND THAT'S JUST THE SORT OF MESSY THINKING ZATANNA'S SPELL CREATES.
SO MY DAMNED FEET KEEP TAKING ME FORWARD, WHETHER I WILL IT OR NOT.
IT'S GETTING DARKER...
BLEEDWOOD SHADOW BLEEDNIGHT
YETNOONFIRE SKYRIDES
WE MUST BE CLOSE.
YES. DO YOU FEEL IT?
THE FOREST ITSELF IS TRYING TO TURN US AWAY!
KEEP MOVING!
NNGH!
THEY'RE NOT WRONG. I'M WOOD FRIENDLY, THANKS TO AN INSPIRED NIGHT OF CARD SHARPING AND DRINK SPIKING WITH A DRUID IN DUBLIN...
RRAH!
...BUT THEY'LL BE PICKING SPLINTERS OUT OF THEIR FACES FOR WEEKS...

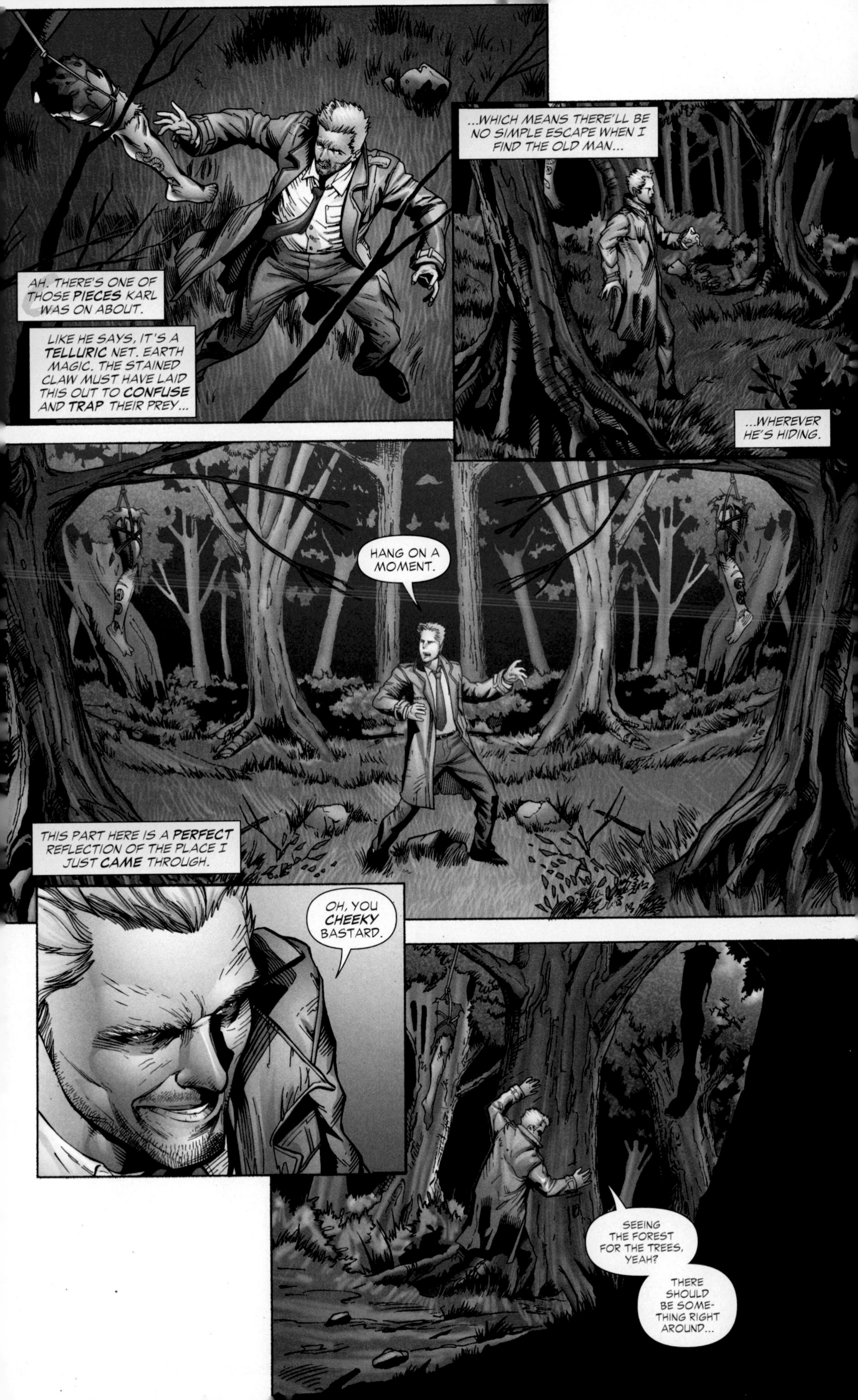
AH. THERE'S ONE OF THOSE PIECES KARL WAS ON ABOUT.
LIKE HE SAYS, IT'S A TELLURIC NET. EARTH MAGIC. THE STAINED CLAW MUST HAVE LAID THIS OUT TO CONFUSE AND TRAP THEIR PREY...
...WHICH MEANS THERE'LL BE NO SIMPLE ESCAPE WHEN I FIND THE OLD MAN...
...WHEREVER HE'S HIDING.
HANG ON A MOMENT.
THIS PART HERE IS A PERFECT REFLECTION OF THE PLACE I JUST CAME THROUGH.
OH, YOU CHEEKY BASTARD.
SEEING THE FOREST FOR THE TREES, YEAH?
THERE SHOULD BE SOME-THING RIGHT AROUND...

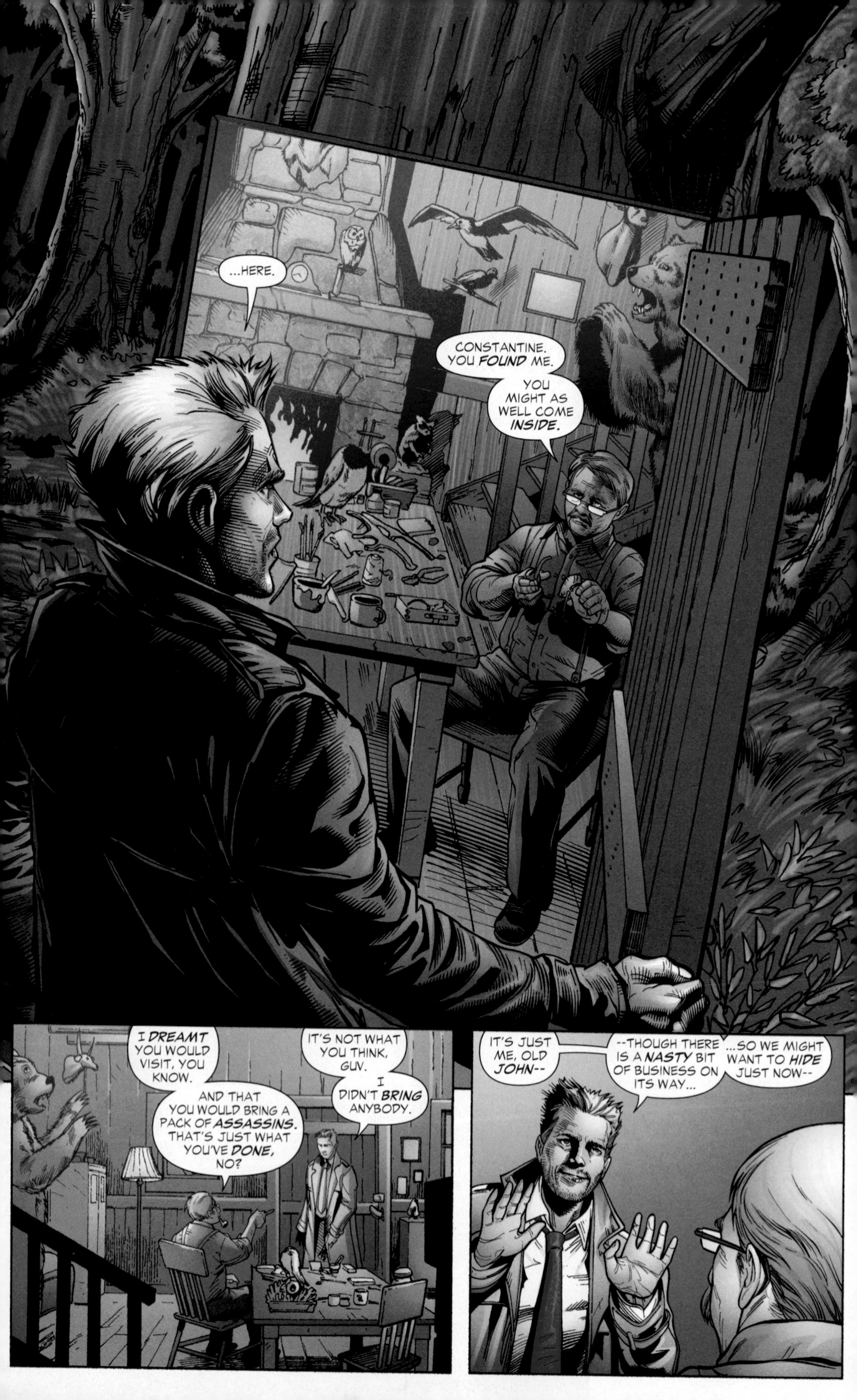
...HERE.
CONSTANTINE. YOU FOUND ME.
YOU MIGHT AS WELL COME INSIDE.
I DREAMT YOU WOULD VISIT, YOU KNOW.
AND THAT YOU WOULD BRING A PACK OF ASSASSINS. THAT'S JUST WHAT YOU'VE DONE, NO?
IT'S NOT WHAT YOU THINK, GUV.
I DIDN'T BRING ANYBODY.
IT'S JUST ME, OLD JOHN--
--THOUGH THERE IS A NASTY BIT OF BUSINESS ON ITS WAY...
...SO WE MIGHT WANT TO HIDE JUST NOW--

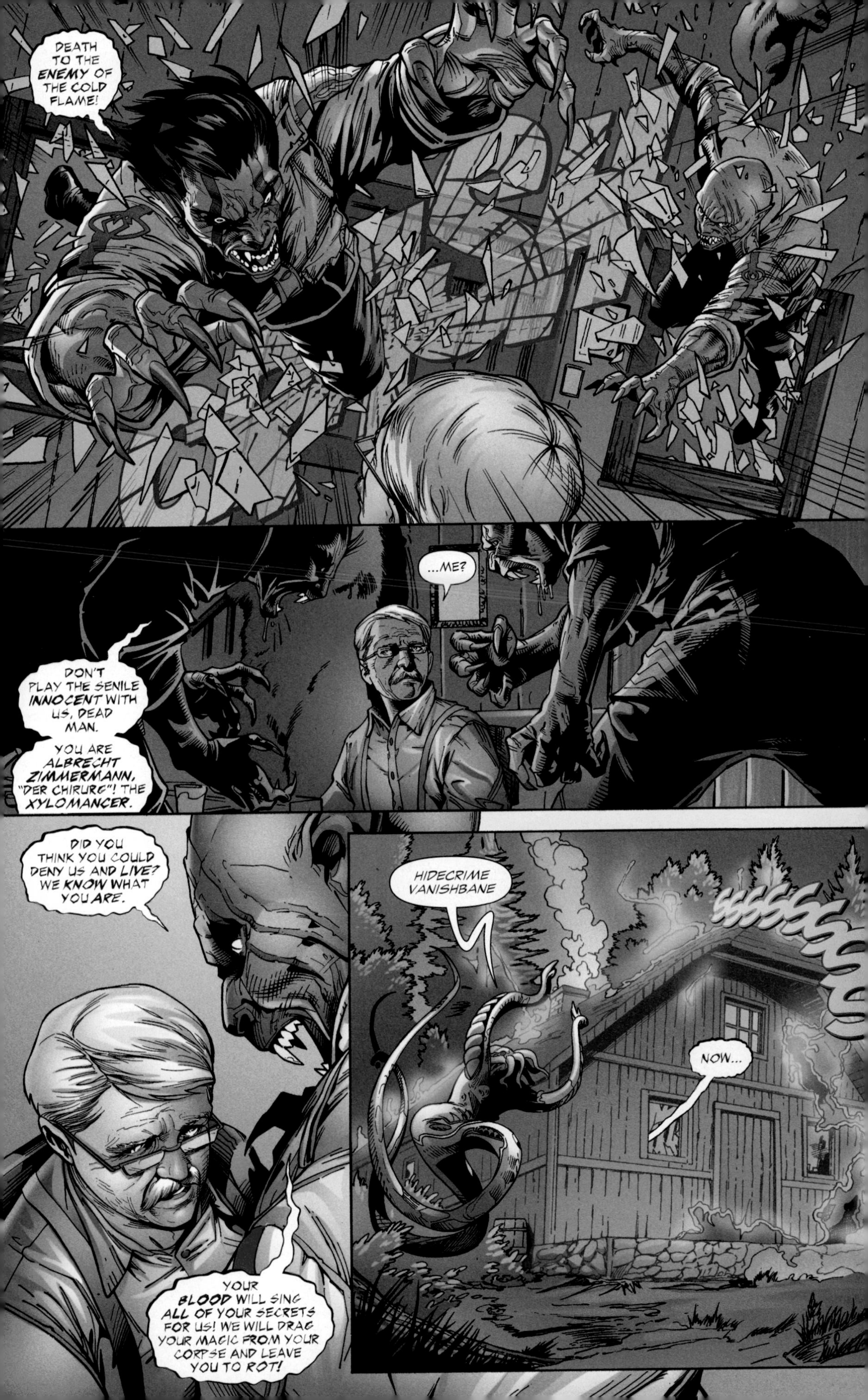
DEATH TO THE ENEMY OF THE COLD FLAME!
...ME?
DON'T PLAY THE SENILE INNOCENT WITH US, DEAD MAN.
YOU ARE ALBRECHT ZIMMERMANN, "DER CHIRURG"! THE XYLOMANCER.
DID YOU THINK YOU COULD DENY US AND LIVE? WE KNOW WHAT YOU ARE.
YOUR BLOOD WILL SING ALL OF YOUR SECRETS FOR US! WE WILL DRAG YOUR MAGIC FROM YOUR CORPSE AND LEAVE YOU TO ROT!
HIDECRIME VANISHBANE
NOW...

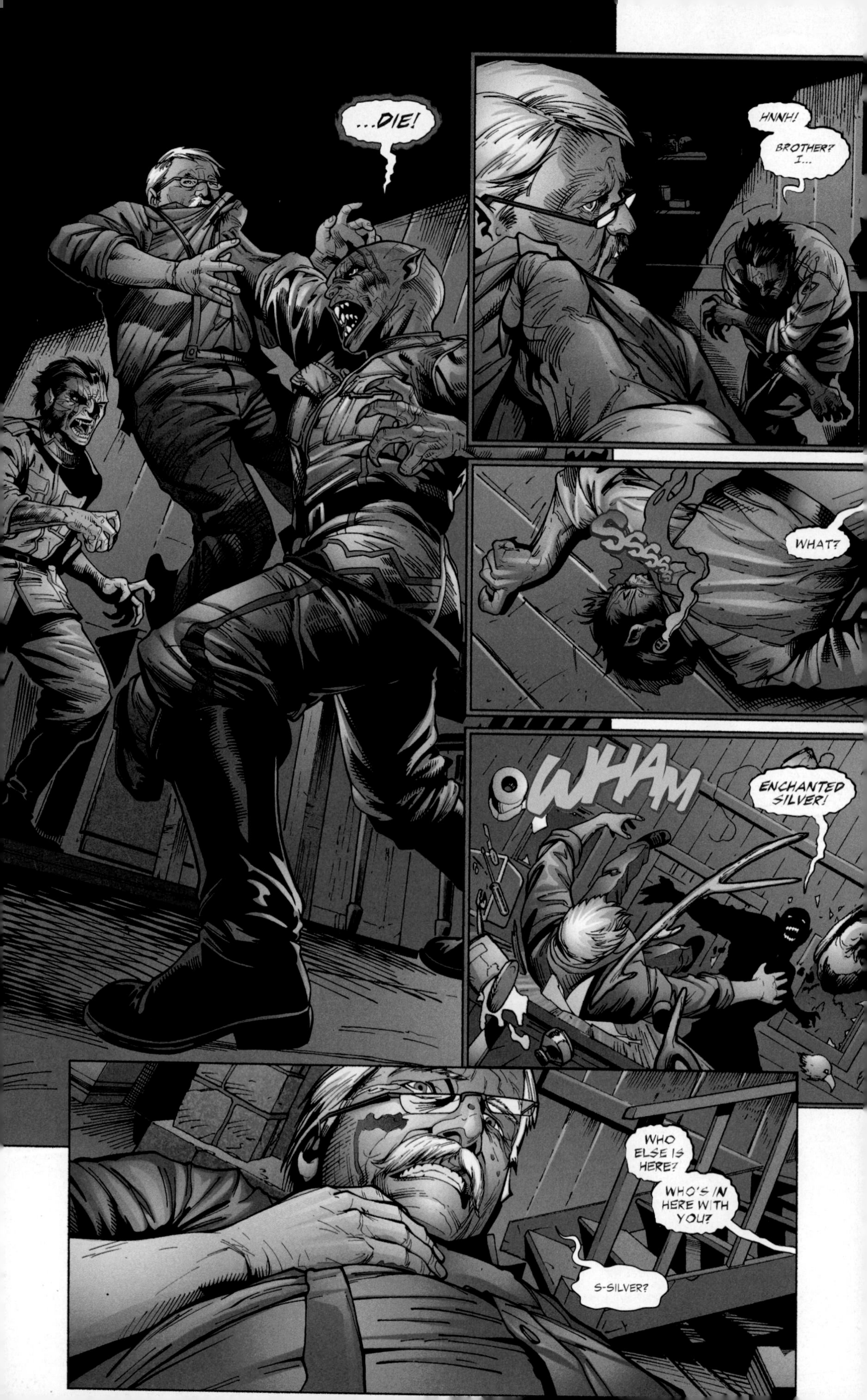
...DIE!
HNNH!
BROTHER? I...
WHAT?
WHAM
ENCHANTED SILVER!
WHO ELSE IS HERE?
WHO'S IN HERE WITH YOU?
S-SILVER?

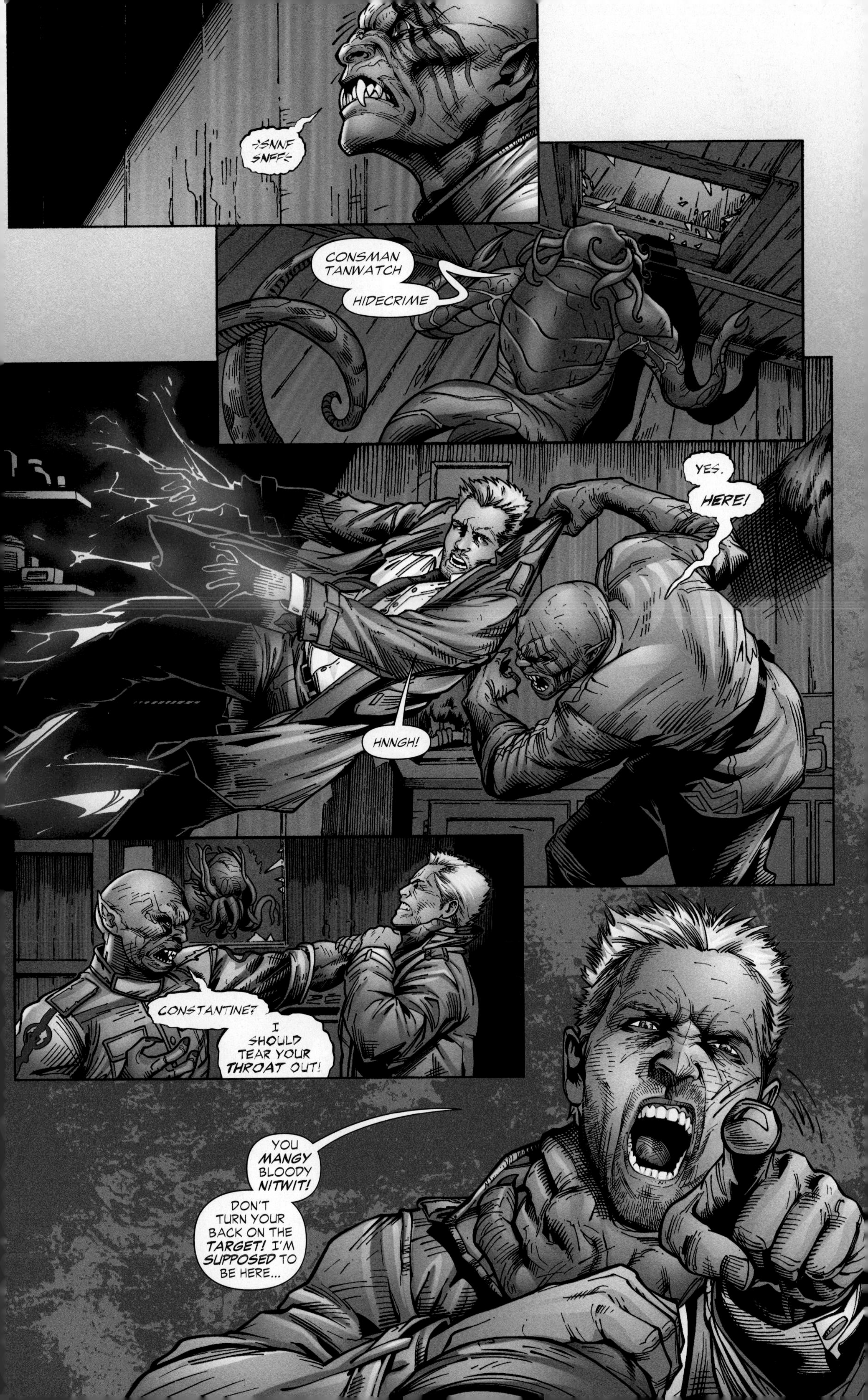

SNNF SNFF
CONSMAN TANWATCH
HIDECRIME
YES.
HERE!
HNNGH!
CONSTANTINE?
I SHOULD TEAR YOUR THROAT OUT!
YOU MANGY BLOODY NITWIT!
DON'T TURN YOUR BACK ON THE TARGET! I'M SUPPOSED TO BE HERE...

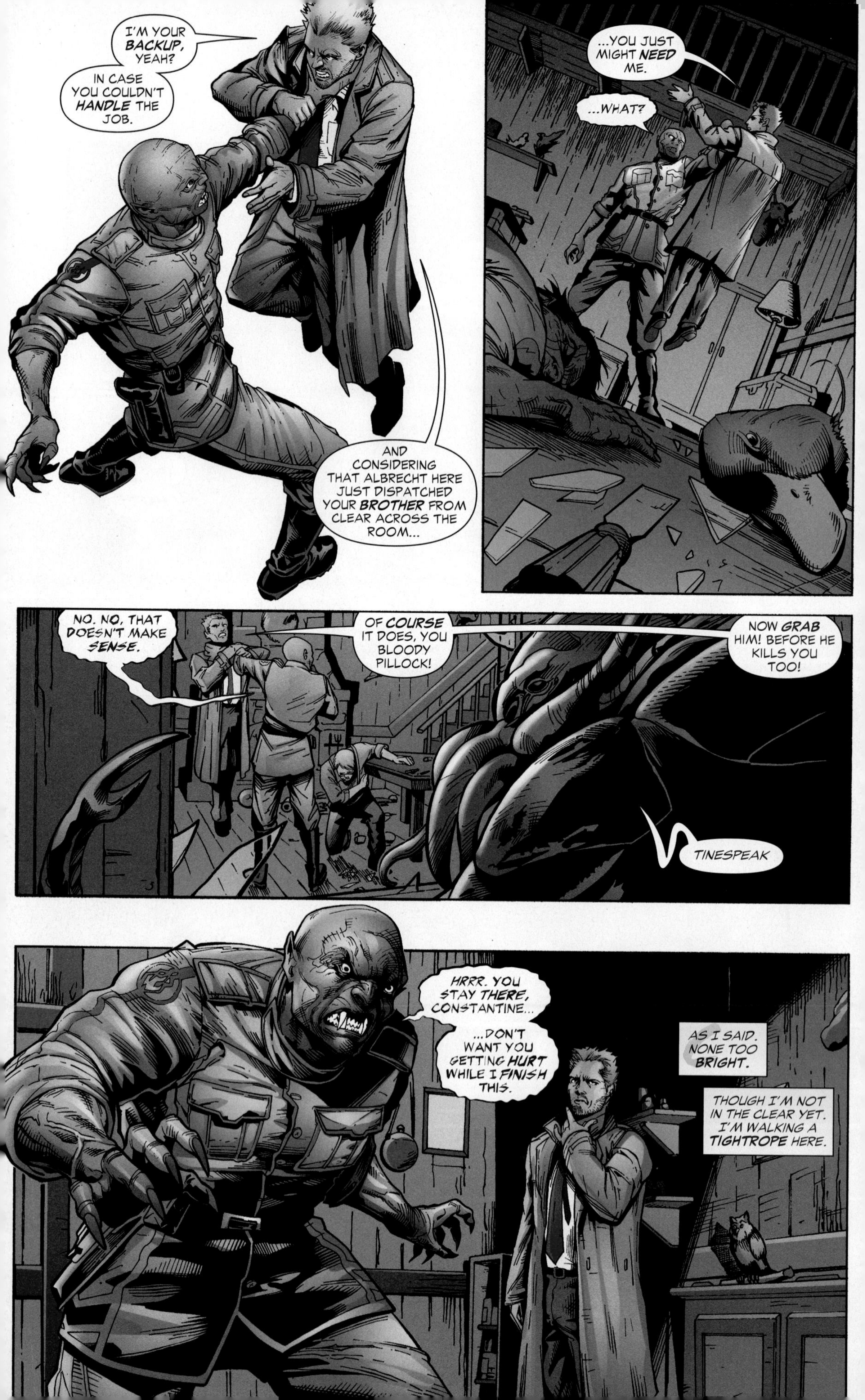
I'M YOUR BACKUP, YEAH?
IN CASE YOU COULDN'T HANDLE THE JOB.
AND CONSIDERING THAT ALBRECHT HERE JUST DISPATCHED YOUR BROTHER FROM CLEAR ACROSS THE ROOM...
...YOU JUST MIGHT NEED ME.
...WHAT?
NO. NO, THAT DOESN'T MAKE SENSE.
OF COURSE IT DOES, YOU BLOODY PILLOCK!
NOW GRAB HIM! BEFORE HE KILLS YOU TOO!
TINESPEAK
HRRR. YOU STAY THERE, CONSTANTINE...
...DON'T WANT YOU GETTING HURT WHILE I FINISH THIS.
AS I SAID. NONE TOO BRIGHT.
THOUGH I'M NOT IN THE CLEAR YET. I'M WALKING A TIGHTROPE HERE.

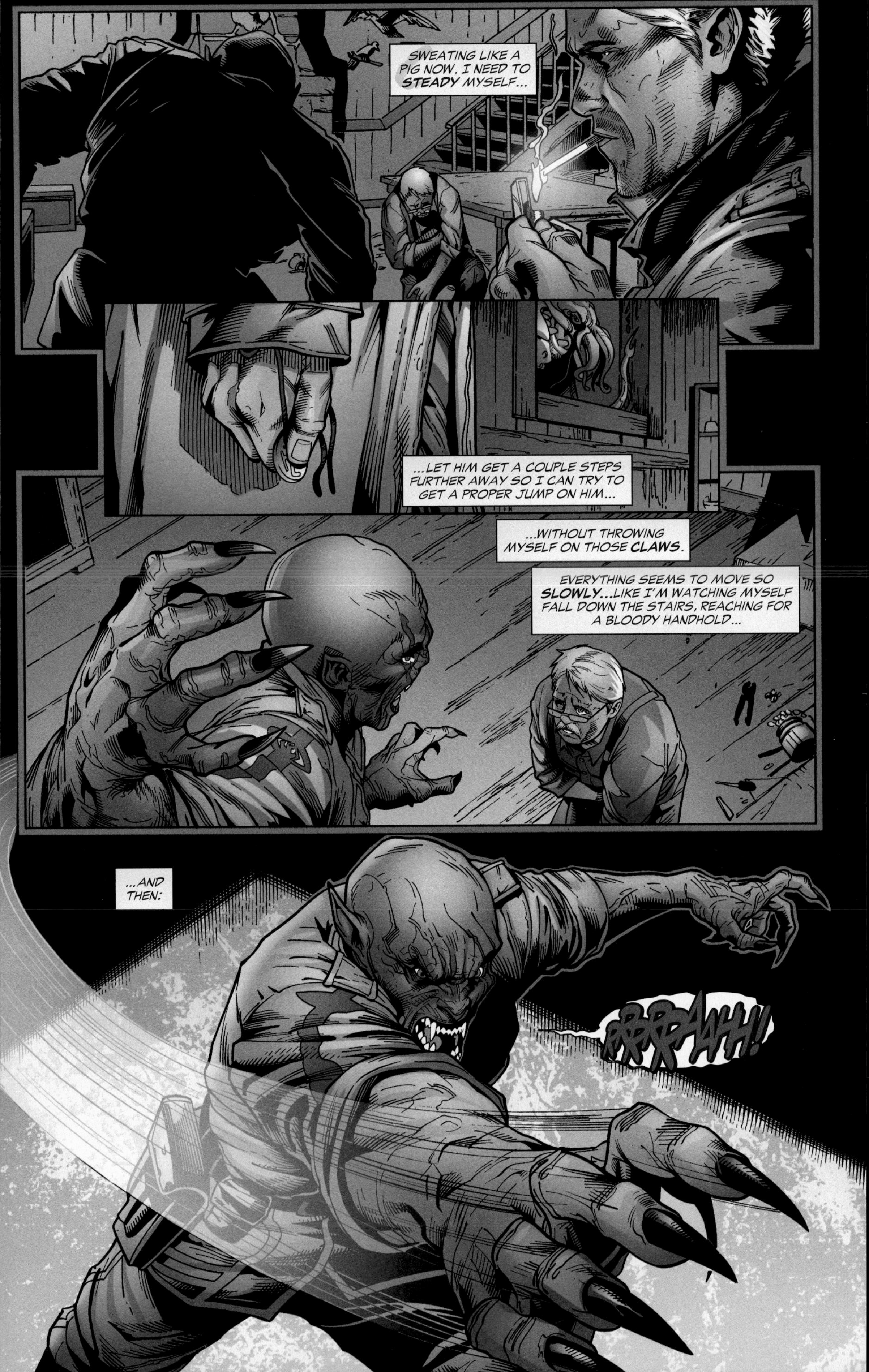

SWEATING LIKE A PIG NOW. I NEED TO STEADY MYSELF...
...LET HIM GET A COUPLE STEPS FURTHER AWAY SO I CAN TRY TO GET A PROPER JUMP ON HIM...
...WITHOUT THROWING MYSELF ON THOSE CLAWS.
EVERYTHING SEEMS TO MOVE SO SLOWLY...LIKE I'M WATCHING MYSELF FALL DOWN THE STAIRS, REACHING FOR A BLOODY HANDHOLD...
...AND THEN:
RRRRAAHH!

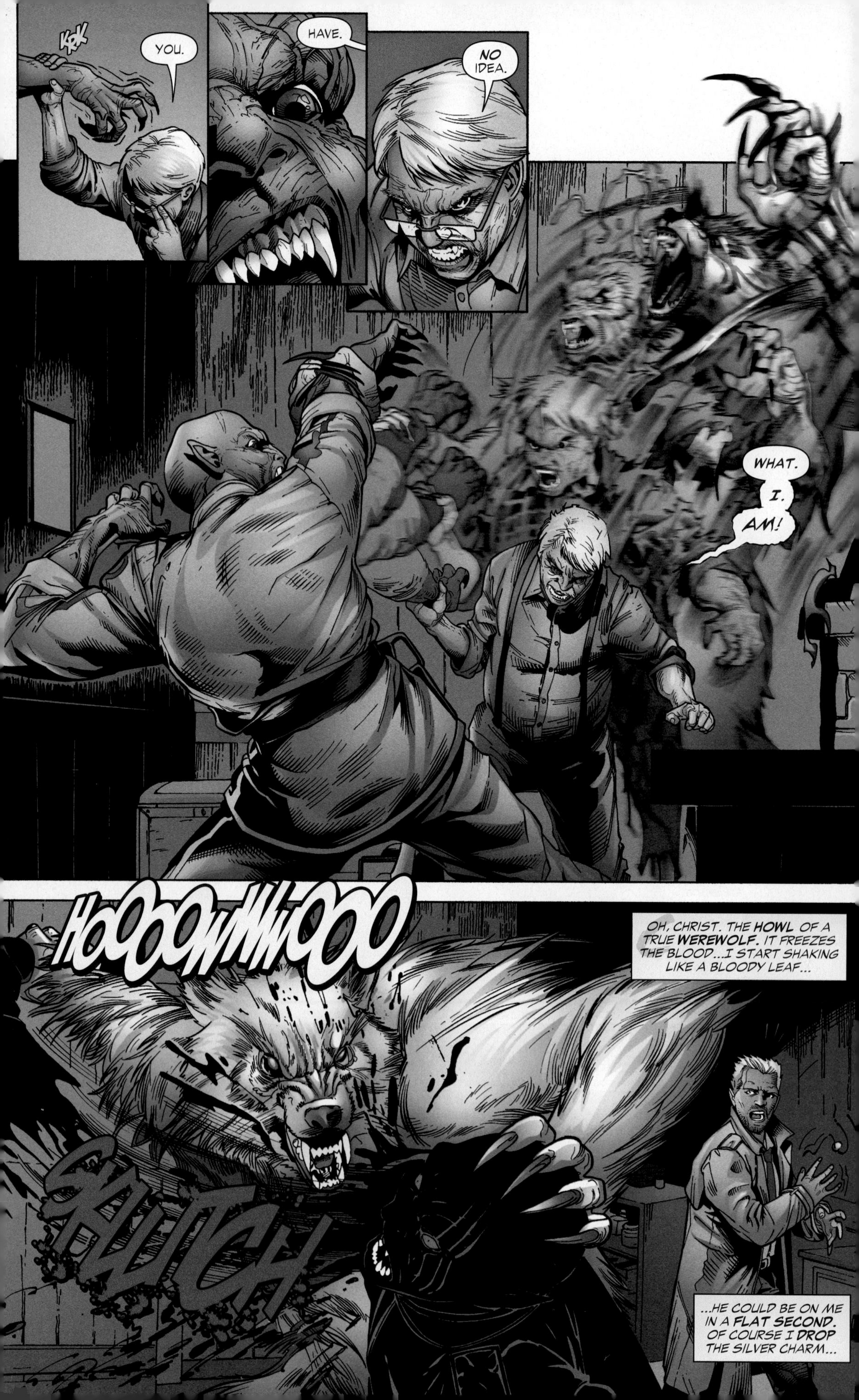
KRK
YOU.
HAVE.
NO IDEA.
WHAT. I. AM!
HOOOOOWWWOOO
OH, CHRIST. THE HOWL OF A TRUE WEREWOLF. IT FREEZES THE BLOOD...I START SHAKING LIKE A BLOODY LEAF...
SHLUTCH
...HE COULD BE ON ME IN A FLAT SECOND. OF COURSE I DROP THE SILVER CHARM...

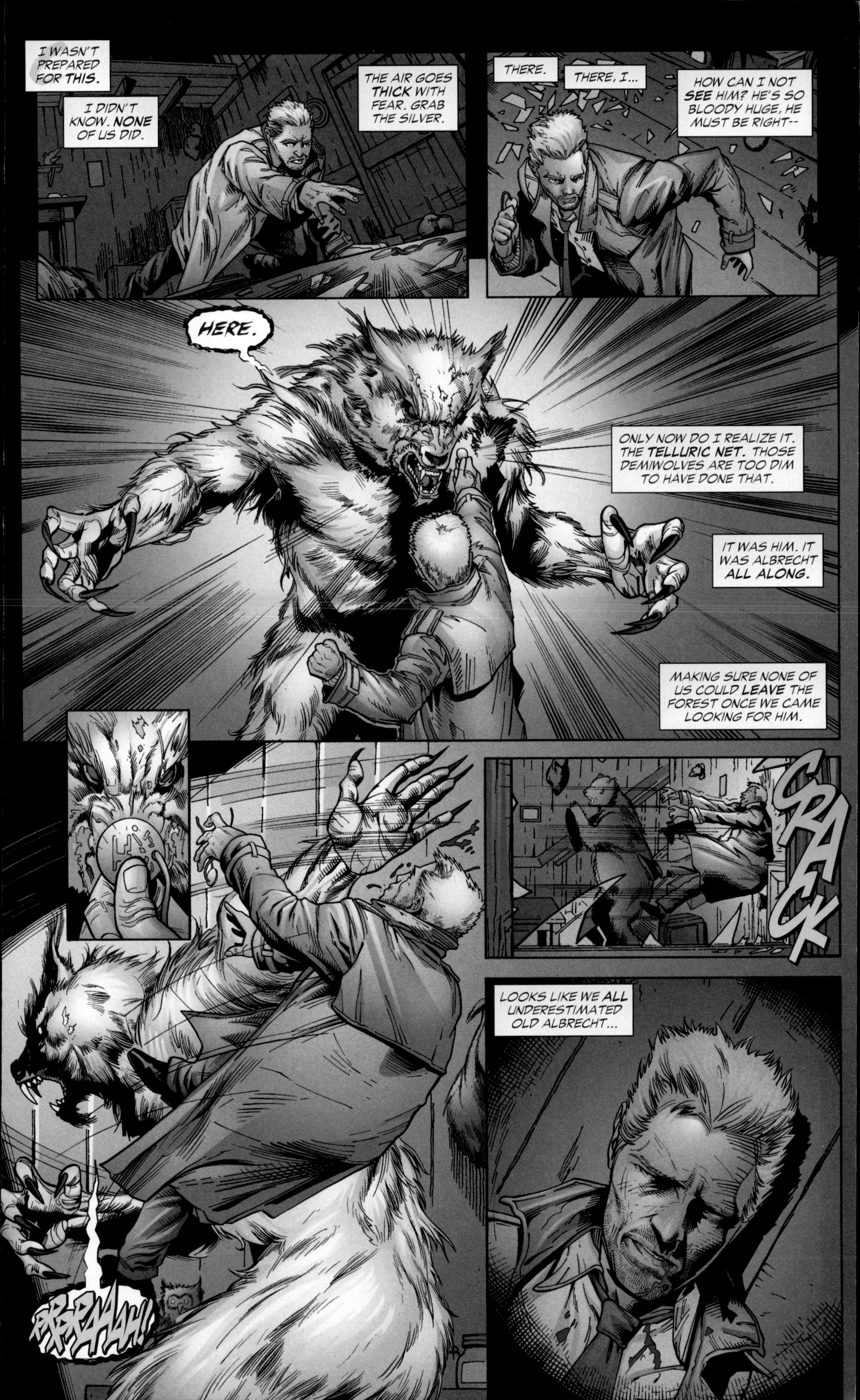
I WASN'T PREPARED FOR THIS.
I DIDN'T KNOW. NONE OF US DID.
THE AIR GOES THICK WITH FEAR. GRAB THE SILVER.
THERE.
THERE, I...
HOW CAN I NOT SEE HIM? HE'S SO BLOODY HUGE, HE MUST BE RIGHT--
HERE.
ONLY NOW DO I REALIZE IT. THE TELLURIC NET. THOSE DEMIWOLVES ARE TOO DIM TO HAVE DONE THAT.
IT WAS HIM. IT WAS ALBRECHT ALL ALONG.
MAKING SURE NONE OF US COULD LEAVE THE FOREST ONCE WE CAME LOOKING FOR HIM.
CRACK
LOOKS LIKE WE ALL UNDERESTIMATED OLD ALBRECHT...

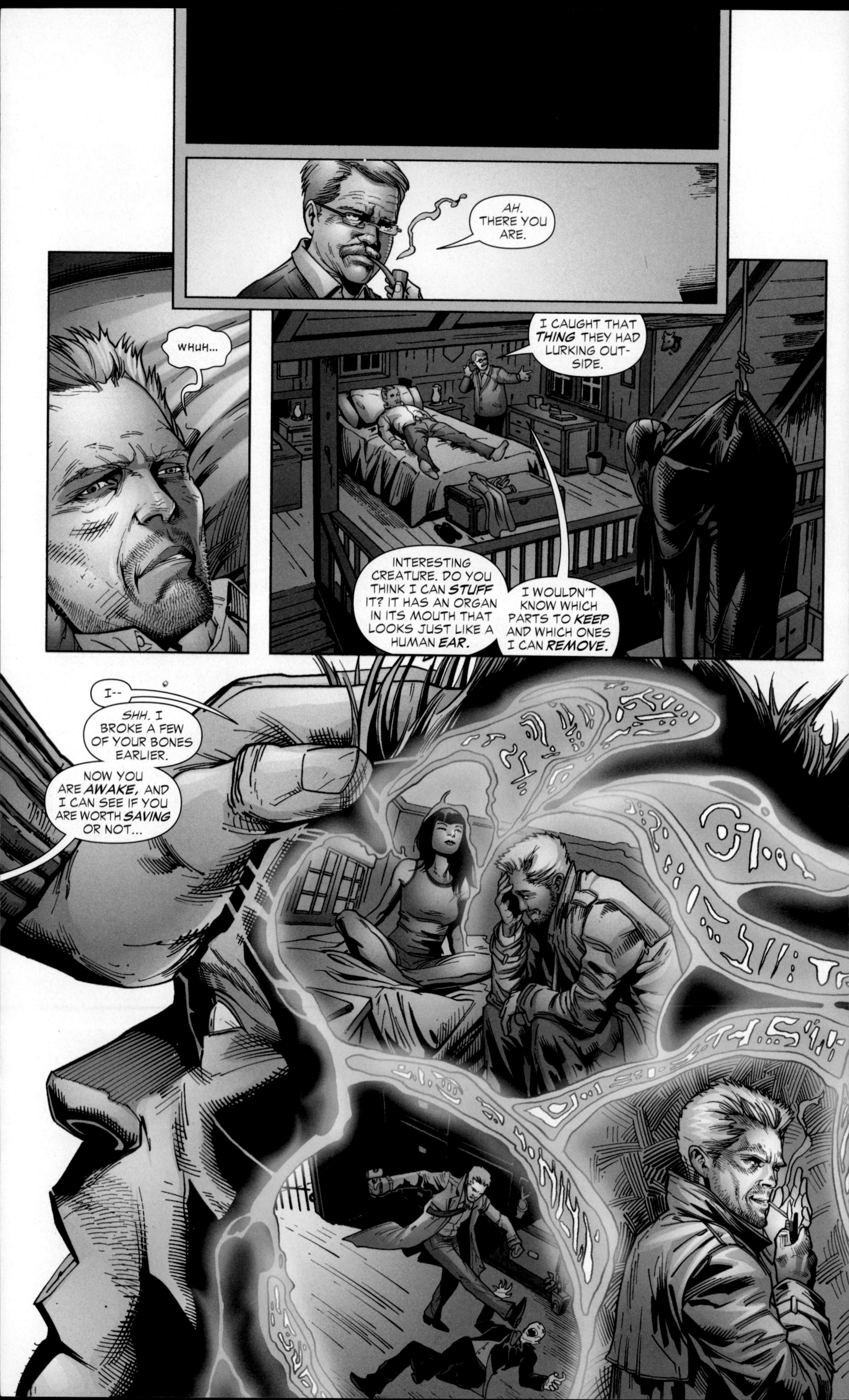
AH. THERE YOU ARE.
WHUH...
I CAUGHT THAT THING THEY HAD LURKING OUT-SIDE.
INTERESTING CREATURE. DO YOU THINK I CAN STUFF IT? IT HAS AN ORGAN IN ITS MOUTH THAT LOOKS JUST LIKE A HUMAN EAR.
I WOULDN'T KNOW WHICH PARTS TO KEEP AND WHICH ONES I CAN REMOVE.
I--
SHH. I BROKE A FEW OF YOUR BONES EARLIER.
NOW YOU ARE AWAKE, AND I CAN SEE IF YOU ARE WORTH SAVING OR NOT...

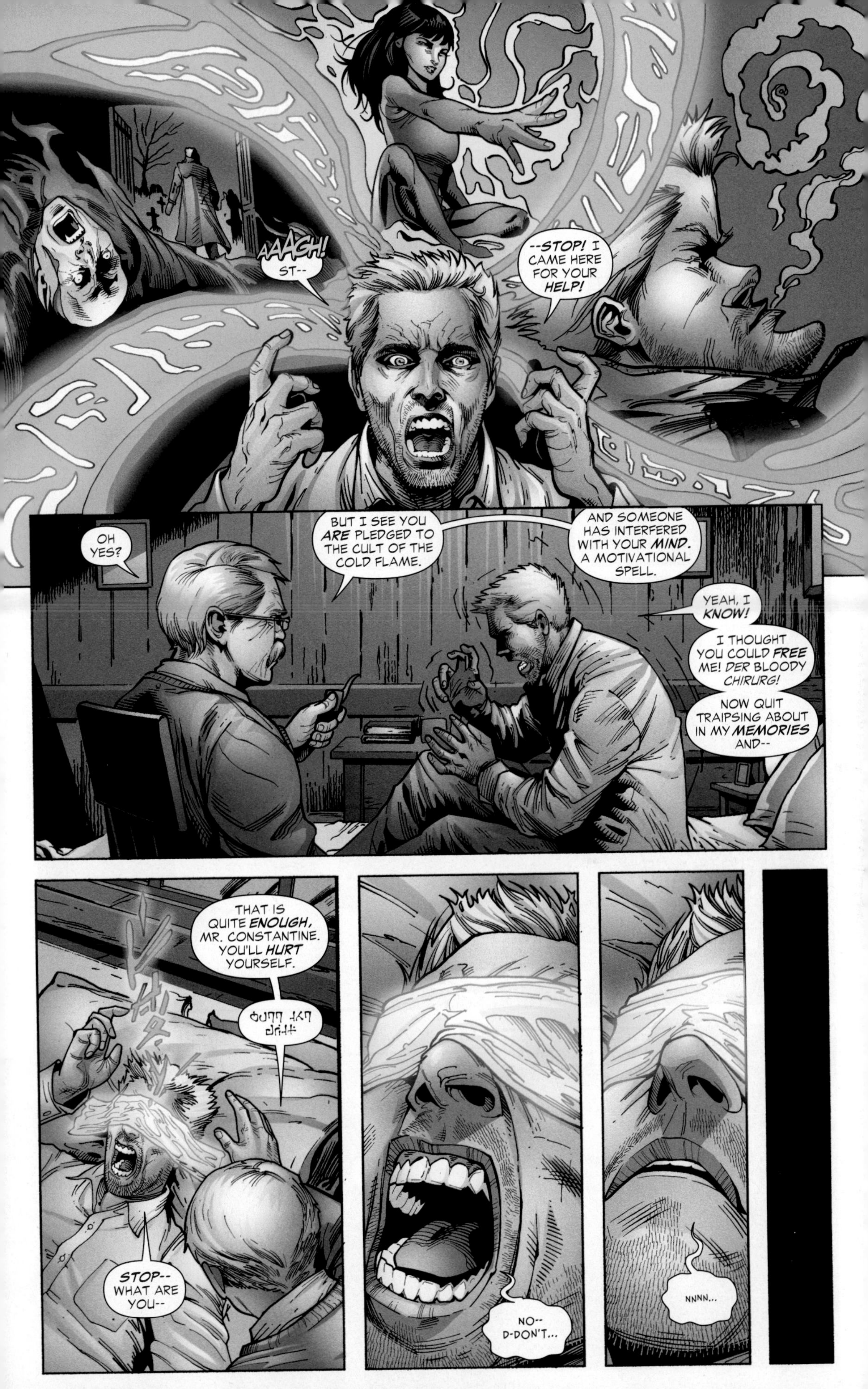
AAAGH!
ST--
--STOP! I CAME HERE FOR YOUR HELP!
OH YES?
BUT I SEE YOU ARE PLEDGED TO THE CULT OF THE COLD FLAME.
AND SOMEONE HAS INTERFERED WITH YOUR MIND. A MOTIVATIONAL SPELL.
YEAH, I KNOW!
I THOUGHT YOU COULD FREE ME! DER BLOODY CHIRURG!
NOW QUIT TRAPSING ABOUT IN MY MEMORIES AND--
THAT IS QUITE ENOUGH, MR. CONSTANTINE. YOU'LL HURT YOURSELF.
STOP-- WHAT ARE YOU--
NO-- D-DON'T...
NNNN...

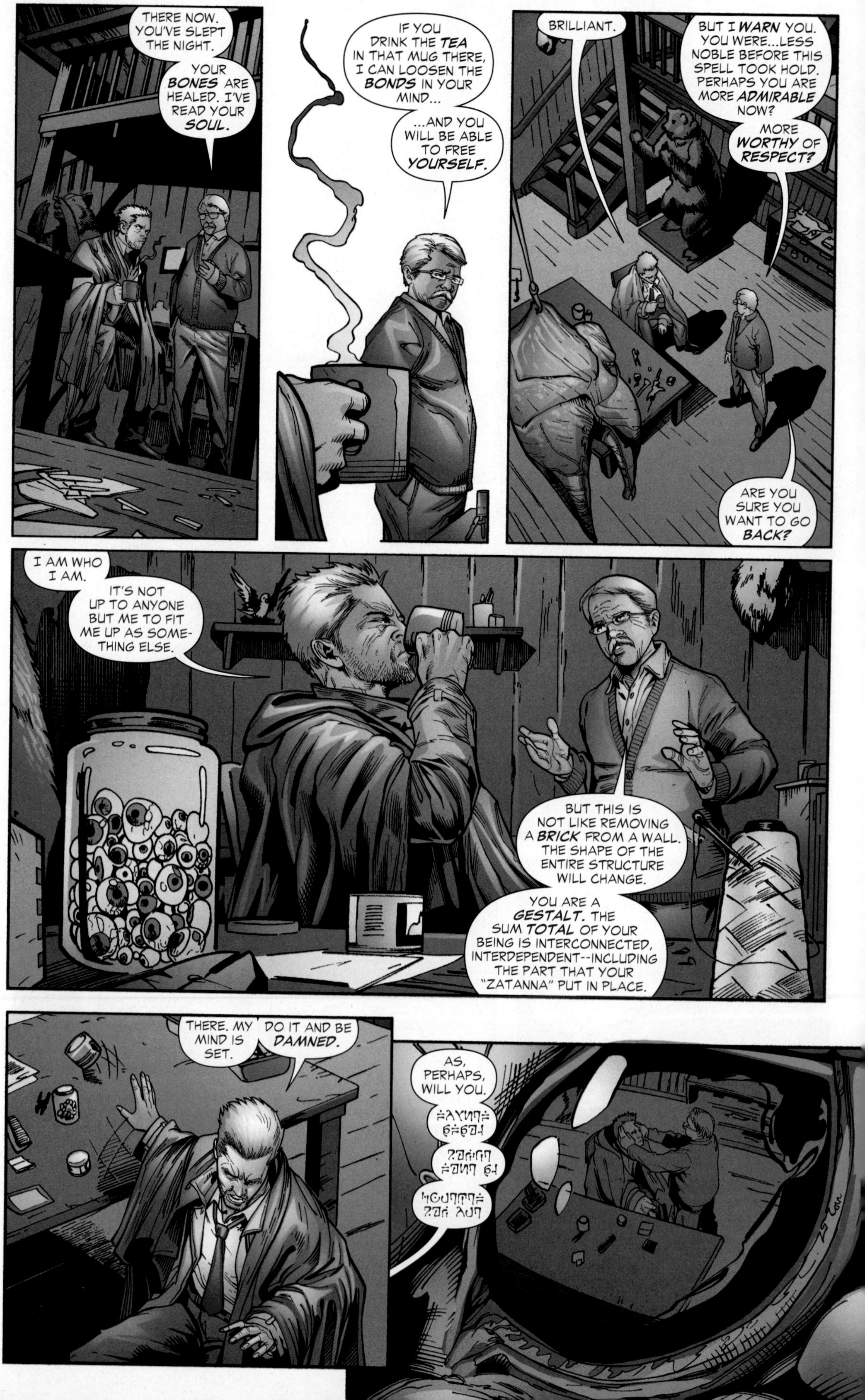

THERE NOW. YOU'VE SLEPT THE NIGHT.
YOUR BONES ARE HEALED. I'VE READ YOUR SOUL.
IF YOU DRINK THE TEA IN THAT MUG THERE, I CAN LOOSEN THE BONDS IN YOUR MIND...
...AND YOU WILL BE ABLE TO FREE YOURSELF.
BRILLIANT.
BUT I WARN YOU. YOU WERE...LESS NOBLE BEFORE THIS SPELL TOOK HOLD. PERHAPS YOU ARE MORE ADMIRABLE NOW?
MORE WORTHY OF RESPECT?
ARE YOU SURE YOU WANT TO GO BACK?
I AM WHO I AM.
IT'S NOT UP TO ANYONE BUT ME TO FIT ME UP AS SOME-THING ELSE.
BUT THIS IS NOT LIKE REMOVING A BRICK FROM A WALL. THE SHAPE OF THE ENTIRE STRUCTURE WILL CHANGE.
YOU ARE A GESTALT. THE SUM TOTAL OF YOUR BEING IS INTERCONNECTED, INTERDEPENDENT--INCLUDING THE PART THAT YOUR "ZATANNA" PUT IN PLACE.
THERE. MY MIND IS SET.
DO IT AND BE DAMNED.
AS, PERHAPS, WILL YOU.

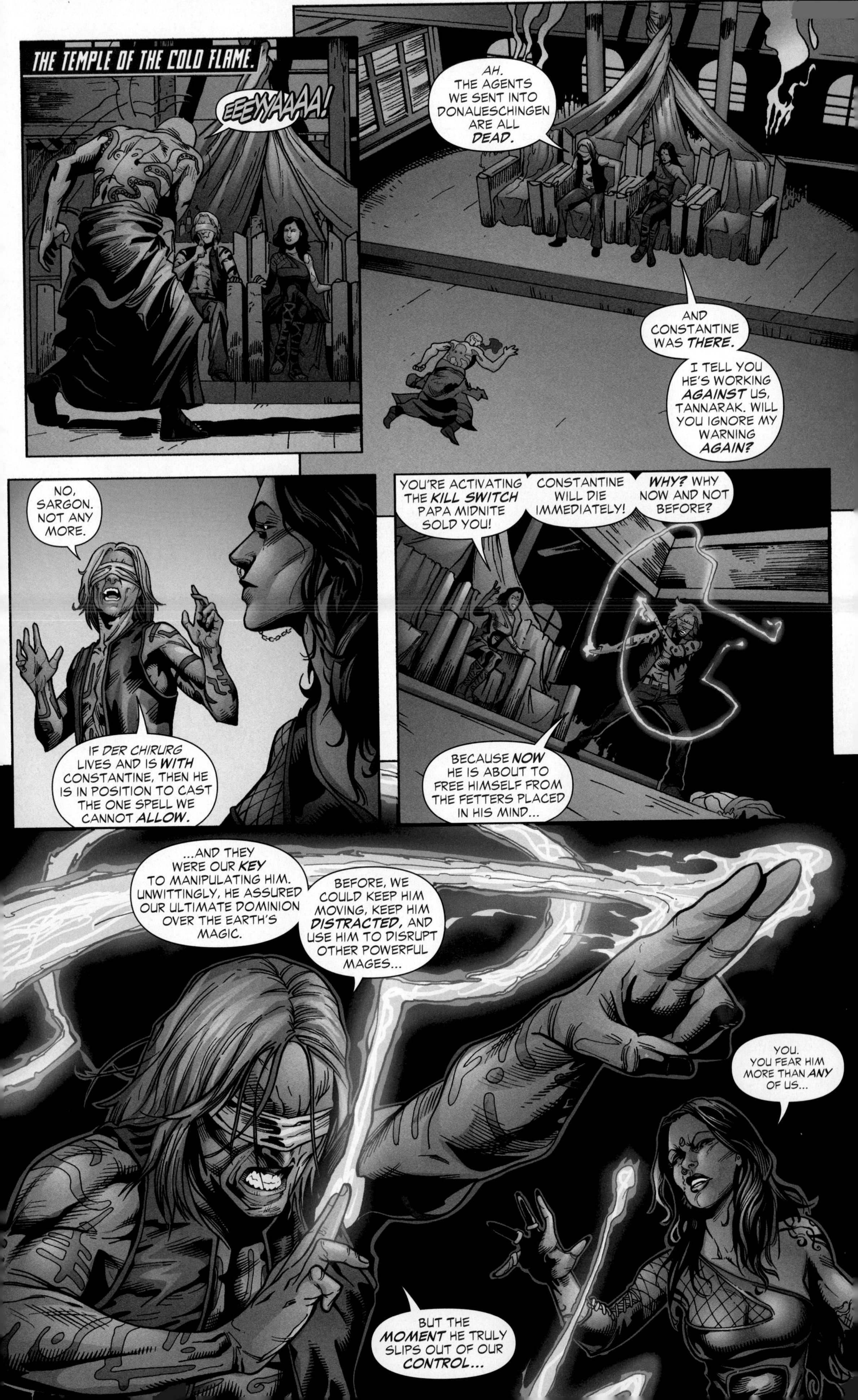
THE TEMPLE OF THE COLD FLAME.
EEEYAAAA!
AH. THE AGENTS WE SENT INTO DONAUESCHINGEN ARE ALL DEAD.
AND CONSTANTINE WAS THERE.
I TELL YOU HE'S WORKING AGAINST US, TANNARAK. WILL YOU IGNORE MY WARNING AGAIN?
NO, SARGON. NOT ANY MORE.
IF DER CHIRURG LIVES AND IS WITH CONSTANTINE, THEN HE IS IN POSITION TO CAST THE ONE SPELL WE CANNOT ALLOW.
YOU'RE ACTIVATING THE KILL SWITCH PAPA MIDNITE SOLD YOU!
CONSTANTINE WILL DIE IMMEDIATELY!
WHY? WHY NOW AND NOT BEFORE?
BECAUSE NOW HE IS ABOUT TO FREE HIMSELF FROM THE FETTERS PLACED IN HIS MIND...
...AND THEY WERE OUR KEY TO MANIPULATING HIM. UNWITTINGLY, HE ASSURED OUR ULTIMATE DOMINION OVER THE EARTH'S MAGIC.
BEFORE, WE COULD KEEP HIM MOVING, KEEP HIM DISTRACTED, AND USE HIM TO DISRUPT OTHER POWERFUL MAGES...
YOU. YOU FEAR HIM MORE THAN ANY OF US...
BUT THE MOMENT HE TRULY SLIPS OUT OF OUR CONTROL...

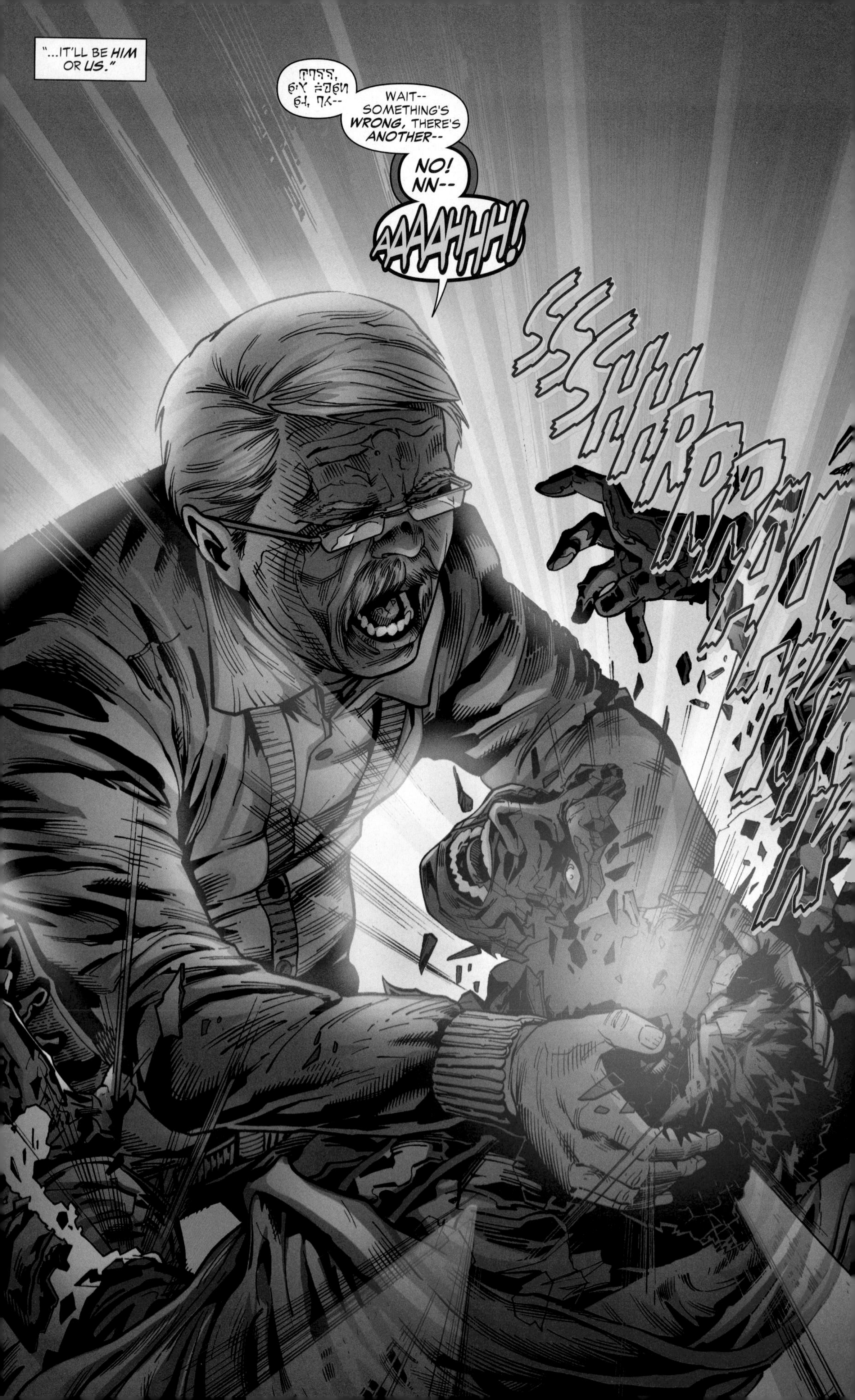
"...IT'LL BE *HIM* OR *US*."
WAIT-- SOMETHING'S *WRONG*, THERE'S *ANOTHER*--
NO! NN--
AAAAHHH!

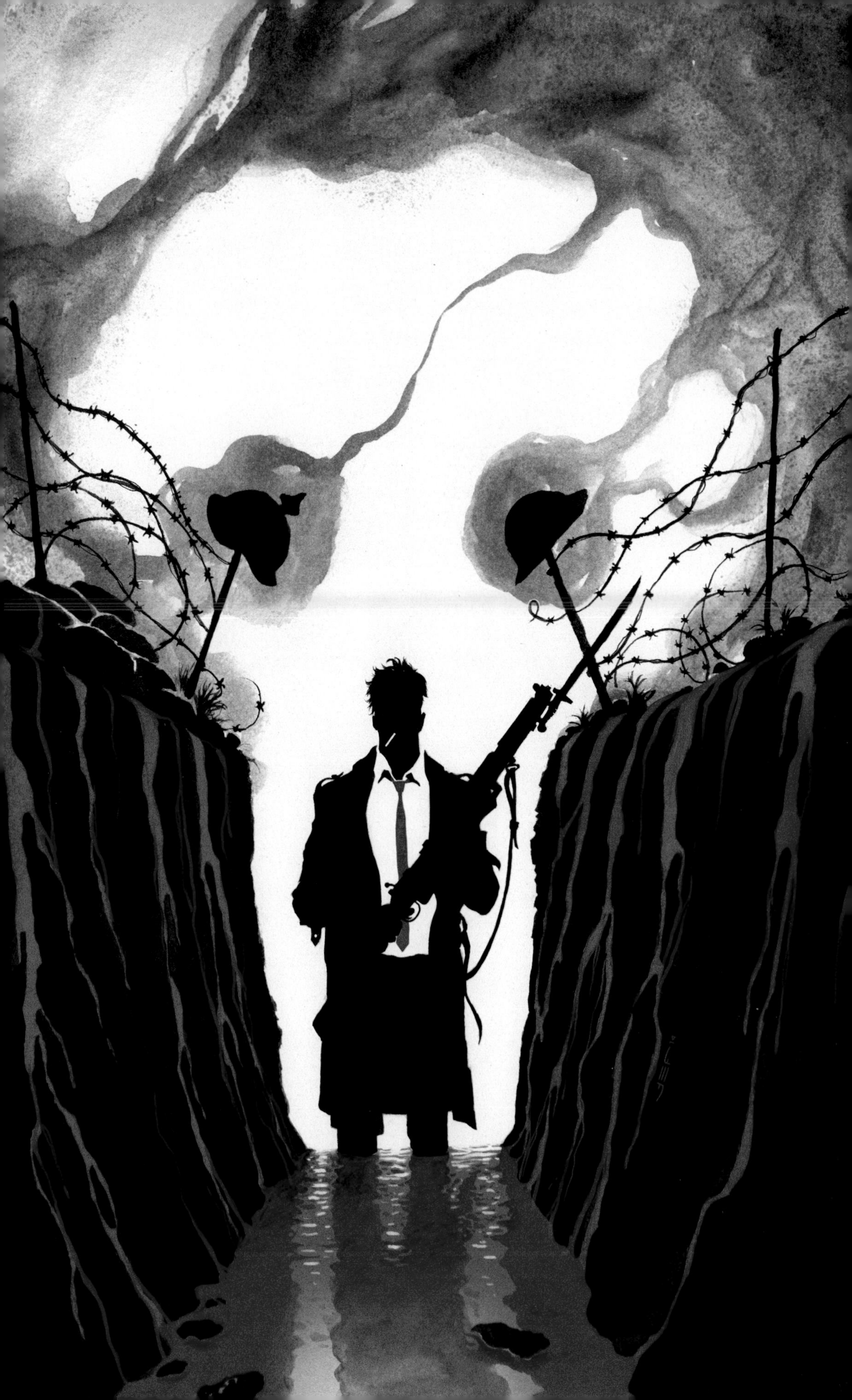

BITS AND PIECES

RAY FAWKES
writer

EDGAR SALAZAR
penciller

JAY LEISTEN
inker

TANYA and RICHARD HORIE
colorists

TAYLOR ESPOSITO
letterer

cover art by
JUAN FERREYRA

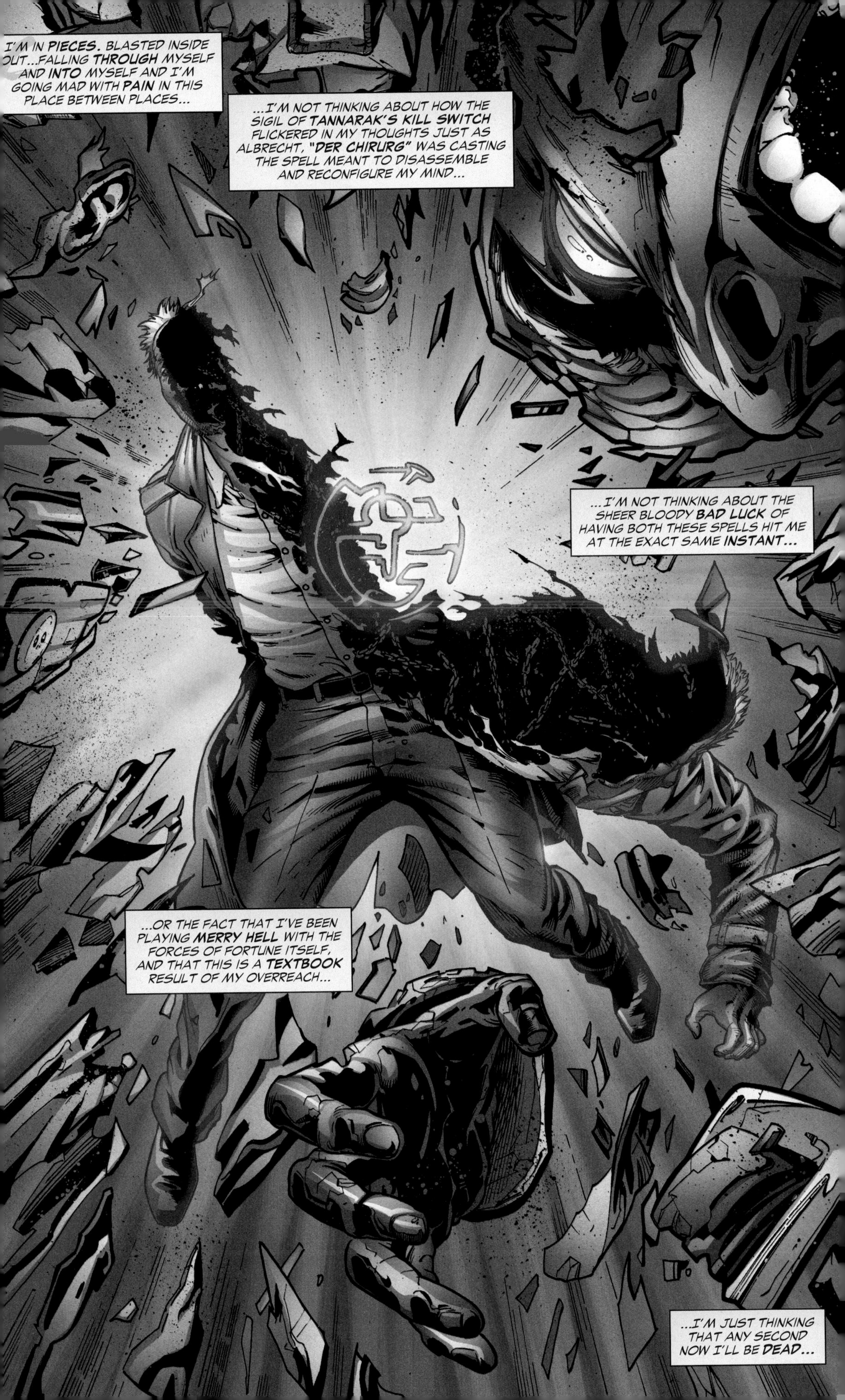
I'M IN PIECES. BLASTED INSIDE OUT...FALLING THROUGH MYSELF AND INTO MYSELF AND I'M GOING MAD WITH PAIN IN THIS PLACE BETWEEN PLACES...
...I'M NOT THINKING ABOUT HOW THE SIGIL OF TANNARAK'S KILL SWITCH FLICKERED IN MY THOUGHTS JUST AS ALBRECHT, "DER CHIRURG" WAS CASTING THE SPELL MEANT TO DISASSEMBLE AND RECONFIGURE MY MIND...
...I'M NOT THINKING ABOUT THE SHEER BLOODY BAD LUCK OF HAVING BOTH THESE SPELLS HIT ME AT THE EXACT SAME INSTANT...
...OR THE FACT THAT I'VE BEEN PLAYING MERRY HELL WITH THE FORCES OF FORTUNE ITSELF, AND THAT THIS IS A TEXTBOOK RESULT OF MY OVERREACH...
...I'M JUST THINKING THAT ANY SECOND NOW I'LL BE DEAD...

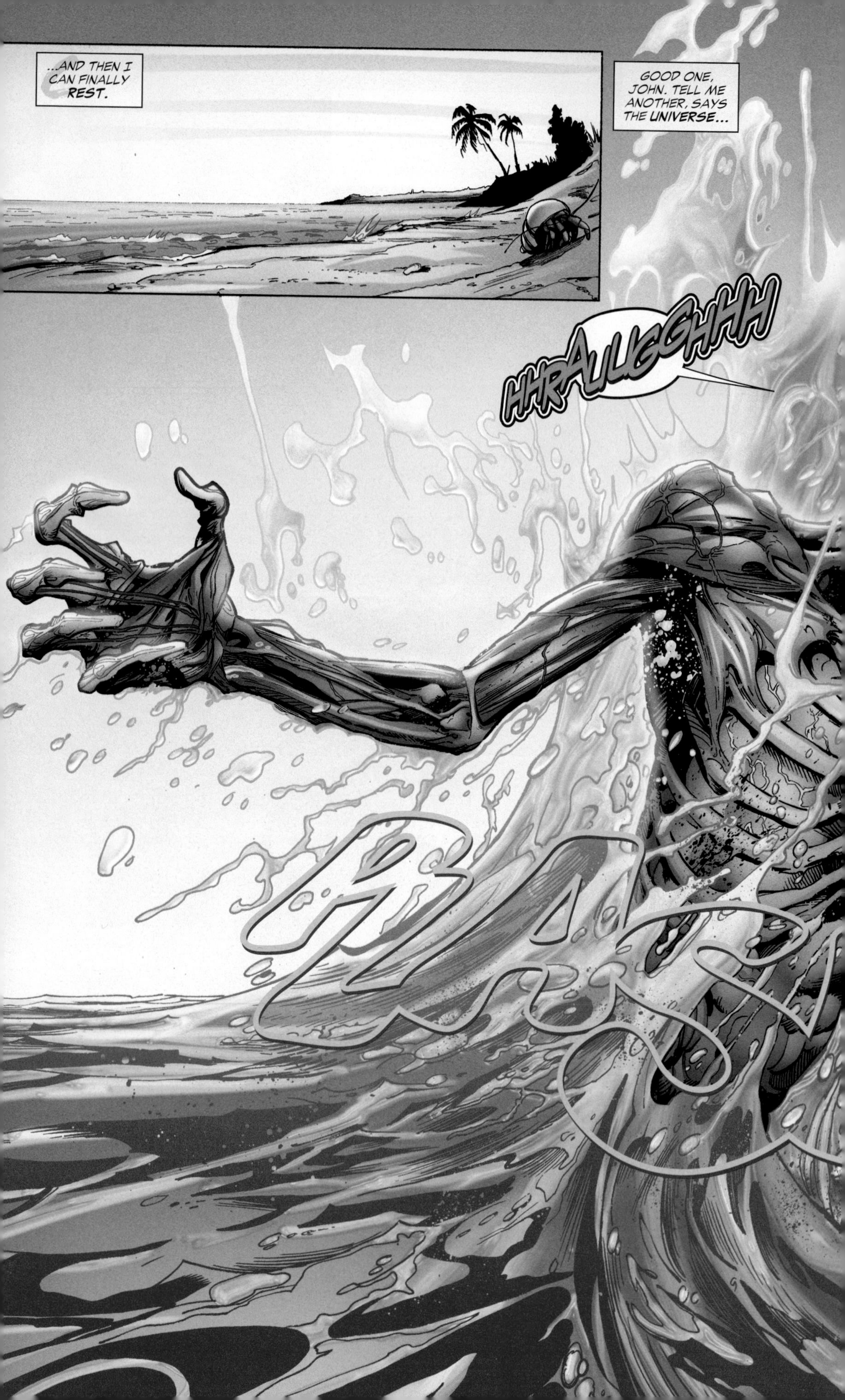
...AND THEN I CAN FINALLY REST.
GOOD ONE, JOHN. TELL ME ANOTHER, SAYS THE UNIVERSE...
HHRAUUGGHHH

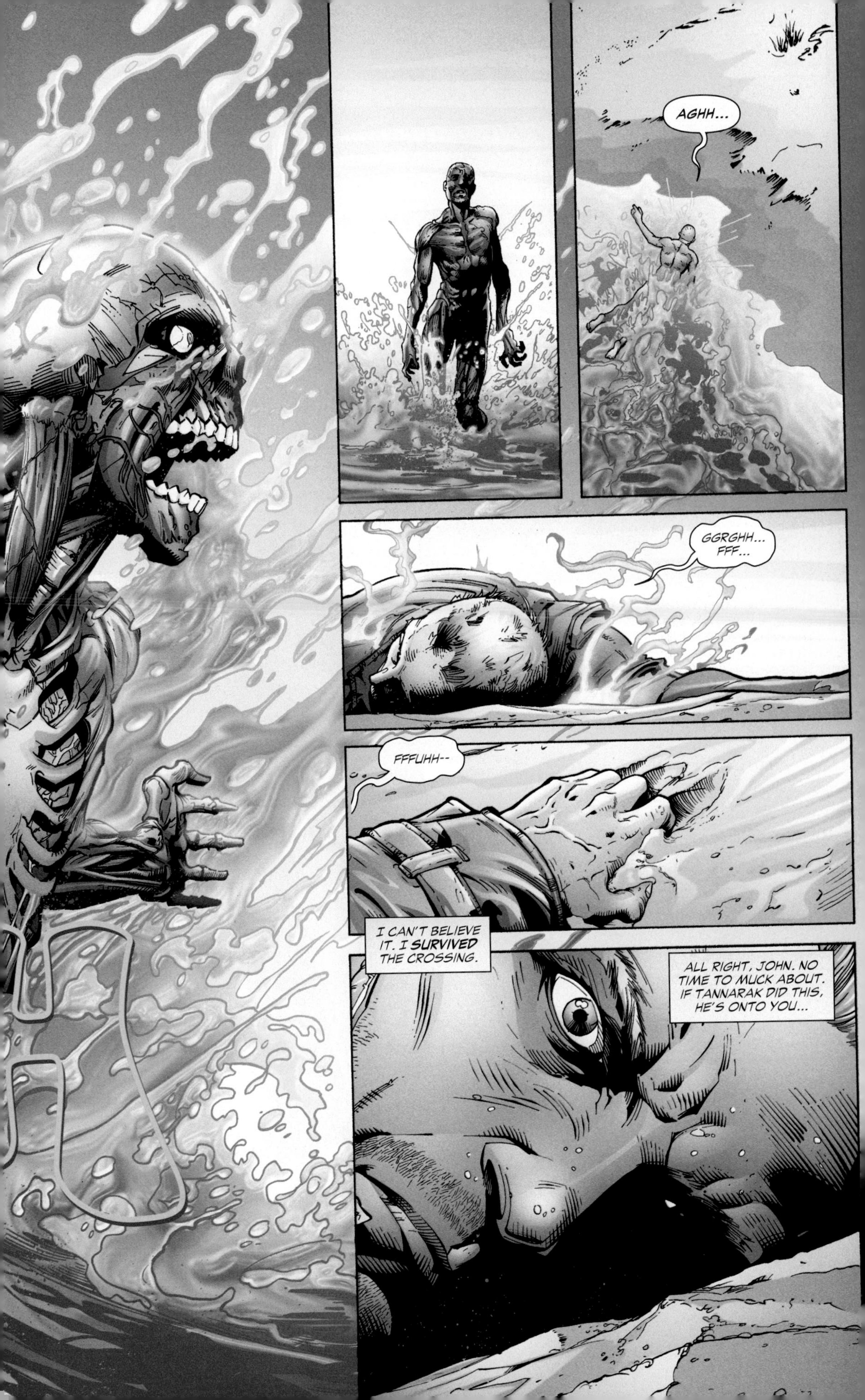
AGHH...
GGRGHH... FFF...
FFFUHH--
I CAN'T BELIEVE IT. I SURVIVED THE CROSSING.
ALL RIGHT, JOHN. NO TIME TO MUCK ABOUT. IF TANNARAK DID THIS, HE'S ONTO YOU...

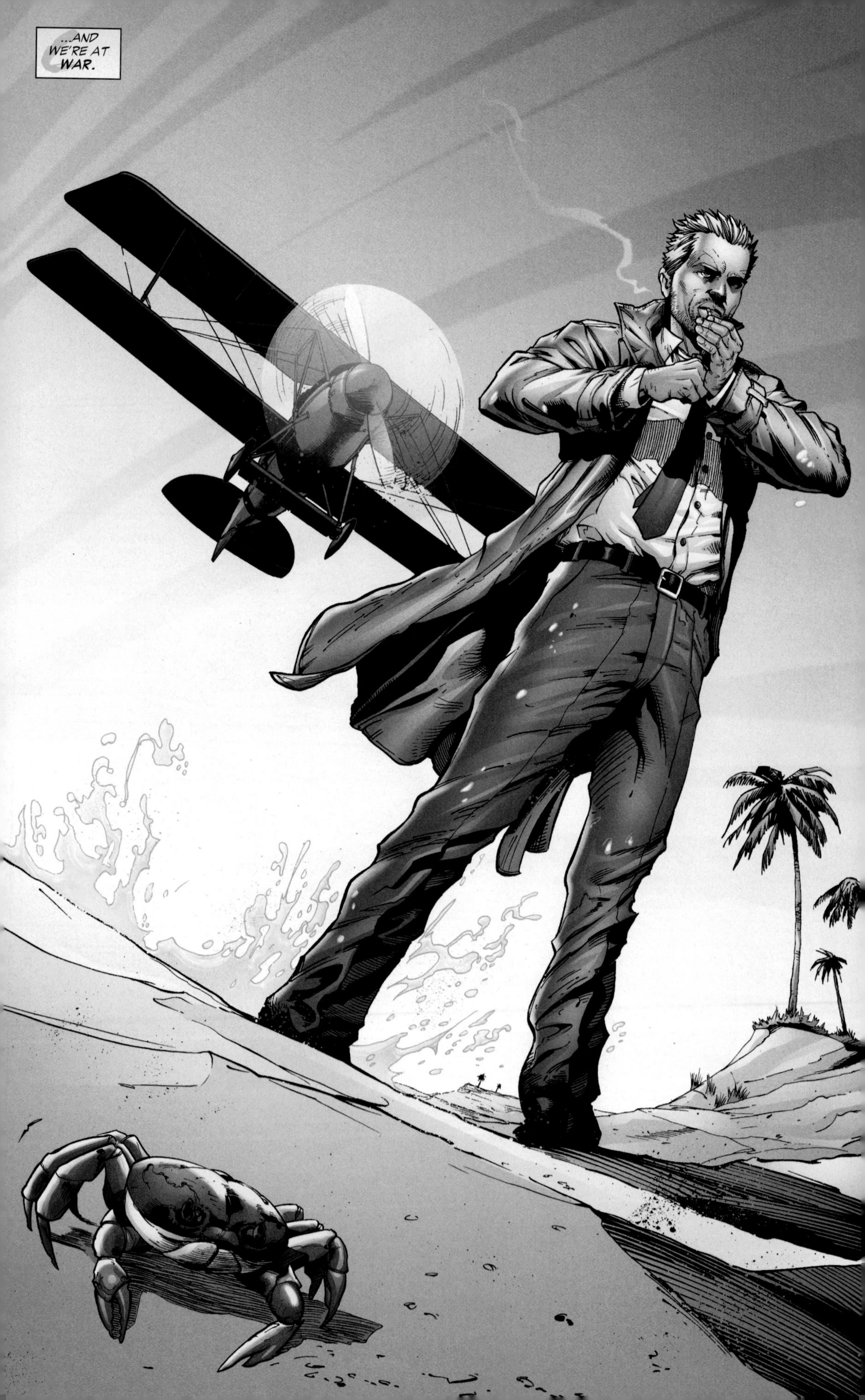
...AND WE'RE AT WAR.

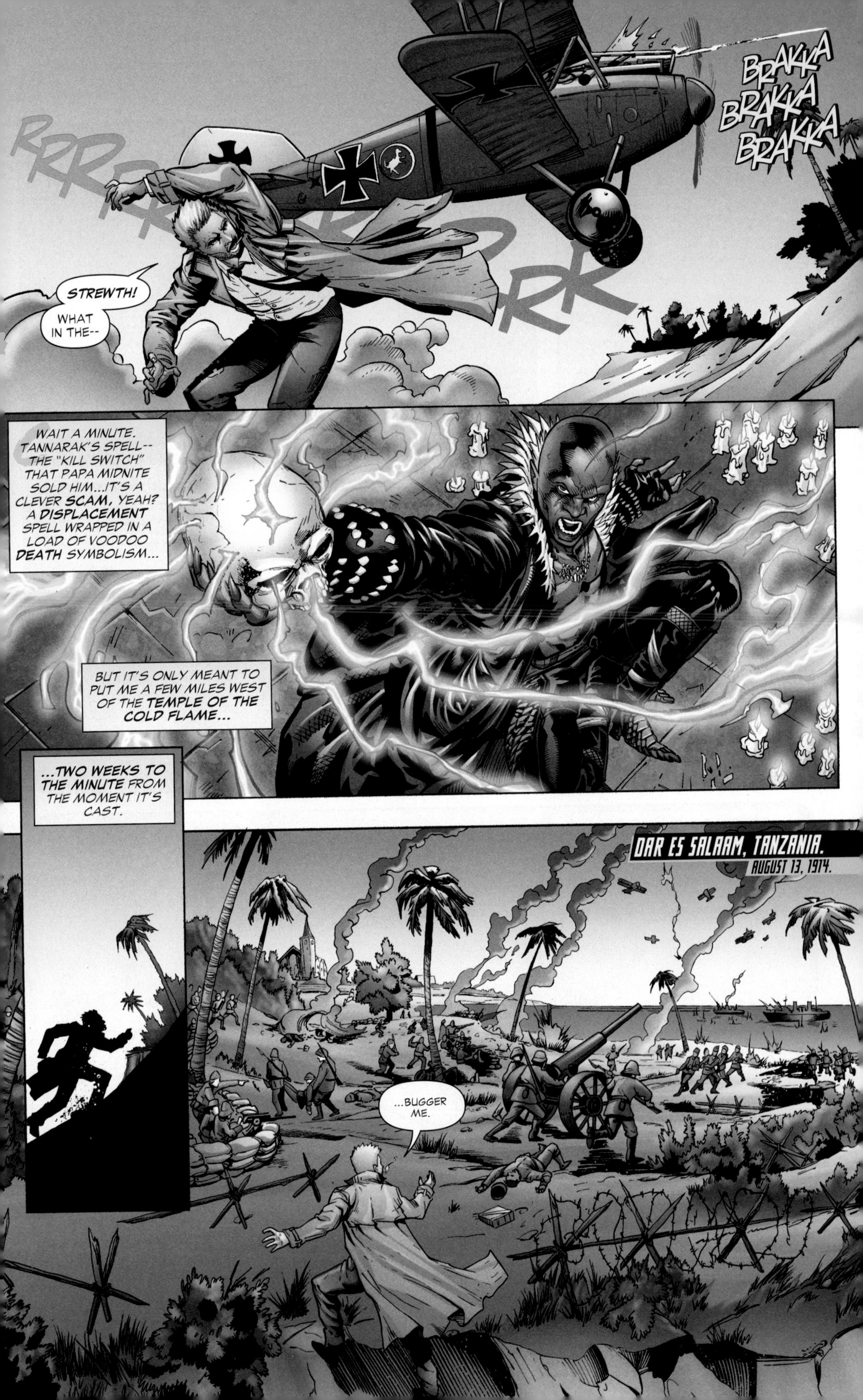
RRRRRRRRRRRRRR
BRAKKA BRAKKA BRAKKA
STREWTH!
WHAT IN THE--
WAIT A MINUTE. TANNARAK'S SPELL-- THE "KILL SWITCH" THAT PAPA MIDNITE SOLD HIM...IT'S A CLEVER SCAM, YEAH? A DISPLACEMENT SPELL WRAPPED IN A LOAD OF VOODOO DEATH SYMBOLISM...
BUT IT'S ONLY MEANT TO PUT ME A FEW MILES WEST OF THE TEMPLE OF THE COLD FLAME...
...TWO WEEKS TO THE MINUTE FROM THE MOMENT IT'S CAST.
DAR ES SALAAM, TANZANIA.
AUGUST 13, 1914.
...BUGGER ME.

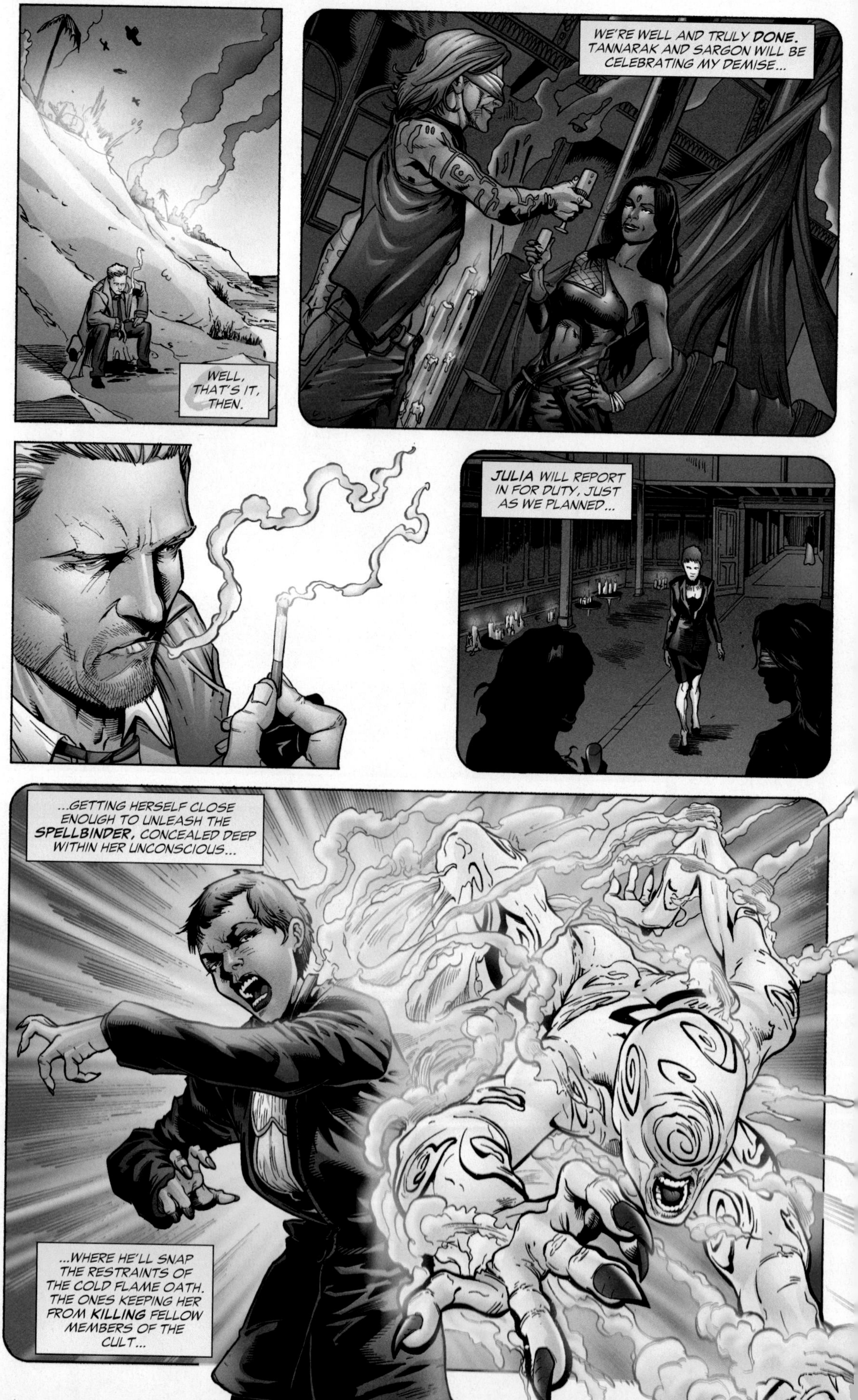
WELL, THAT'S IT, THEN.
WE'RE WELL AND TRULY DONE. TANNARAK AND SARGON WILL BE CELEBRATING MY DEMISE...
JULIA WILL REPORT IN FOR DUTY, JUST AS WE PLANNED...
...GETTING HERSELF CLOSE ENOUGH TO UNLEASH THE SPELLBINDER, CONCEALED DEEP WITHIN HER UNCONSCIOUS...
...WHERE HE'LL SNAP THE RESTRAINTS OF THE COLD FLAME OATH. THE ONES KEEPING HER FROM KILLING FELLOW MEMBERS OF THE CULT...

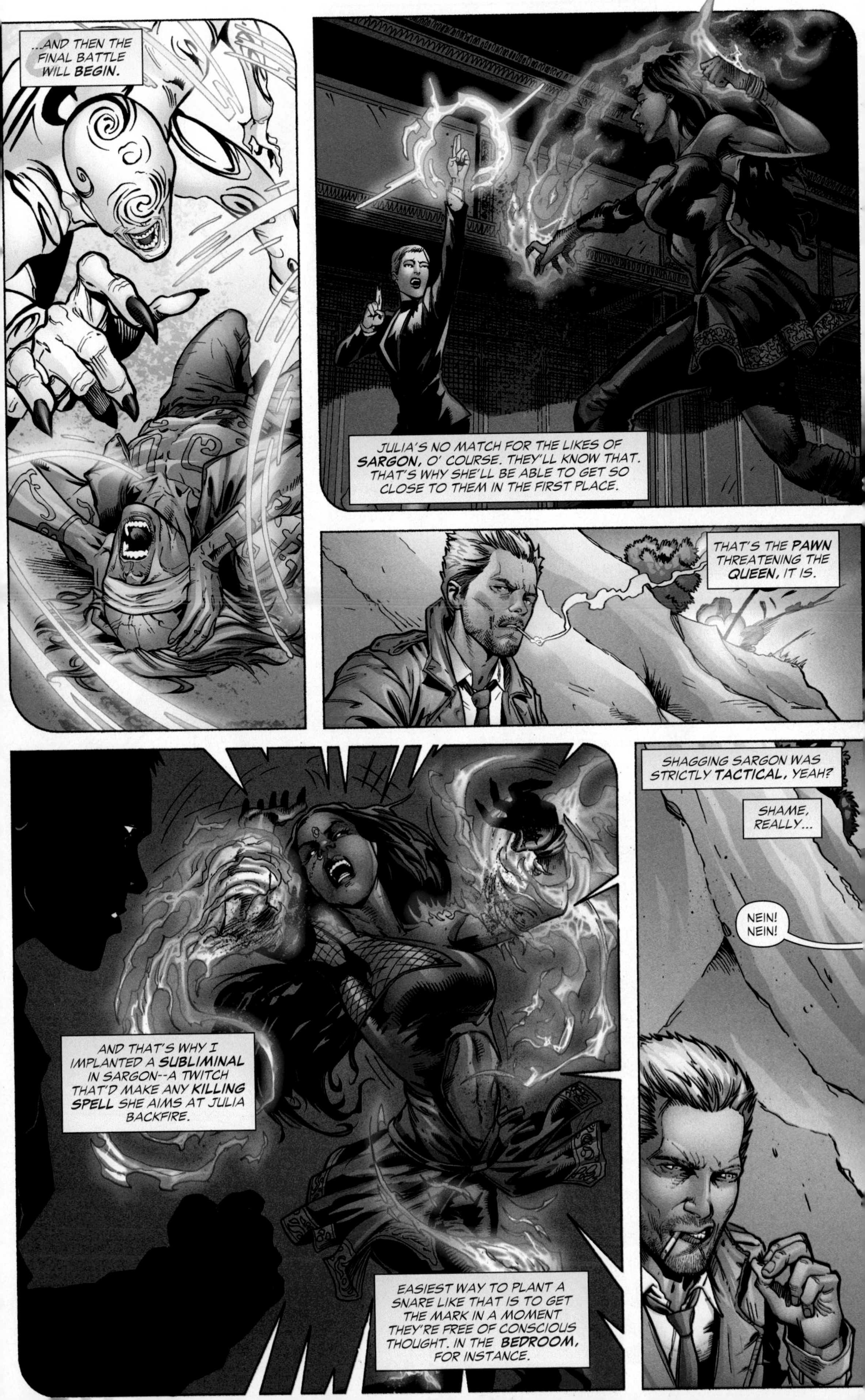
...AND THEN THE FINAL BATTLE WILL BEGIN.
JULIA'S NO MATCH FOR THE LIKES OF SARGON, O' COURSE. THEY'LL KNOW THAT. THAT'S WHY SHE'LL BE ABLE TO GET SO CLOSE TO THEM IN THE FIRST PLACE.
THAT'S THE PAWN THREATENING THE QUEEN, IT IS.
AND THAT'S WHY I IMPLANTED A SUBLIMINAL IN SARGON--A TWITCH THAT'D MAKE ANY KILLING SPELL SHE AIMS AT JULIA BACKFIRE.
EASIEST WAY TO PLANT A SNARE LIKE THAT IS TO GET THE MARK IN A MOMENT THEY'RE FREE OF CONSCIOUS THOUGHT. IN THE BEDROOM, FOR INSTANCE.
SHAGGING SARGON WAS STRICTLY TACTICAL, YEAH?
SHAME, REALLY...
NEIN! NEIN!

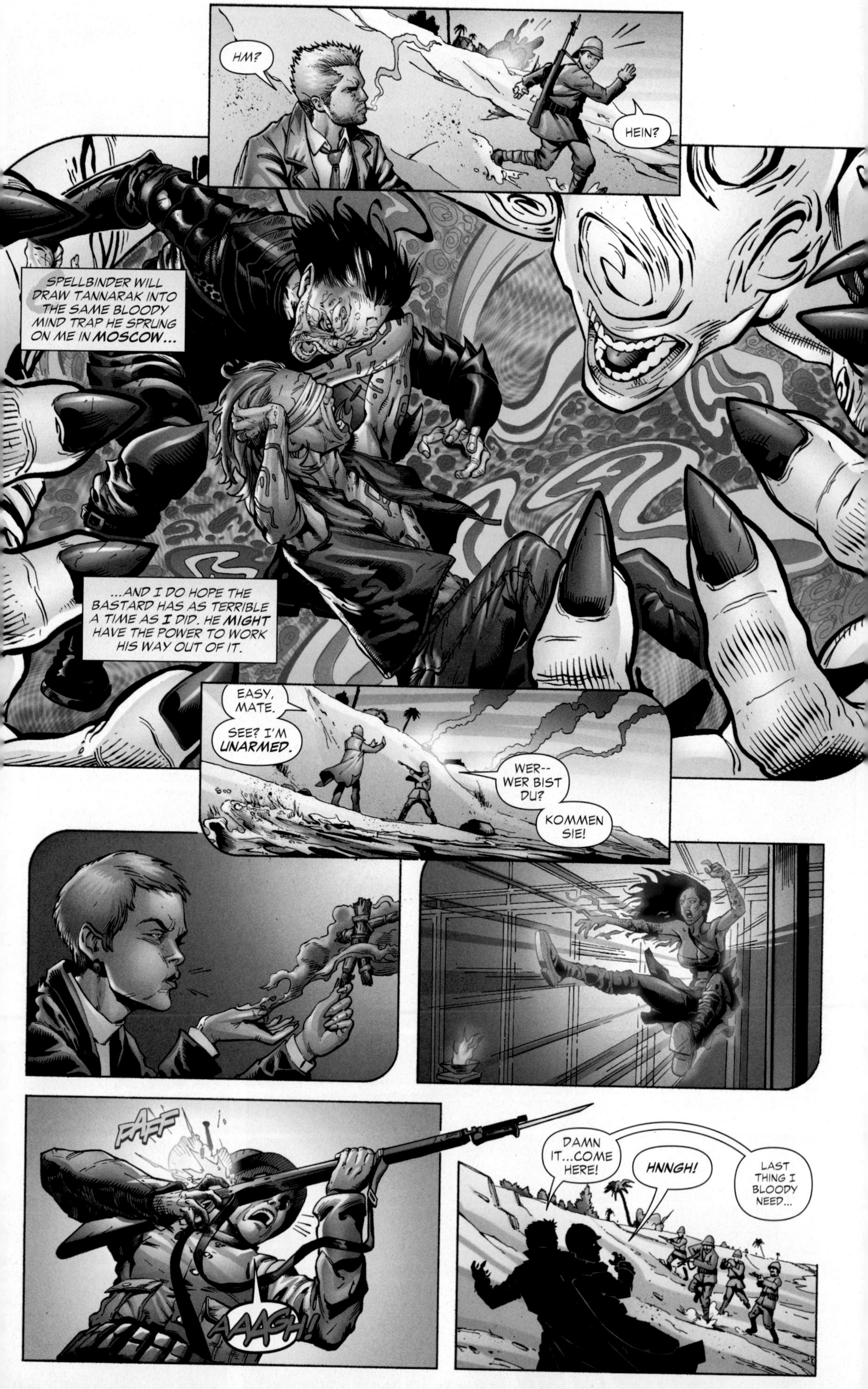
HM?
HEIN?
SPELLBINDER WILL DRAW TANNARAK INTO THE SAME BLOODY MIND TRAP HE SPRUNG ON ME IN MOSCOW...
...AND I DO HOPE THE BASTARD HAS AS TERRIBLE A TIME AS I DID. HE MIGHT HAVE THE POWER TO WORK HIS WAY OUT OF IT.
EASY, MATE.
SEE? I'M UNARMED.
WER-- WER BIST DU?
KOMMEN SIE!
PAFF
AAAGH!
DAMN IT...COME HERE!
HNNGH!
LAST THING I BLOODY NEED...

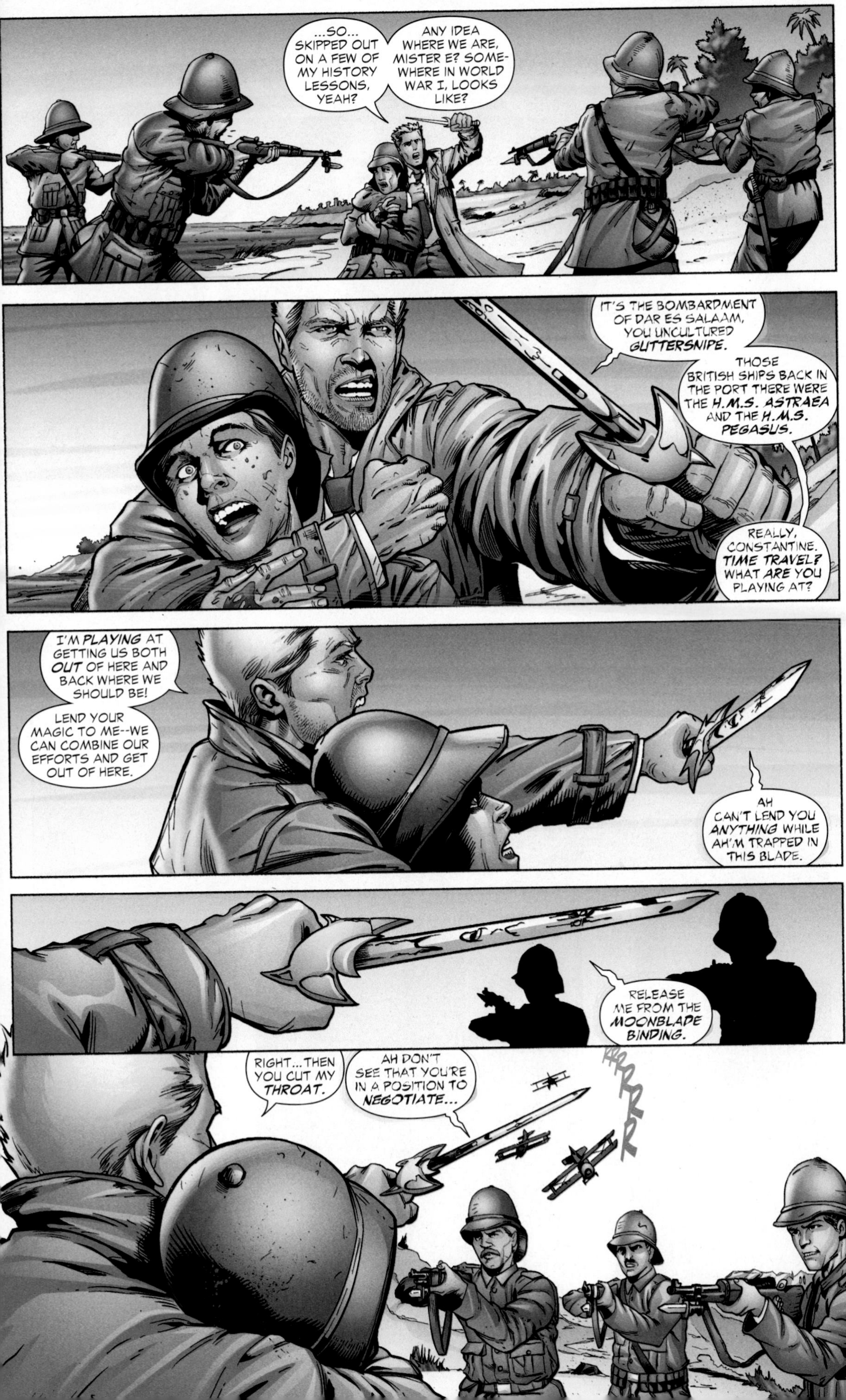
...SO... SKIPPED OUT ON A FEW OF MY HISTORY LESSONS, YEAH?
ANY IDEA WHERE WE ARE, MISTER E? SOMEWHERE IN WORLD WAR I, LOOKS LIKE?
IT'S THE BOMBARDMENT OF DAR ES SALAAM, YOU UNCULTURED GUTTERSNIPE.
THOSE BRITISH SHIPS BACK IN THE PORT THERE WERE THE H.M.S. ASTRAEA AND THE H.M.S. PEGASUS.
REALLY, CONSTANTINE. TIME TRAVEL? WHAT ARE YOU PLAYING AT?
I'M PLAYING AT GETTING US BOTH OUT OF HERE AND BACK WHERE WE SHOULD BE!
LEND YOUR MAGIC TO ME--WE CAN COMBINE OUR EFFORTS AND GET OUT OF HERE.
AH CAN'T LEND YOU ANYTHING WHILE AH'M TRAPPED IN THIS BLADE.
RELEASE ME FROM THE MOONBLADE BINDING.
RIGHT... THEN YOU CUT MY THROAT.
AH DON'T SEE THAT YOU'RE IN A POSITION TO NEGOTIATE...
RRRRRRR

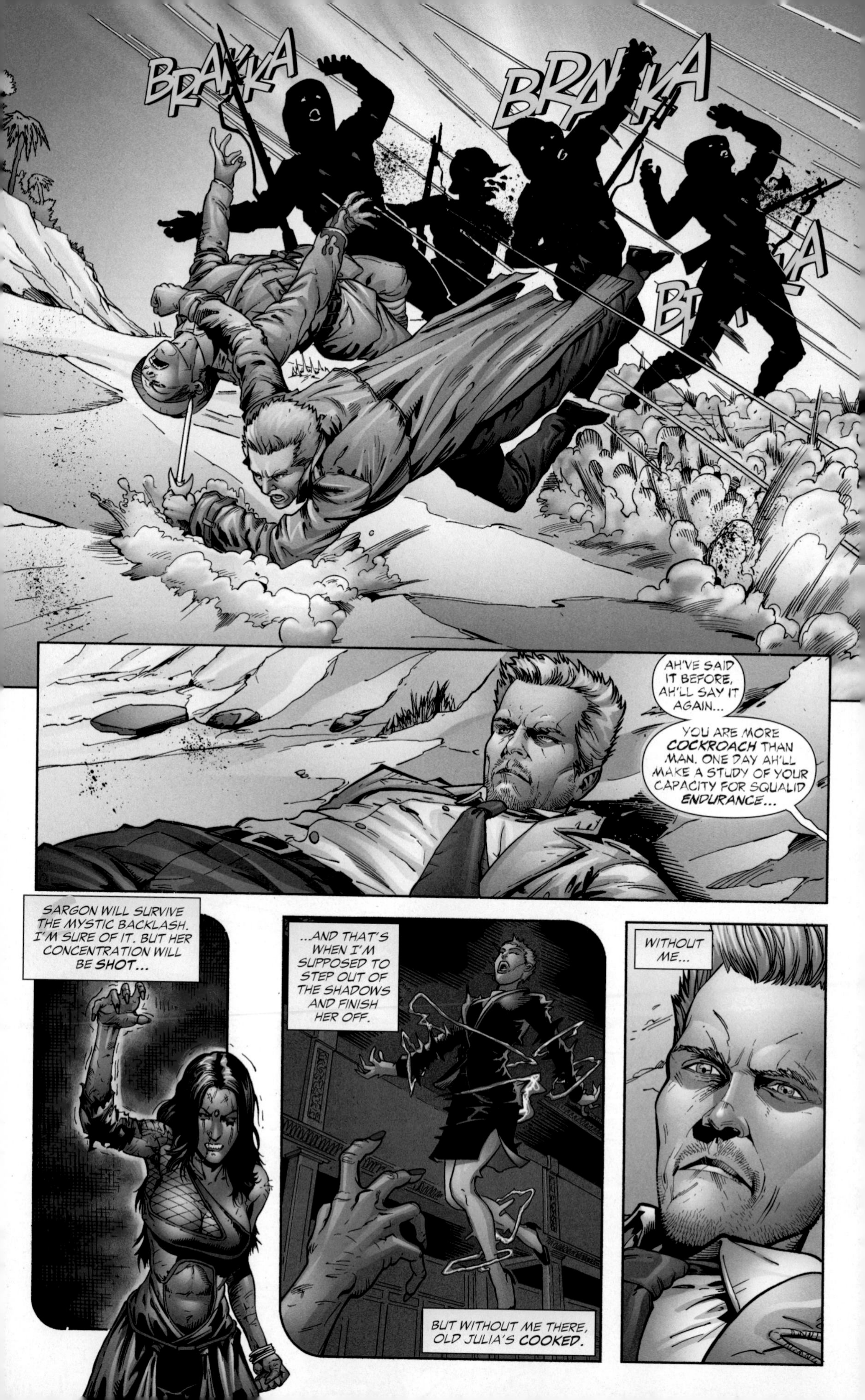
BRAKKA
BRAKKA
BRAKKA
AH'VE SAID IT BEFORE, AH'LL SAY IT AGAIN...
YOU ARE MORE COCKROACH THAN MAN. ONE DAY AH'LL MAKE A STUDY OF YOUR CAPACITY FOR SQUALID ENDURANCE...
SARGON WILL SURVIVE THE MYSTIC BACKLASH. I'M SURE OF IT. BUT HER CONCENTRATION WILL BE SHOT...
...AND THAT'S WHEN I'M SUPPOSED TO STEP OUT OF THE SHADOWS AND FINISH HER OFF.
BUT WITHOUT ME THERE, OLD JULIA'S COOKED.
WITHOUT ME...

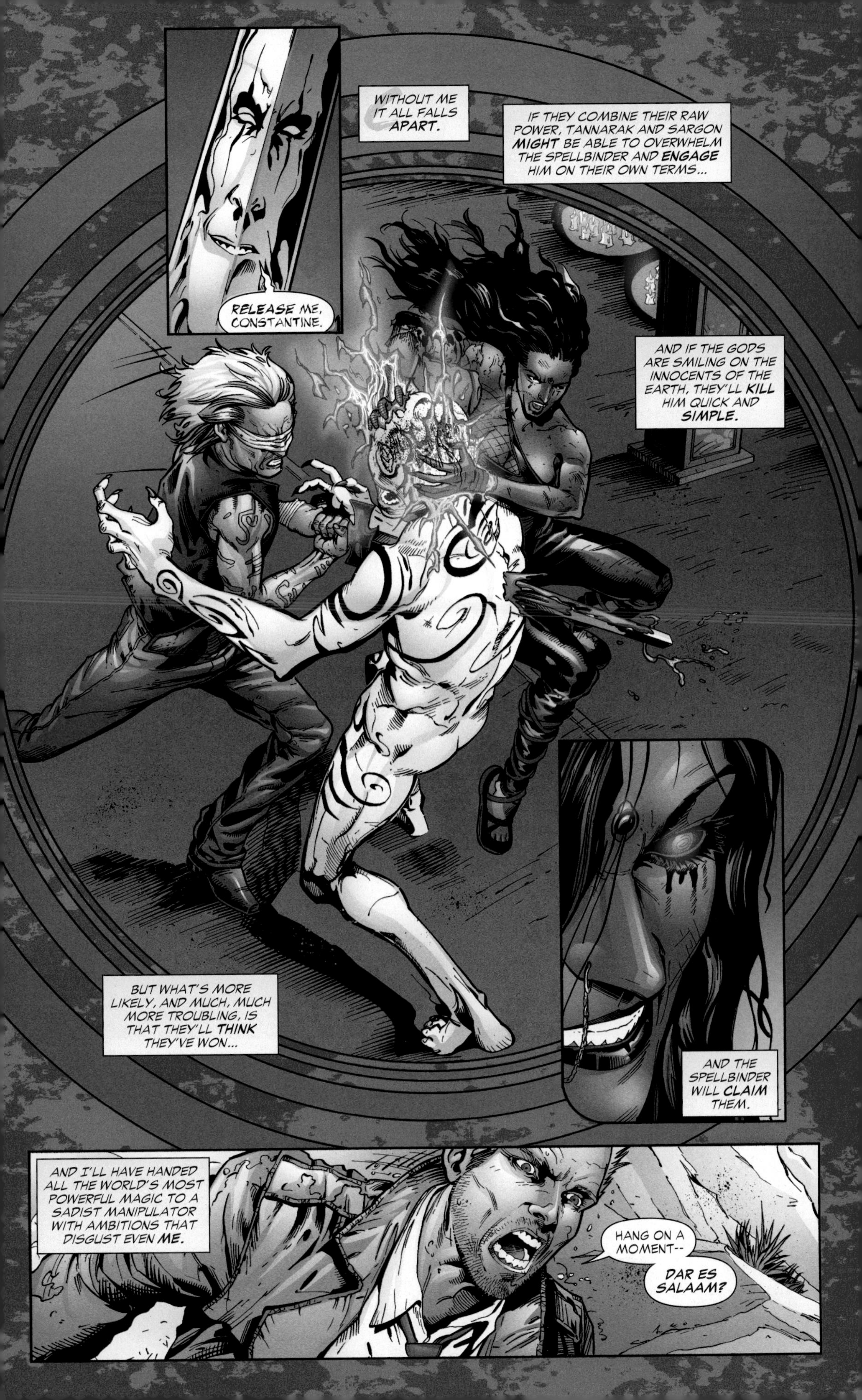
WITHOUT ME IT ALL FALLS APART.
RELEASE ME, CONSTANTINE.
IF THEY COMBINE THEIR RAW POWER, TANNARAK AND SARGON MIGHT BE ABLE TO OVERWHELM THE SPELLBINDER AND ENGAGE HIM ON THEIR OWN TERMS...
AND IF THE GODS ARE SMILING ON THE INNOCENTS OF THE EARTH, THEY'LL KILL HIM QUICK AND SIMPLE.
BUT WHAT'S MORE LIKELY, AND MUCH, MUCH MORE TROUBLING, IS THAT THEY'LL THINK THEY'VE WON...
AND THE SPELLBINDER WILL CLAIM THEM.
AND I'LL HAVE HANDED ALL THE WORLD'S MOST POWERFUL MAGIC TO A SADIST MANIPULATOR WITH AMBITIONS THAT DISGUST EVEN ME.
HANG ON A MOMENT--
DAR ES SALAAM?

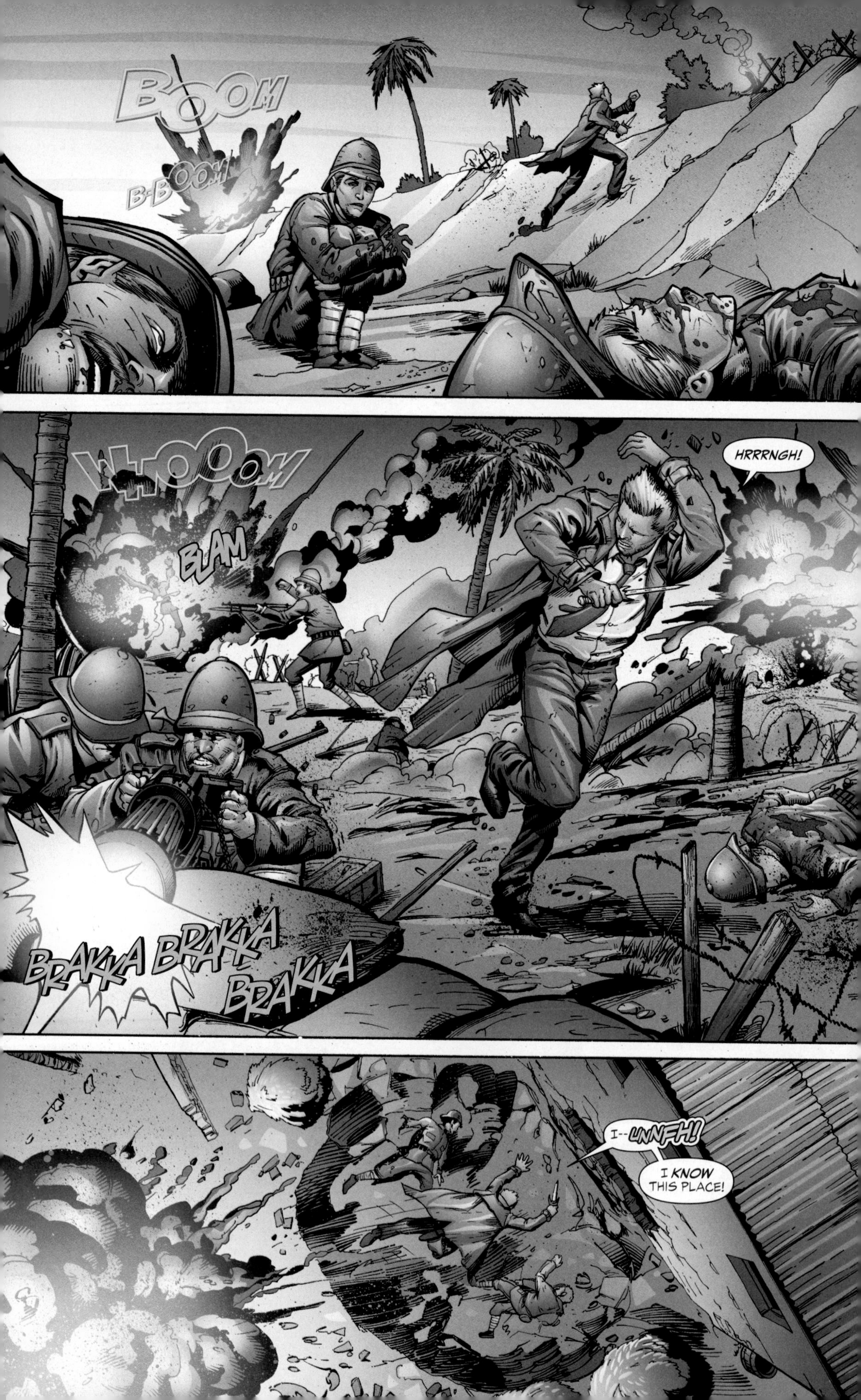
BOOOM
B-BOOM
WHOOOOM
HRRRNGH!
BLAM
BRAKKA BRAKKA
BRAKKA
I--UNNFH!
I KNOW THIS PLACE!

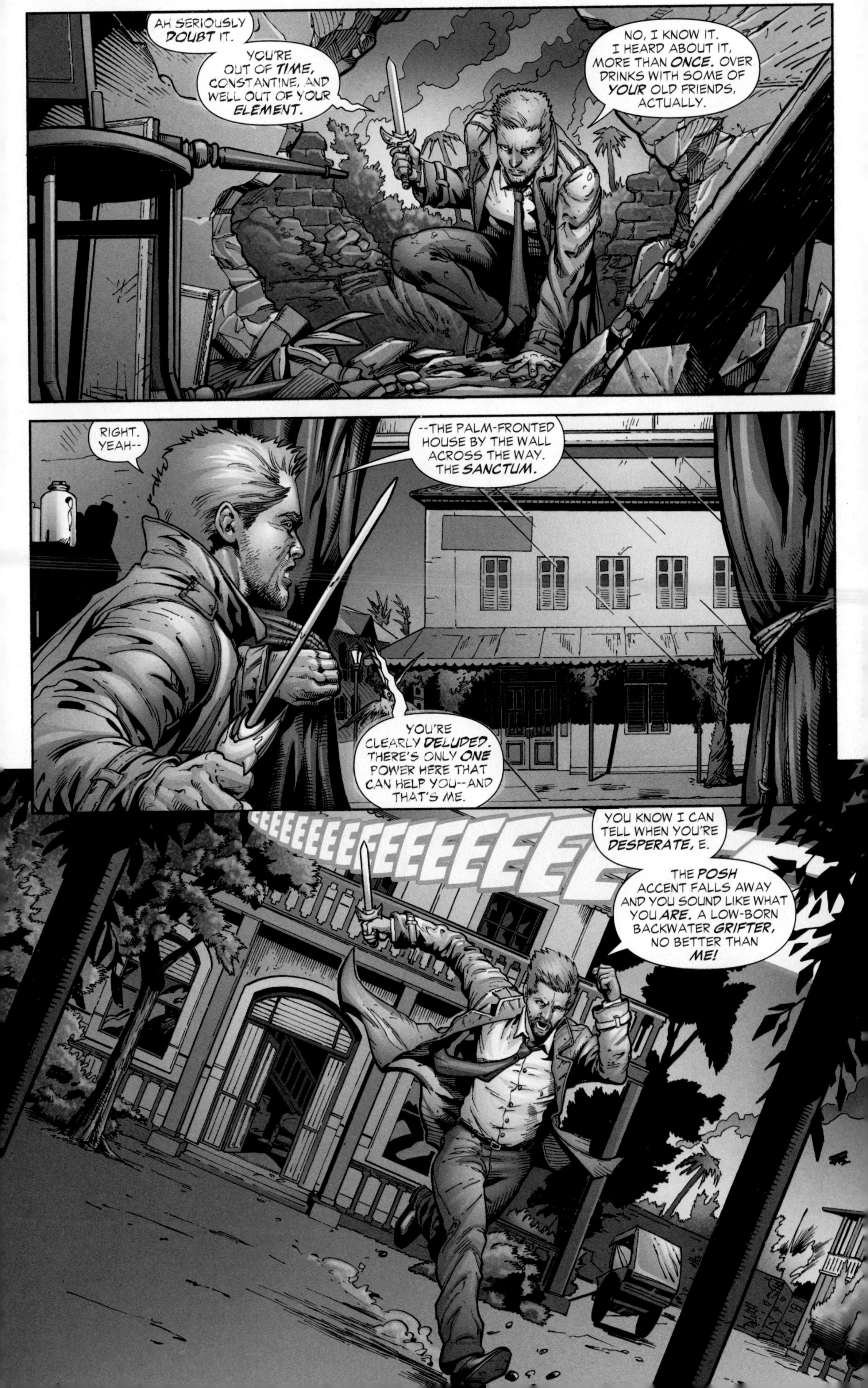
AH SERIOUSLY DOUBT IT.
YOU'RE OUT OF TIME, CONSTANTINE, AND WELL OUT OF YOUR ELEMENT.
NO, I KNOW IT. I HEARD ABOUT IT, MORE THAN ONCE. OVER DRINKS WITH SOME OF YOUR OLD FRIENDS, ACTUALLY.
RIGHT. YEAH--
--THE PALM-FRONTED HOUSE BY THE WALL ACROSS THE WAY. THE SANCTUM.
YOU'RE CLEARLY DELUDED. THERE'S ONLY ONE POWER HERE THAT CAN HELP YOU--AND THAT'S ME.
EEEEEEEEEEEEEEEEEE
YOU KNOW I CAN TELL WHEN YOU'RE DESPERATE, E.
THE POSH ACCENT FALLS AWAY AND YOU SOUND LIKE WHAT YOU ARE. A LOW-BORN BACKWATER GRIFTER, NO BETTER THAN ME!

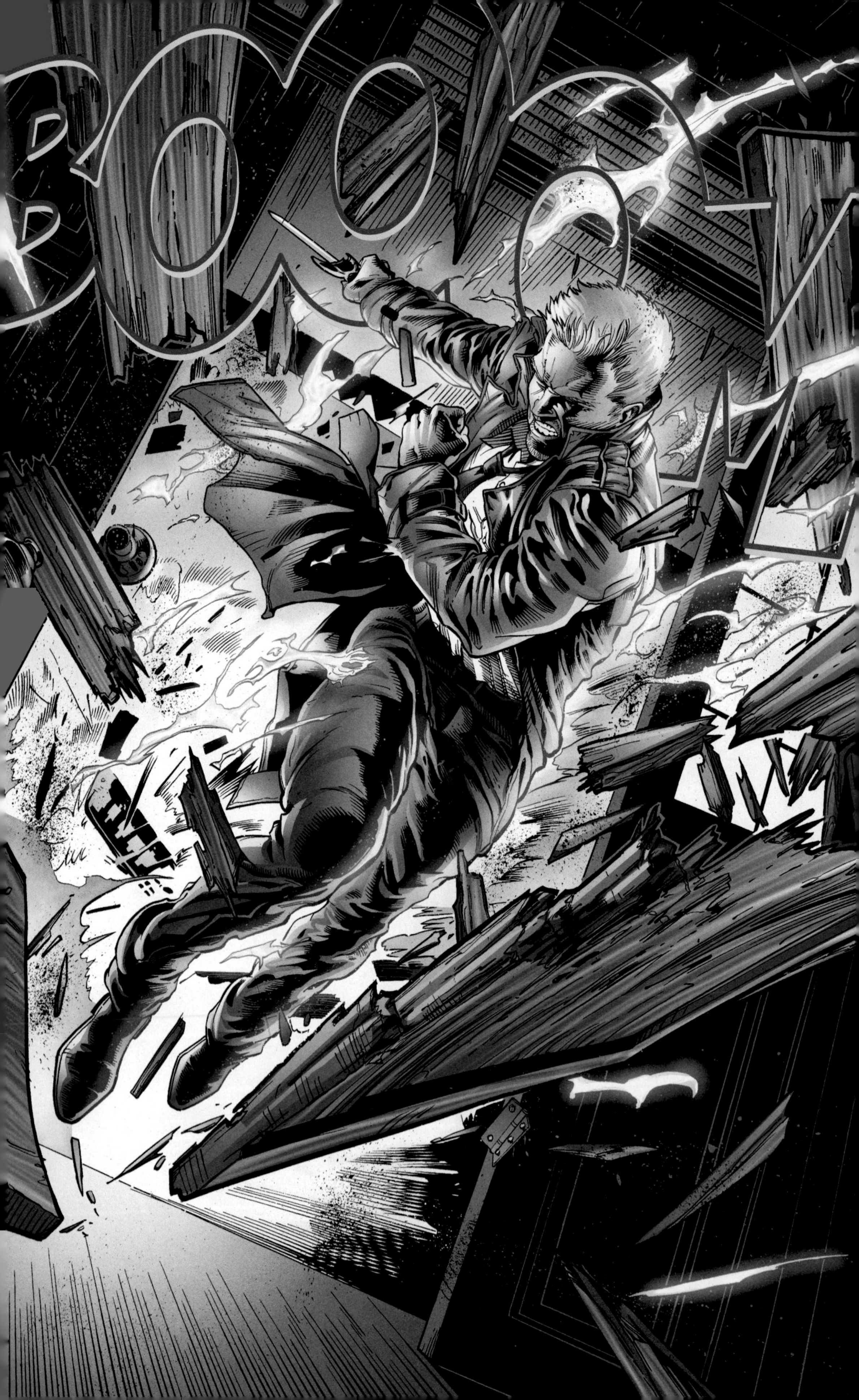
BOOOM

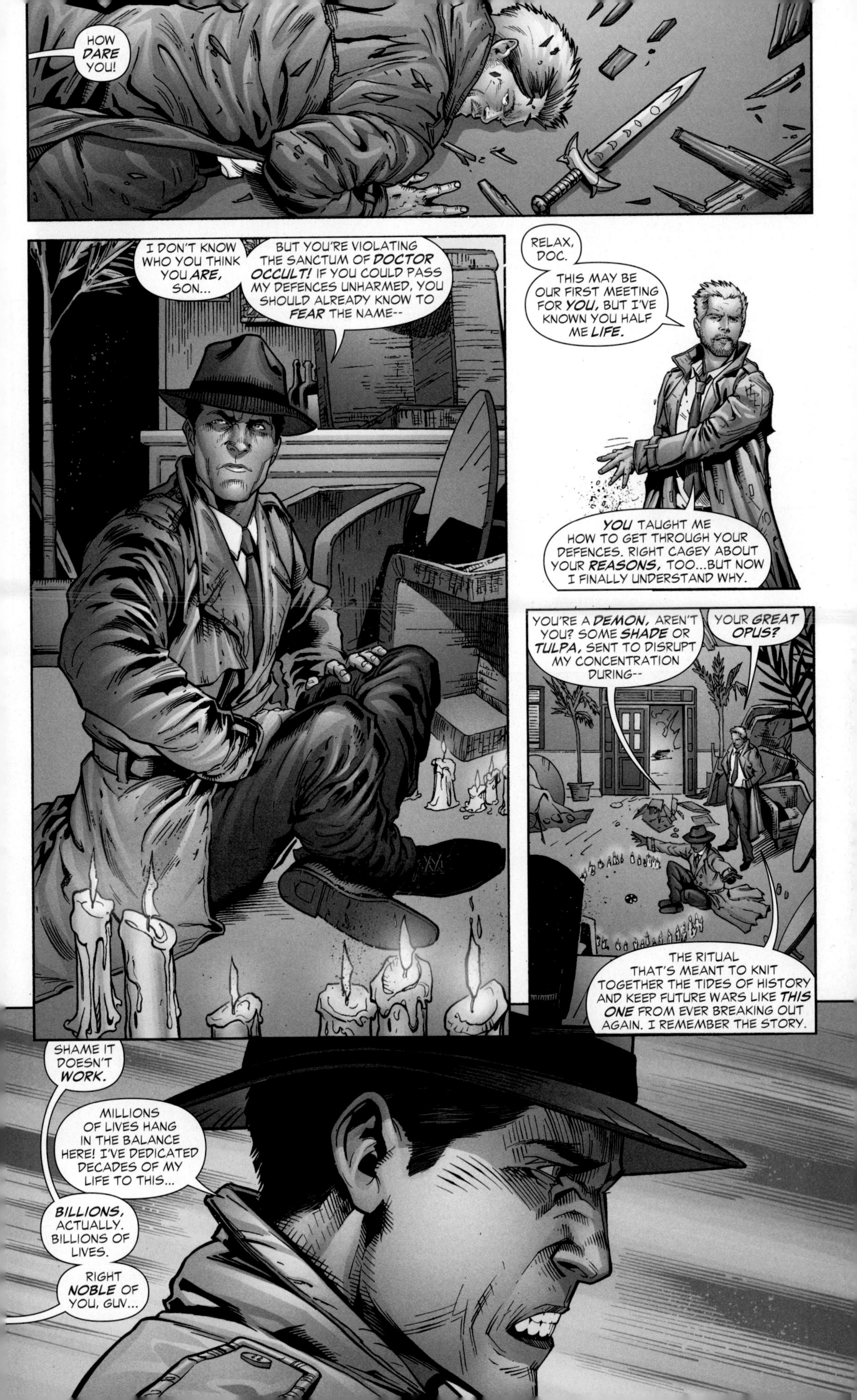
HOW DARE YOU!
I DON'T KNOW WHO YOU THINK YOU ARE, SON...
BUT YOU'RE VIOLATING THE SANCTUM OF DOCTOR OCCULT! IF YOU COULD PASS MY DEFENCES UNHARMED, YOU SHOULD ALREADY KNOW TO FEAR THE NAME--
RELAX, DOC.
THIS MAY BE OUR FIRST MEETING FOR YOU, BUT I'VE KNOWN YOU HALF ME LIFE.
YOU TAUGHT ME HOW TO GET THROUGH YOUR DEFENCES. RIGHT CAGEY ABOUT YOUR REASONS, TOO...BUT NOW I FINALLY UNDERSTAND WHY.
YOU'RE A DEMON, AREN'T YOU? SOME SHADE OR TULPA, SENT TO DISRUPT MY CONCENTRATION DURING--
YOUR GREAT OPUS?
THE RITUAL THAT'S MEANT TO KNIT TOGETHER THE TIDES OF HISTORY AND KEEP FUTURE WARS LIKE THIS ONE FROM EVER BREAKING OUT AGAIN. I REMEMBER THE STORY.
SHAME IT DOESN'T WORK.
MILLIONS OF LIVES HANG IN THE BALANCE HERE! I'VE DEDICATED DECADES OF MY LIFE TO THIS...
BILLIONS, ACTUALLY. BILLIONS OF LIVES.
RIGHT NOBLE OF YOU, GUV...

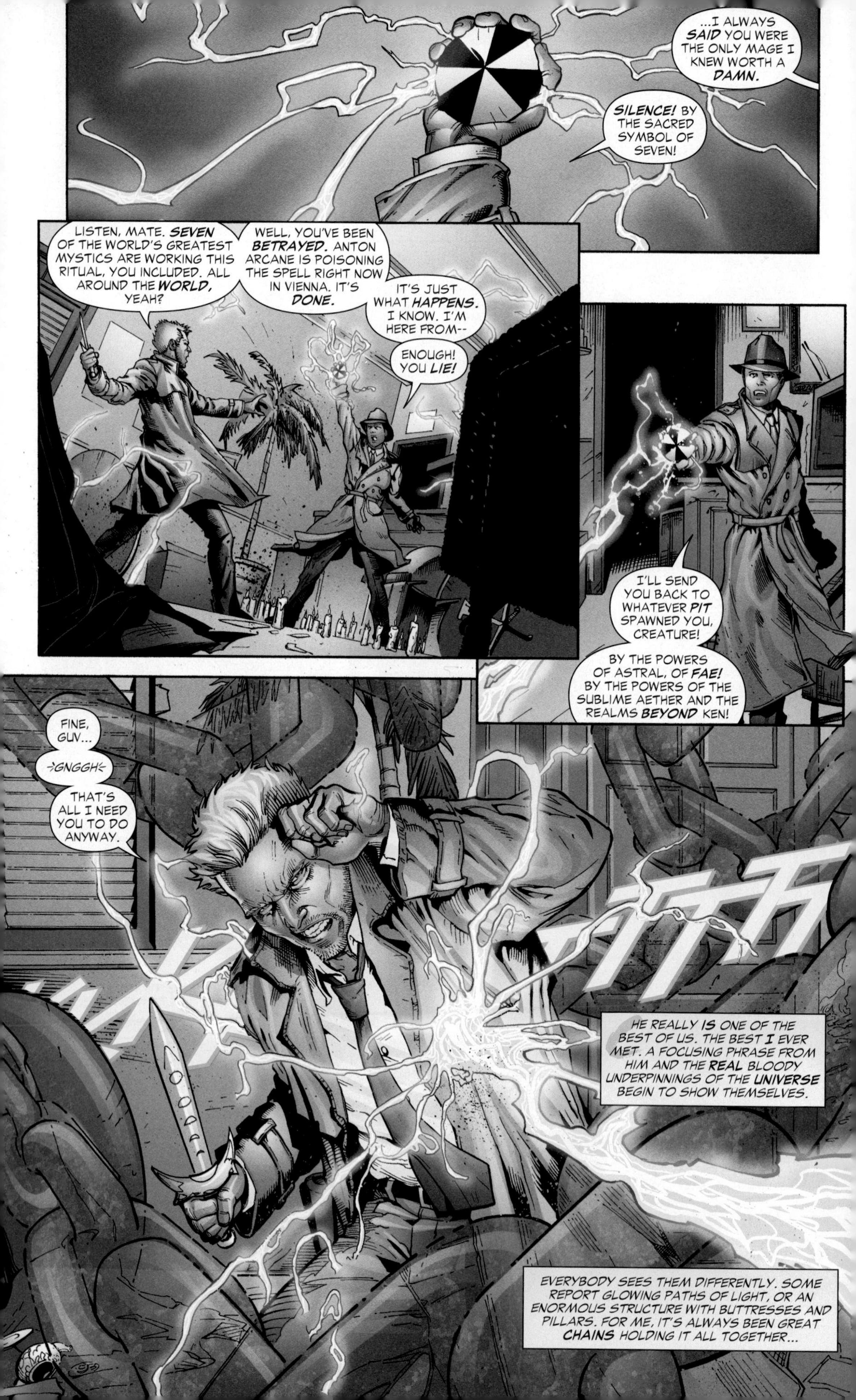
...I ALWAYS SAID YOU WERE THE ONLY MAGE I KNEW WORTH A DAMN.
SILENCE! BY THE SACRED SYMBOL OF SEVEN!
LISTEN, MATE. SEVEN OF THE WORLD'S GREATEST MYSTICS ARE WORKING THIS RITUAL, YOU INCLUDED. ALL AROUND THE WORLD, YEAH?
WELL, YOU'VE BEEN BETRAYED. ANTON ARCANE IS POISONING THE SPELL RIGHT NOW IN VIENNA. IT'S DONE.
IT'S JUST WHAT HAPPENS. I KNOW. I'M HERE FROM--
ENOUGH! YOU LIE!
I'LL SEND YOU BACK TO WHATEVER PIT SPAWNED YOU, CREATURE!
BY THE POWERS OF ASTRAL, OF FAE! BY THE POWERS OF THE SUBLIME AETHER AND THE REALMS BEYOND KEN!
FINE, GUV...
GNGGH
THAT'S ALL I NEED YOU TO DO ANYWAY.
HE REALLY IS ONE OF THE BEST OF US. THE BEST I EVER MET. A FOCUSING PHRASE FROM HIM AND THE REAL BLOODY UNDERPINNINGS OF THE UNIVERSE BEGIN TO SHOW THEMSELVES.
EVERYBODY SEES THEM DIFFERENTLY. SOME REPORT GLOWING PATHS OF LIGHT, OR AN ENORMOUS STRUCTURE WITH BUTTRESSES AND PILLARS. FOR ME, IT'S ALWAYS BEEN GREAT CHAINS HOLDING IT ALL TOGETHER...

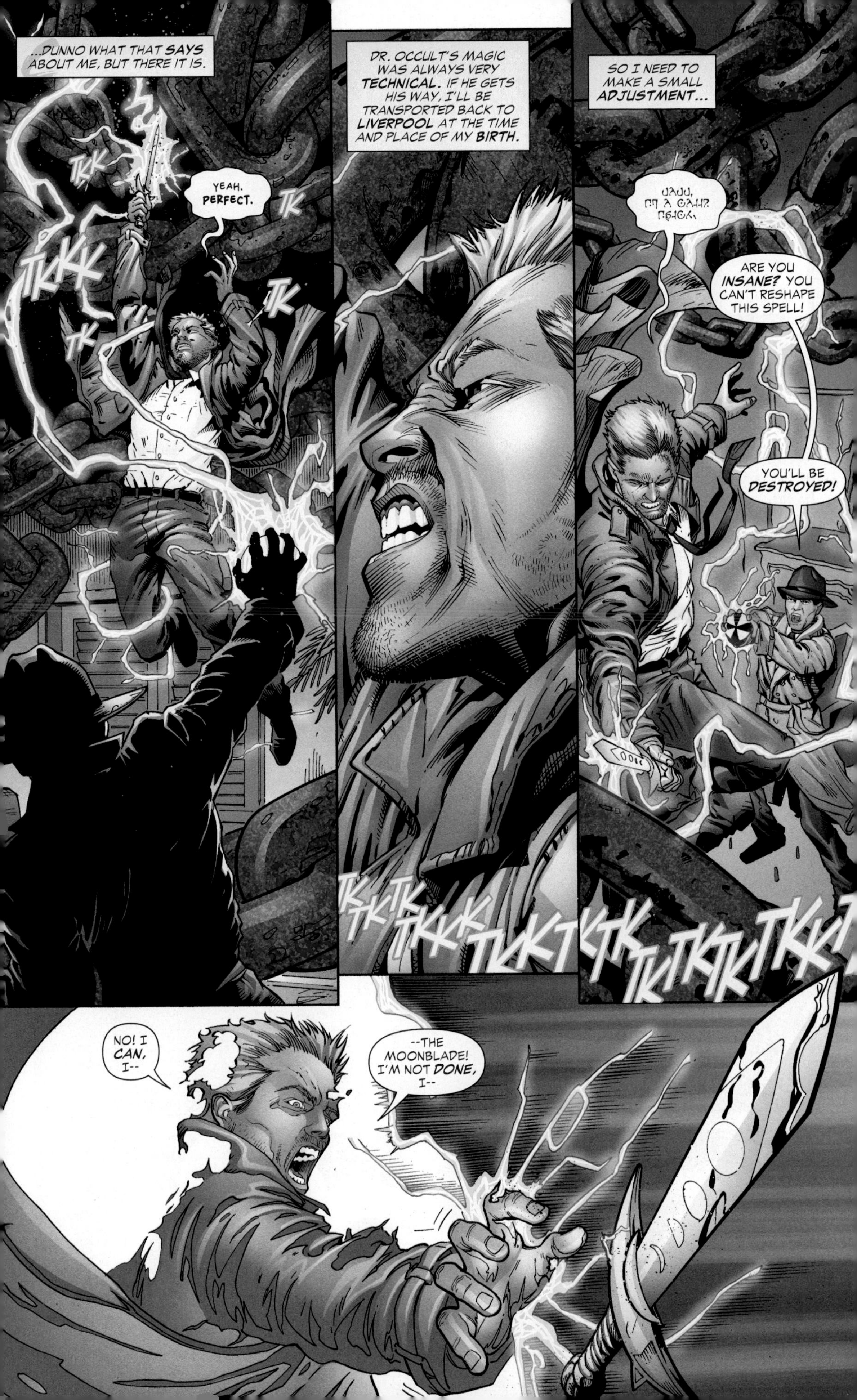
...DUNNO WHAT THAT SAYS ABOUT ME, BUT THERE IT IS.
TKK
YEAH. PERFECT.
TK
TKKK
TK
TK
DR. OCCULT'S MAGIC WAS ALWAYS VERY TECHNICAL. IF HE GETS HIS WAY, I'LL BE TRANSPORTED BACK TO LIVERPOOL AT THE TIME AND PLACE OF MY BIRTH.
SO I NEED TO MAKE A SMALL ADJUSTMENT...
ARE YOU INSANE? YOU CAN'T RESHAPE THIS SPELL!
YOU'LL BE DESTROYED!
TKTKTK TKKKK TKKTKTK TKTKTKTKTKKK
NO! I CAN, I--
--THE MOONBLADE! I'M NOT DONE, I--

SHHHRAAAKKRKKK

IN THIS PLACE **BETWEEN** PLACES...

...BLASTED INSIDE OUT...WAIT, ARE THESE MY THOUGHTS FROM **NOW** OR **BEFORE**--

--ARE THESE MY THOUGHTS OR SOMEONE **ELSE'S**?

FALLING **INTO** MYSELF AND **THROUGH** MYSELF AND I'M GOING BLOODY MAD WITH THE **PAIN**--

--THE BROKEN CHAINS...HAVEN'T I SEEN THIS **BEFORE**?

WHERE AM I? **WHEN** AM I?

I'M IN BLOODY **PIECES** AND I--AND I--

--AND I--

BOOOOOM

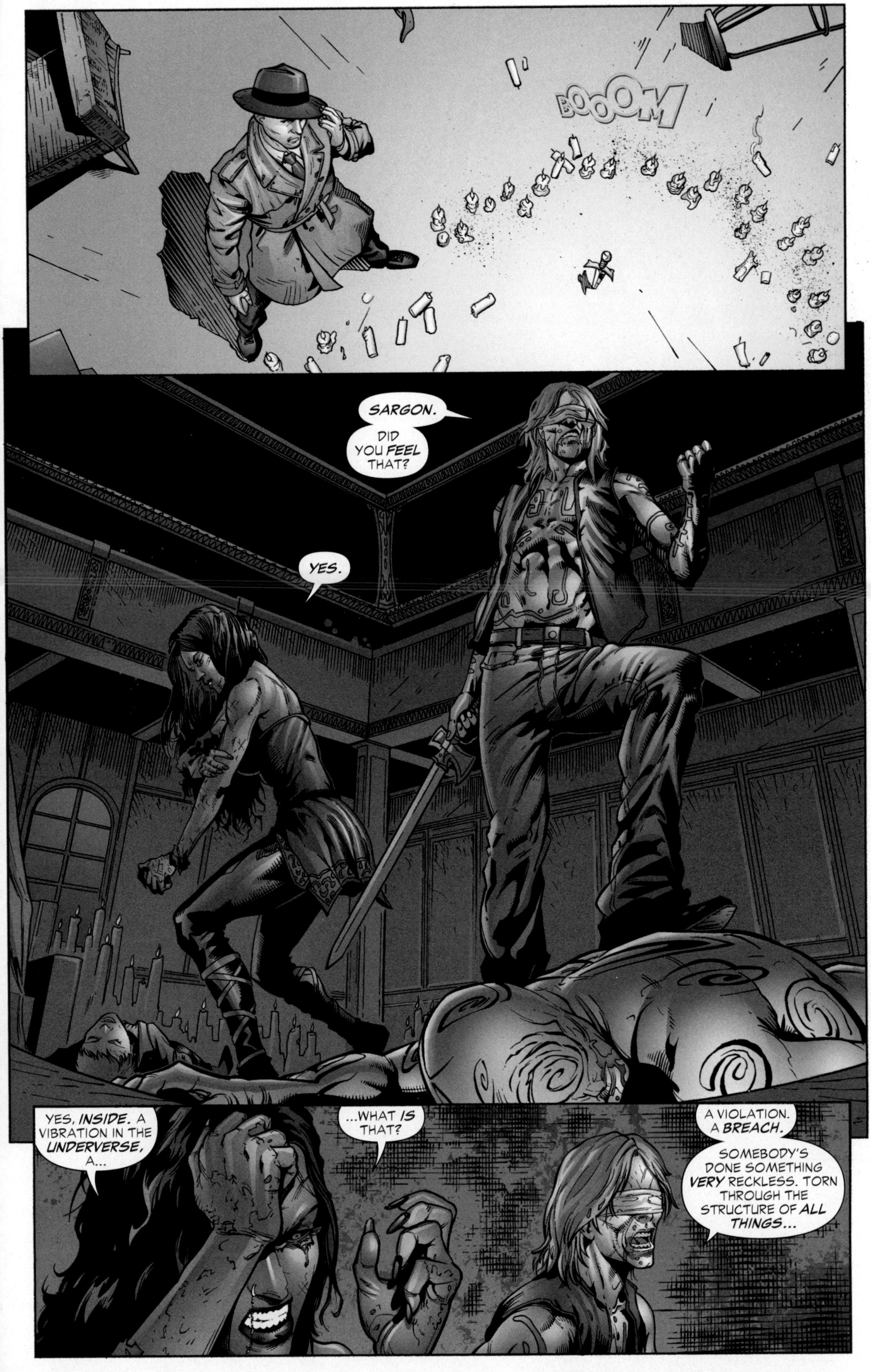
BOOOOM
SARGON.
DID YOU FEEL THAT?
YES.
YES, INSIDE. A VIBRATION IN THE UNDERVERSE, A...
...WHAT IS THAT?
A VIOLATION. A BREACH.
SOMEBODY'S DONE SOMETHING VERY RECKLESS. TORN THROUGH THE STRUCTURE OF ALL THINGS...

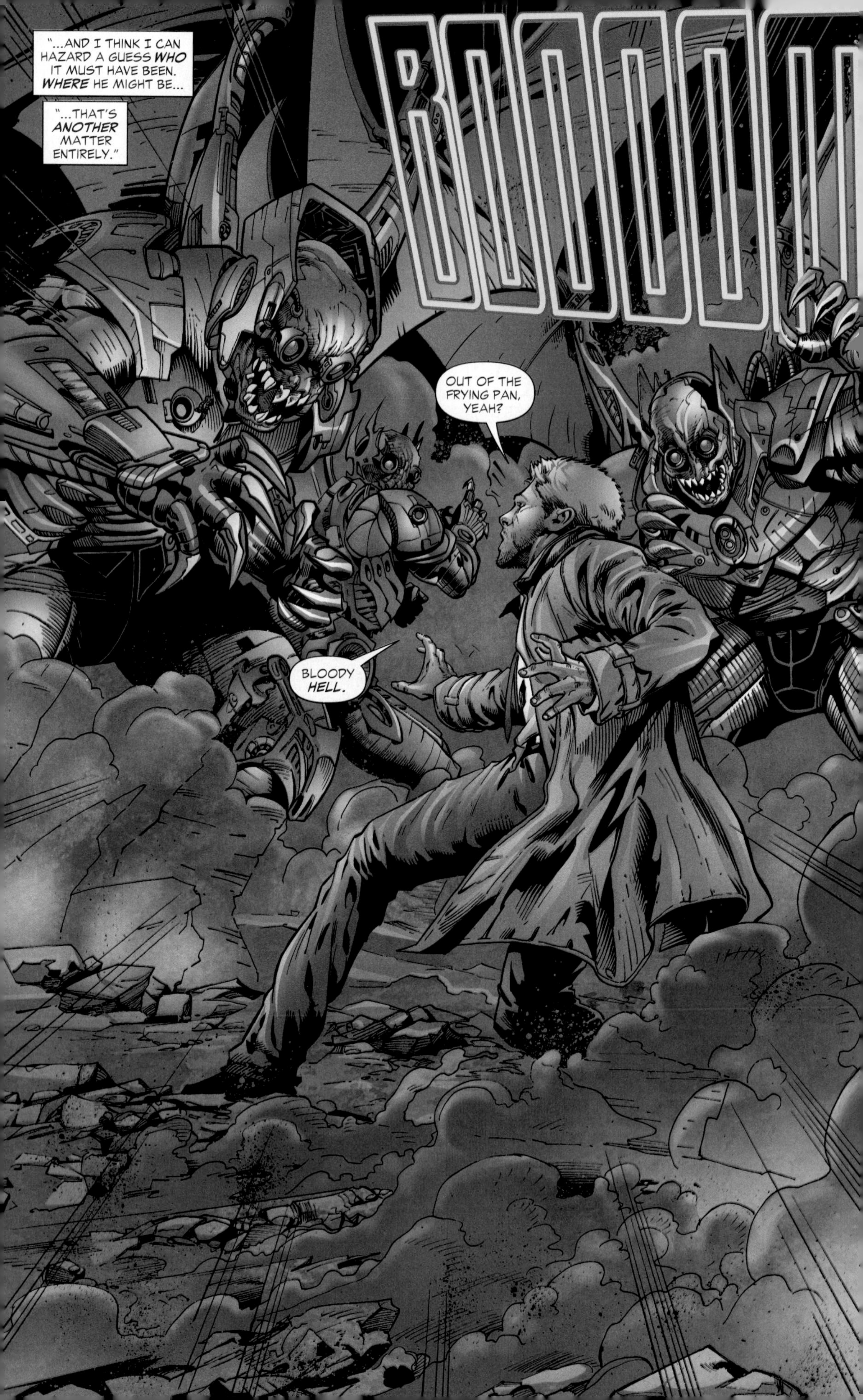
"...AND I THINK I CAN HAZARD A GUESS WHO IT MUST HAVE BEEN. WHERE HE MIGHT BE...
"...THAT'S ANOTHER MATTER ENTIRELY."
BOOOOOM
OUT OF THE FRYING PAN, YEAH?
BLOODY HELL.

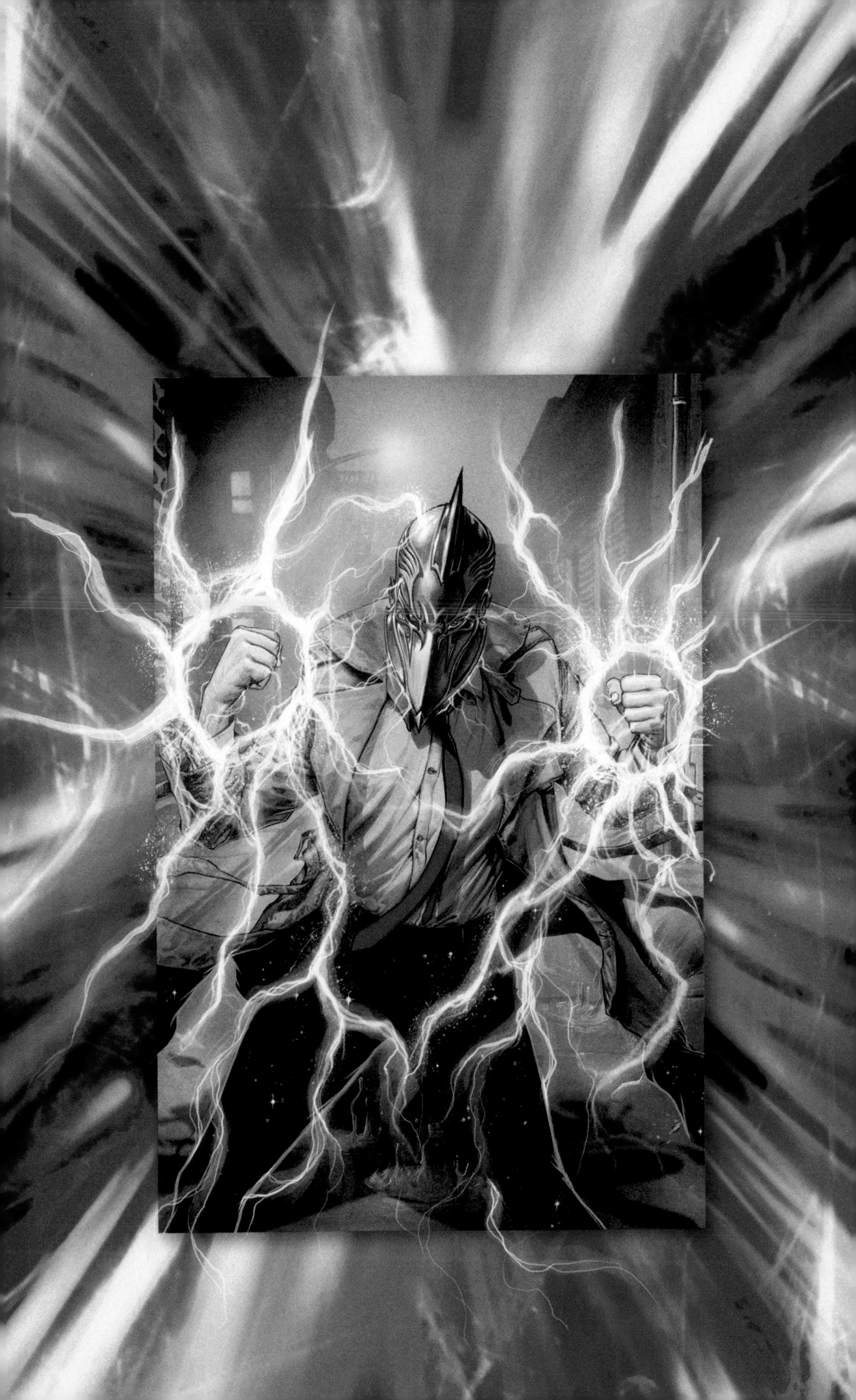

WEIGHING THE HEART

RAY FAWKES
writer

JUAN FERREYRA
artist

TANYA and RICHARD HORIE
colorists

PAT BROSSEAU
letterer

cover art by
JUAN FERREYRA

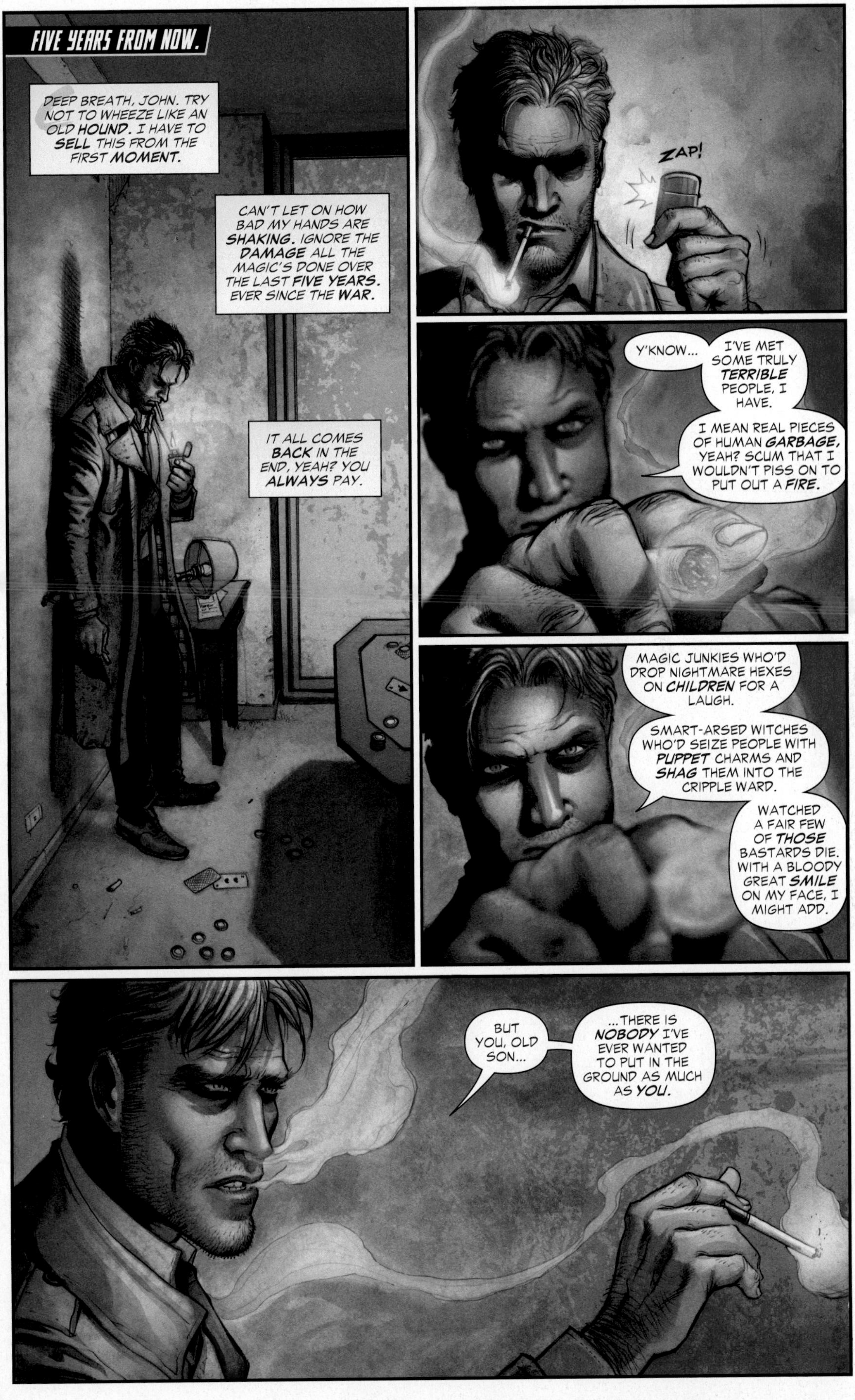
FIVE YEARS FROM NOW.
DEEP BREATH, JOHN. TRY NOT TO WHEEZE LIKE AN OLD HOUND. I HAVE TO SELL THIS FROM THE FIRST MOMENT.
CAN'T LET ON HOW BAD MY HANDS ARE SHAKING. IGNORE THE DAMAGE ALL THE MAGIC'S DONE OVER THE LAST FIVE YEARS. EVER SINCE THE WAR.
IT ALL COMES BACK IN THE END, YEAH? YOU ALWAYS PAY.
ZAP!
Y'KNOW...
I'VE MET SOME TRULY TERRIBLE PEOPLE, I HAVE.
I MEAN REAL PIECES OF HUMAN GARBAGE, YEAH? SCUM THAT I WOULDN'T PISS ON TO PUT OUT A FIRE.
MAGIC JUNKIES WHO'D DROP NIGHTMARE HEXES ON CHILDREN FOR A LAUGH.
SMART-ARSED WITCHES WHO'D SEIZE PEOPLE WITH PUPPET CHARMS AND SHAG THEM INTO THE CRIPPLE WARD.
WATCHED A FAIR FEW OF THOSE BASTARDS DIE. WITH A BLOODY GREAT SMILE ON MY FACE, I MIGHT ADD.
BUT YOU, OLD SON...
...THERE IS NOBODY I'VE EVER WANTED TO PUT IN THE GROUND AS MUCH AS YOU.

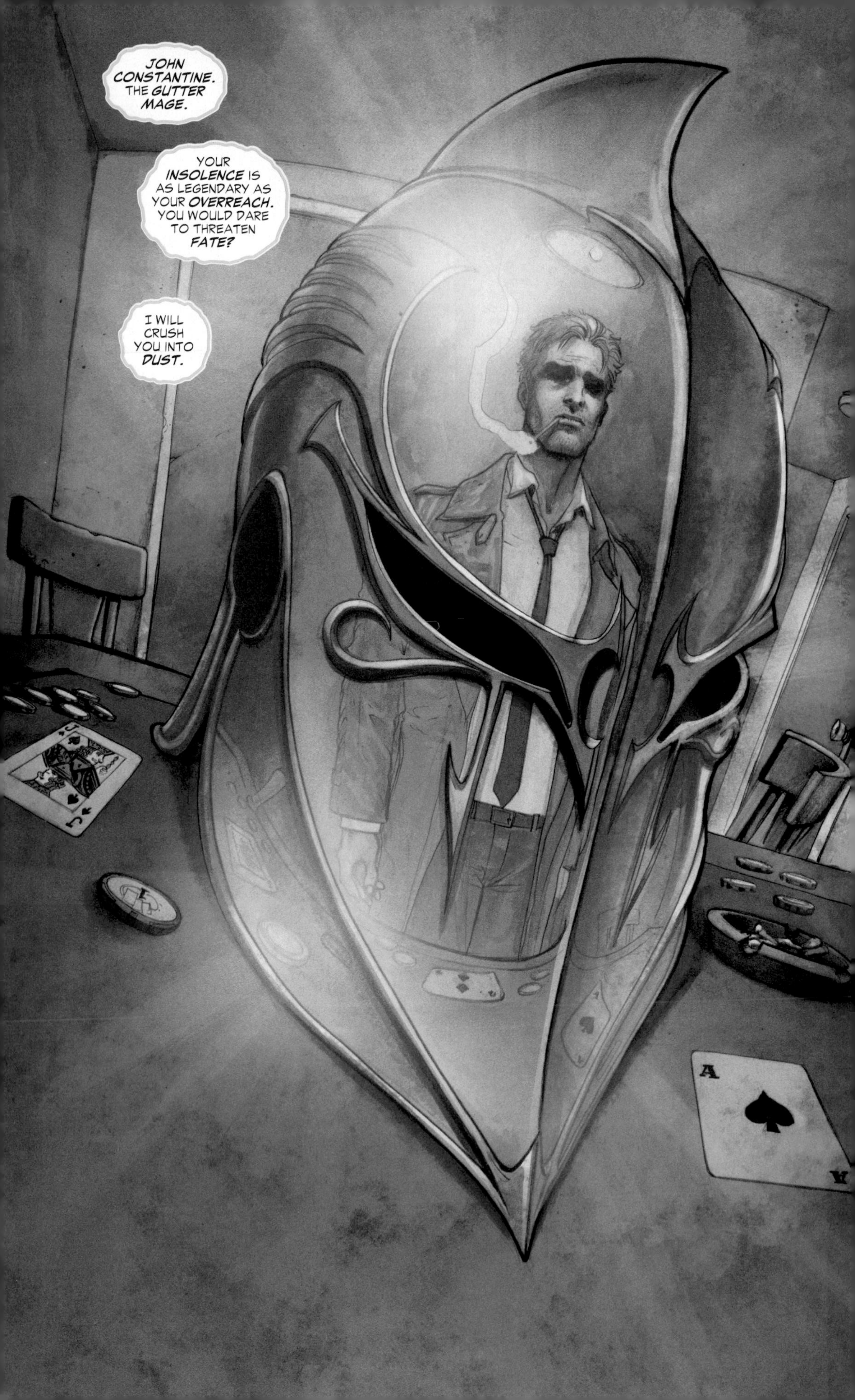

JOHN CONSTANTINE. THE GUTTER MAGE.
YOUR INSOLENCE IS AS LEGENDARY AS YOUR OVERREACH. YOU WOULD DARE TO THREATEN FATE?
I WILL CRUSH YOU INTO DUST.

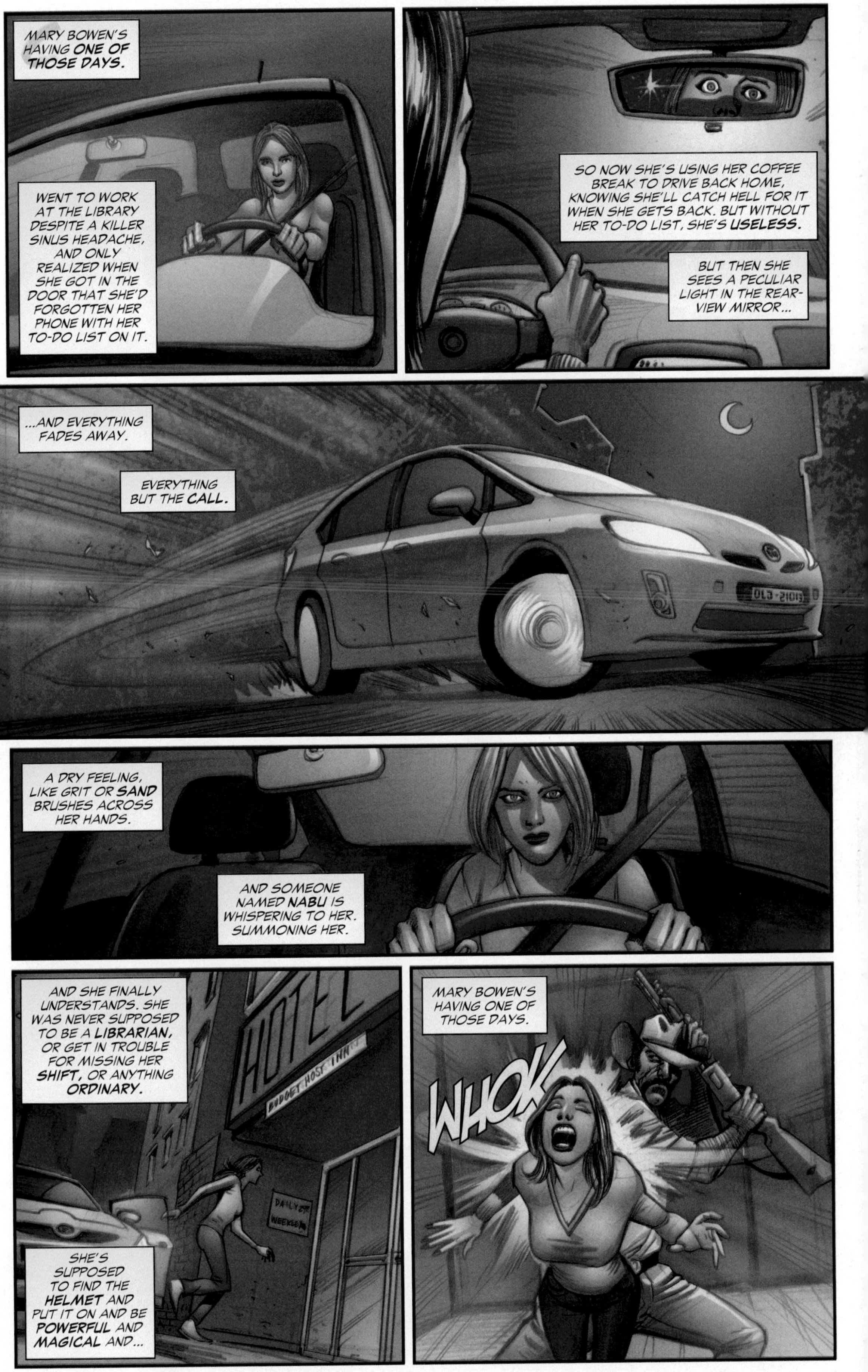

MARY BOWEN'S HAVING ONE OF THOSE DAYS.
WENT TO WORK AT THE LIBRARY DESPITE A KILLER SINUS HEADACHE, AND ONLY REALIZED WHEN SHE GOT IN THE DOOR THAT SHE'D FORGOTTEN HER PHONE WITH HER TO-DO LIST ON IT.
SO NOW SHE'S USING HER COFFEE BREAK TO DRIVE BACK HOME, KNOWING SHE'LL CATCH HELL FOR IT WHEN SHE GETS BACK. BUT WITHOUT HER TO-DO LIST, SHE'S USELESS.
BUT THEN SHE SEES A PECULIAR LIGHT IN THE REAR-VIEW MIRROR...
...AND EVERYTHING FADES AWAY.
EVERYTHING BUT THE CALL.
A DRY FEELING, LIKE GRIT OR SAND BRUSHES ACROSS HER HANDS.
AND SOMEONE NAMED NABU IS WHISPERING TO HER. SUMMONING HER.
AND SHE FINALLY UNDERSTANDS. SHE WAS NEVER SUPPOSED TO BE A LIBRARIAN, OR GET IN TROUBLE FOR MISSING HER SHIFT, OR ANYTHING ORDINARY.
HOTEL
BUDGET HOST INN
SHE'S SUPPOSED TO FIND THE HELMET AND PUT IT ON AND BE POWERFUL AND MAGICAL AND...
MARY BOWEN'S HAVING ONE OF THOSE DAYS.
WHOK

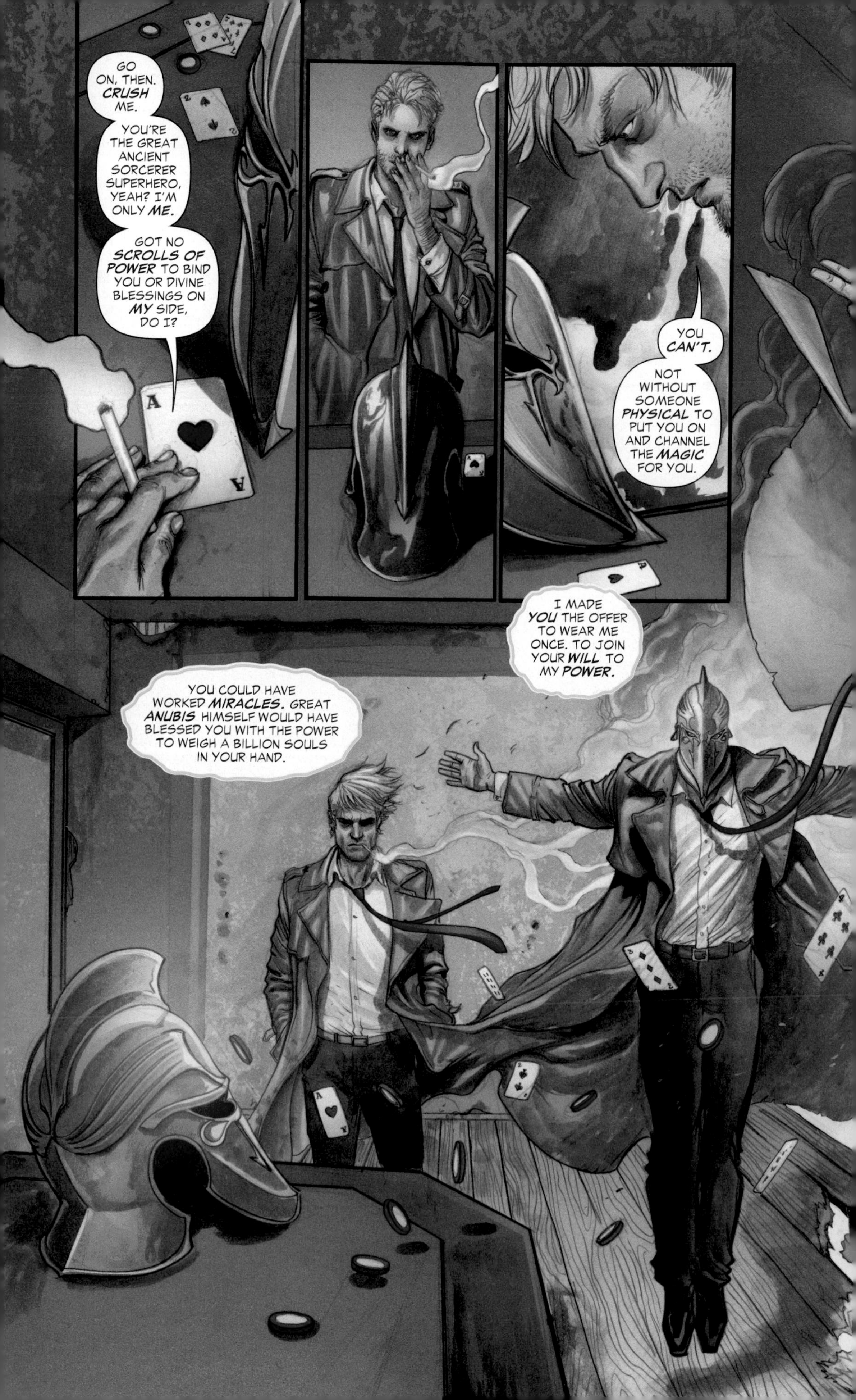
GO ON, THEN. CRUSH ME.
YOU'RE THE GREAT ANCIENT SORCERER SUPERHERO, YEAH? I'M ONLY ME.
GOT NO SCROLLS OF POWER TO BIND YOU OR DIVINE BLESSINGS ON MY SIDE, DO I?
YOU CAN'T.
NOT WITHOUT SOMEONE PHYSICAL TO PUT YOU ON AND CHANNEL THE MAGIC FOR YOU.
I MADE YOU THE OFFER TO WEAR ME ONCE. TO JOIN YOUR WILL TO MY POWER.
YOU COULD HAVE WORKED MIRACLES. GREAT ANUBIS HIMSELF WOULD HAVE BLESSED YOU WITH THE POWER TO WEIGH A BILLION SOULS IN YOUR HAND.

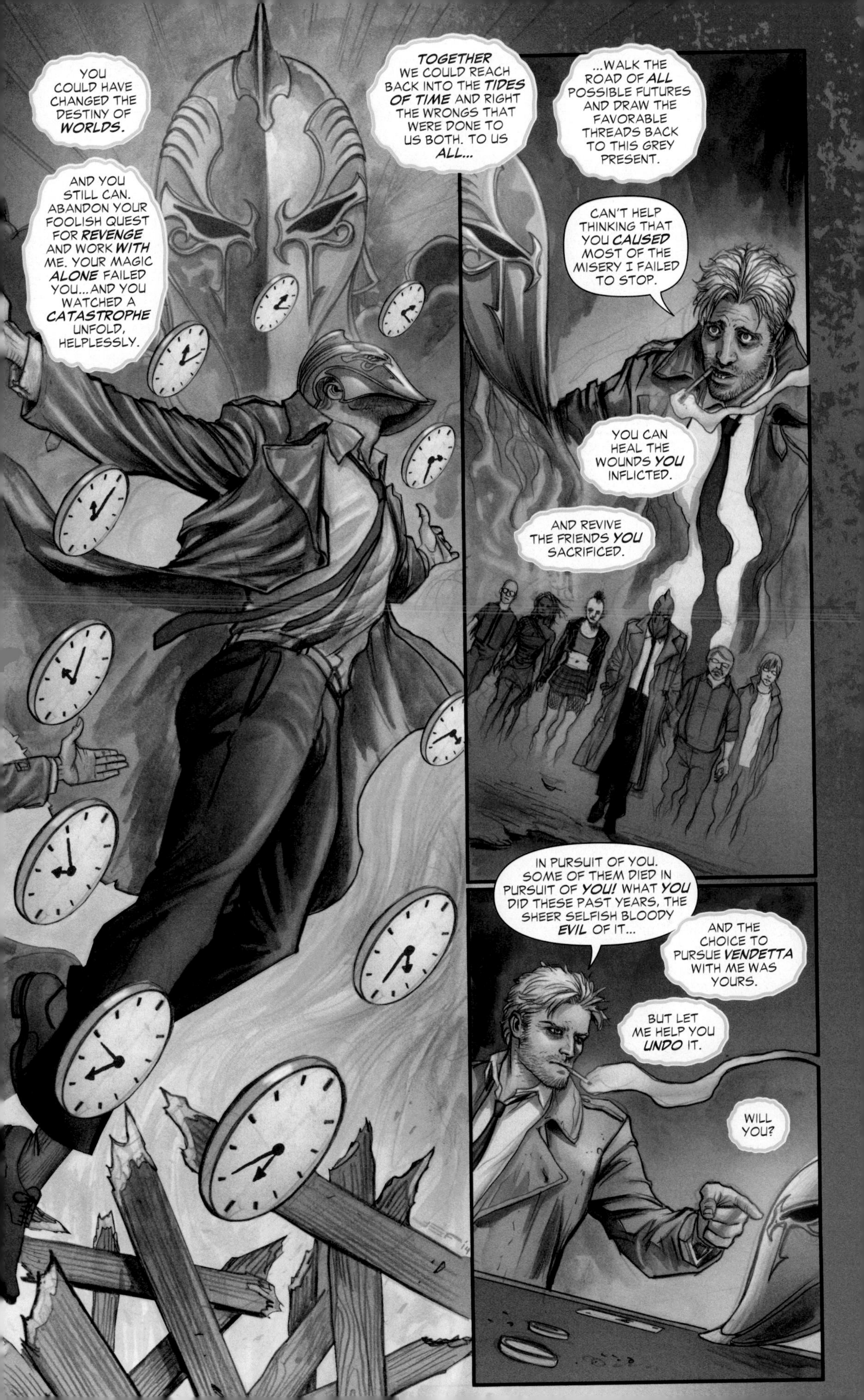

YOU COULD HAVE CHANGED THE DESTINY OF *WORLDS.*
AND YOU STILL CAN. ABANDON YOUR FOOLISH QUEST FOR *REVENGE* AND WORK *WITH* ME. YOUR MAGIC *ALONE* FAILED YOU...AND YOU WATCHED A *CATASTROPHE* UNFOLD, HELPLESSLY.
TOGETHER WE COULD REACH BACK INTO THE *TIDES OF TIME* AND RIGHT THE WRONGS THAT WERE DONE TO US BOTH. TO US *ALL...*
...WALK THE ROAD OF *ALL* POSSIBLE FUTURES AND DRAW THE FAVORABLE THREADS BACK TO THIS GREY PRESENT.
CAN'T HELP THINKING THAT YOU *CAUSED* MOST OF THE MISERY I FAILED TO STOP.
YOU CAN HEAL THE WOUNDS *YOU* INFLICTED.
AND REVIVE THE FRIENDS *YOU* SACRIFICED.
IN PURSUIT OF YOU. SOME OF THEM DIED IN PURSUIT OF *YOU!* WHAT *YOU* DID THESE PAST YEARS, THE SHEER SELFISH BLOODY *EVIL* OF IT...
AND THE CHOICE TO PURSUE *VENDETTA* WITH ME WAS YOURS.
BUT LET ME HELP YOU *UNDO* IT.
WILL YOU?

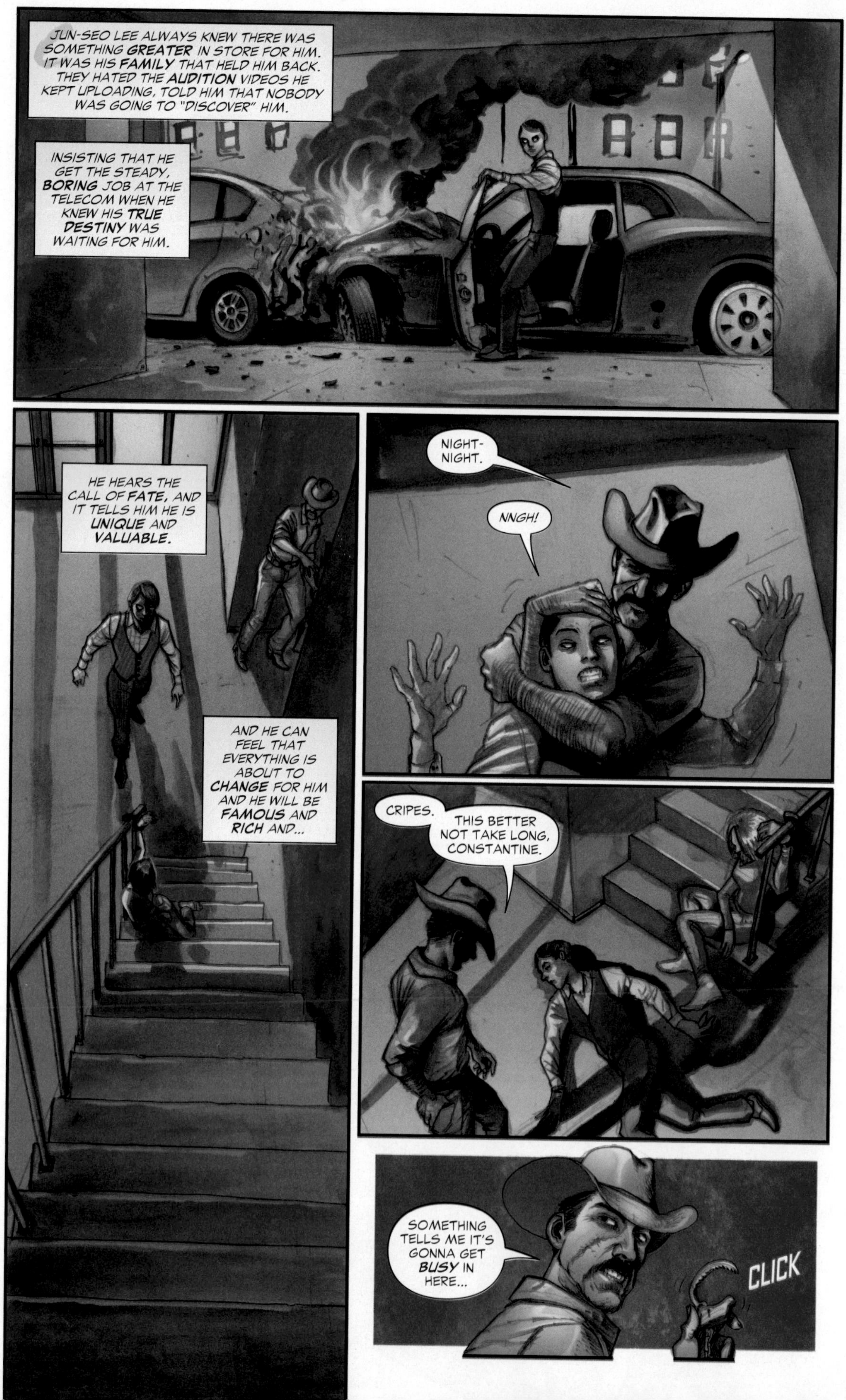
JUN-SEO LEE ALWAYS KNEW THERE WAS SOMETHING GREATER IN STORE FOR HIM. IT WAS HIS FAMILY THAT HELD HIM BACK. THEY HATED THE AUDITION VIDEOS HE KEPT UPLOADING, TOLD HIM THAT NOBODY WAS GOING TO "DISCOVER" HIM.
INSISTING THAT HE GET THE STEADY, BORING JOB AT THE TELECOM WHEN HE KNEW HIS TRUE DESTINY WAS WAITING FOR HIM.
HE HEARS THE CALL OF FATE, AND IT TELLS HIM HE IS UNIQUE AND VALUABLE.
AND HE CAN FEEL THAT EVERYTHING IS ABOUT TO CHANGE FOR HIM AND HE WILL BE FAMOUS AND RICH AND...
NIGHT-NIGHT.
NNGH!
CRIPES.
THIS BETTER NOT TAKE LONG, CONSTANTINE.
SOMETHING TELLS ME IT'S GONNA GET BUSY IN HERE...
CLICK

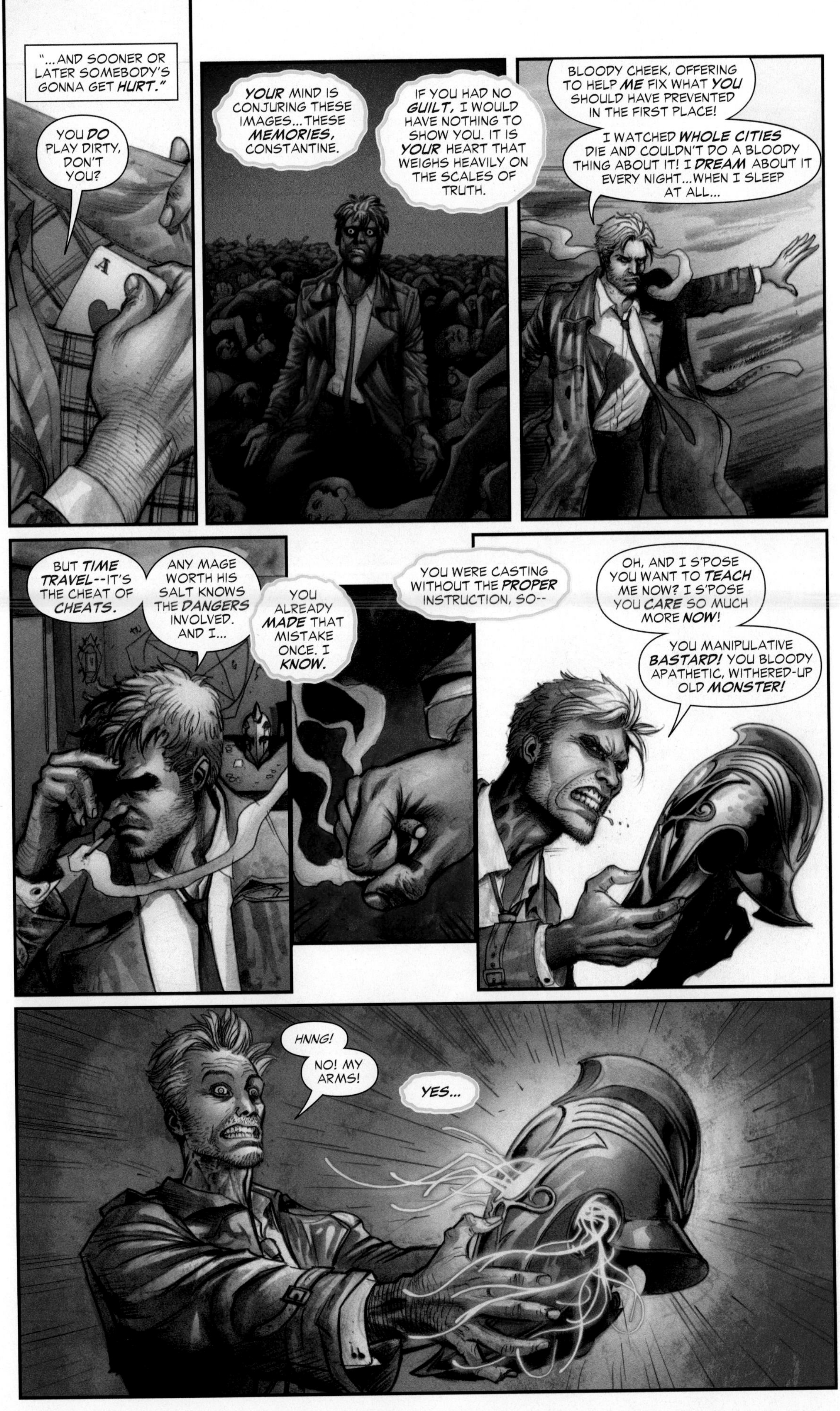
"...AND SOONER OR LATER SOMEBODY'S GONNA GET HURT."
YOU DO PLAY DIRTY, DON'T YOU?
YOUR MIND IS CONJURING THESE IMAGES...THESE MEMORIES, CONSTANTINE.
IF YOU HAD NO GUILT, I WOULD HAVE NOTHING TO SHOW YOU. IT IS YOUR HEART THAT WEIGHS HEAVILY ON THE SCALES OF TRUTH.
BLOODY CHEEK, OFFERING TO HELP ME FIX WHAT YOU SHOULD HAVE PREVENTED IN THE FIRST PLACE!
I WATCHED WHOLE CITIES DIE AND COULDN'T DO A BLOODY THING ABOUT IT! I DREAM ABOUT IT EVERY NIGHT...WHEN I SLEEP AT ALL...
BUT TIME TRAVEL--IT'S THE CHEAT OF CHEATS.
ANY MAGE WORTH HIS SALT KNOWS THE DANGERS INVOLVED. AND I...
YOU ALREADY MADE THAT MISTAKE ONCE. I KNOW.
YOU WERE CASTING WITHOUT THE PROPER INSTRUCTION, SO--
OH, AND I S'POSE YOU WANT TO TEACH ME NOW? I S'POSE YOU CARE SO MUCH MORE NOW!
YOU MANIPULATIVE BASTARD! YOU BLOODY APATHETIC, WITHERED-UP OLD MONSTER!
HNNG!
NO! MY ARMS!
YES...

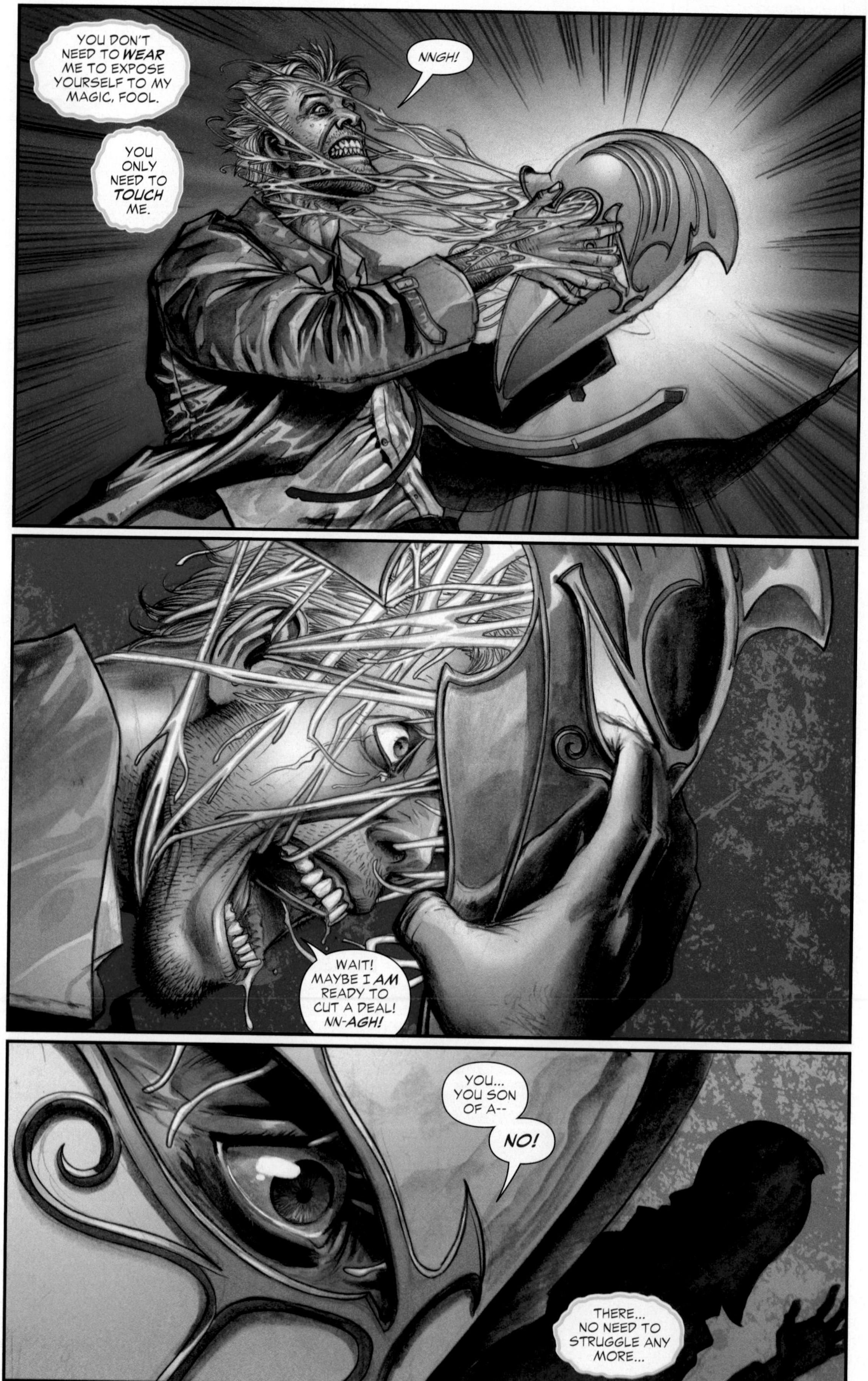
YOU DON'T NEED TO *WEAR* ME TO EXPOSE YOURSELF TO MY MAGIC, FOOL.
YOU ONLY NEED TO *TOUCH* ME.
NNGH!
WAIT! MAYBE I *AM* READY TO CUT A DEAL! *NN-AGH!*
YOU... YOU SON OF A--
NO!
THERE... NO NEED TO STRUGGLE ANY MORE...

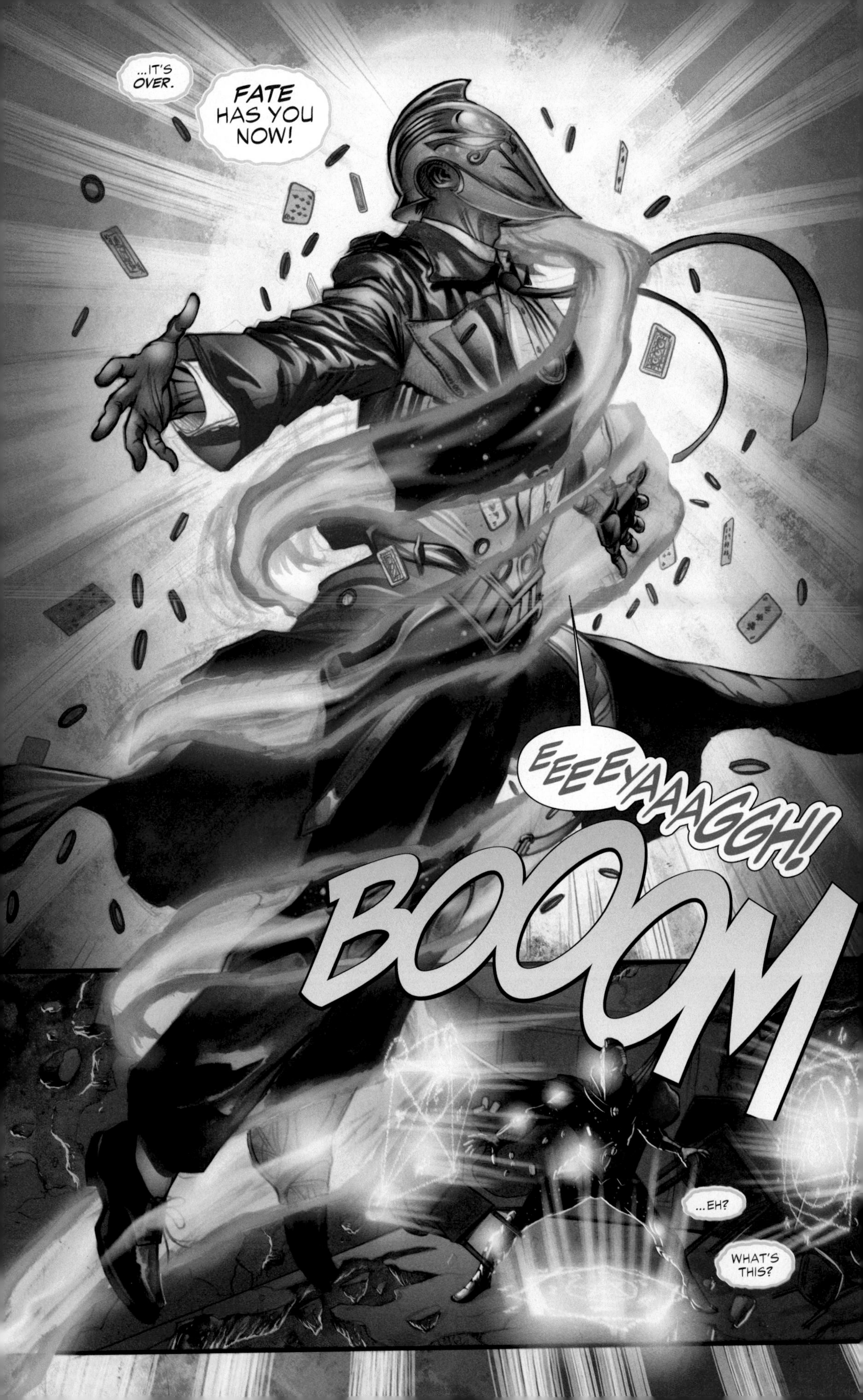
...IT'S OVER.
FATE HAS YOU NOW!
EEEEYAAAGGH!
BOOOM
...EH?
WHAT'S THIS?

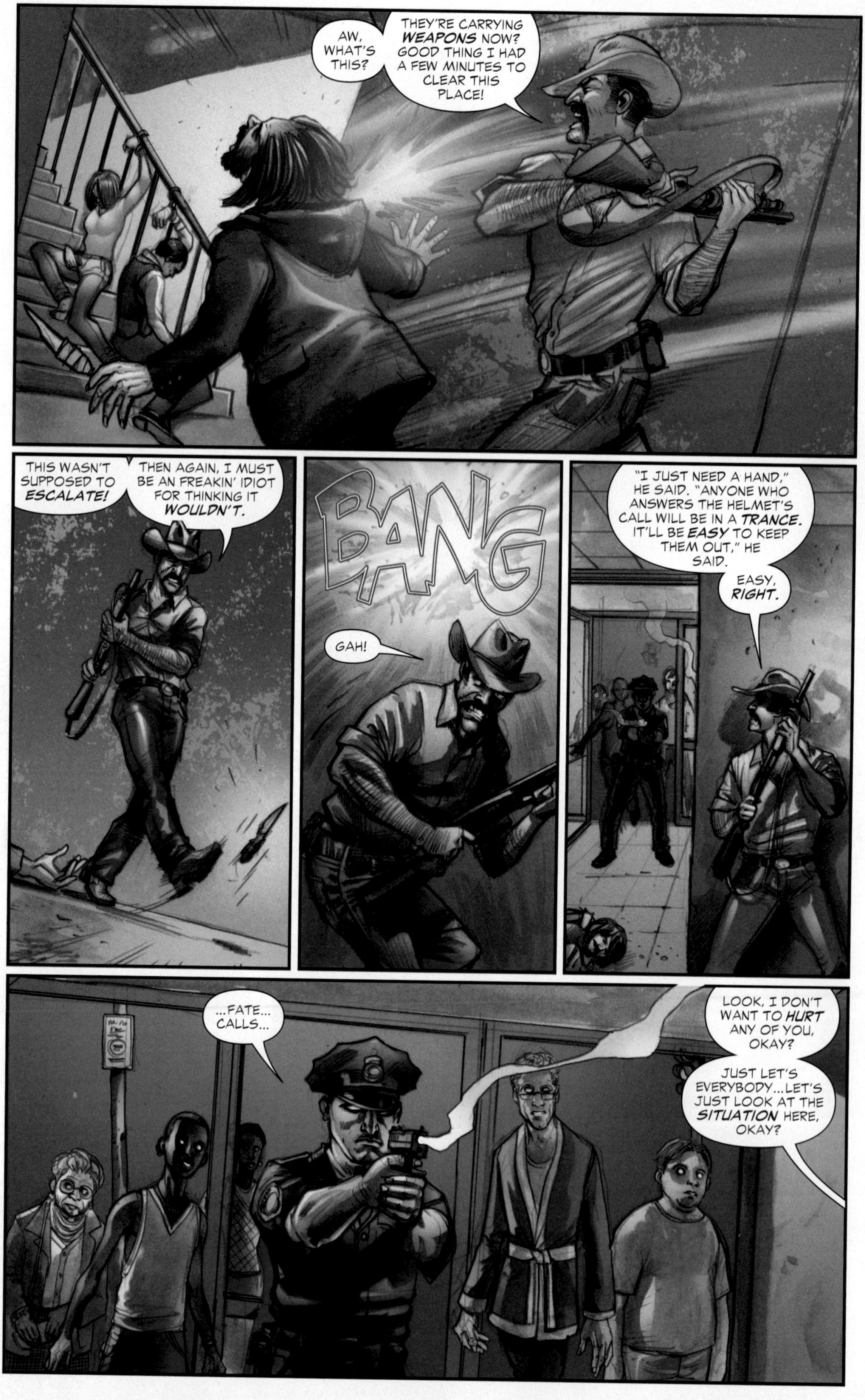
AW, WHAT'S THIS?
THEY'RE CARRYING WEAPONS NOW? GOOD THING I HAD A FEW MINUTES TO CLEAR THIS PLACE!
THIS WASN'T SUPPOSED TO ESCALATE!
THEN AGAIN, I MUST BE AN FREAKIN' IDIOT FOR THINKING IT WOULDN'T.
BANG
GAH!
"I JUST NEED A HAND," HE SAID. "ANYONE WHO ANSWERS THE HELMET'S CALL WILL BE IN A TRANCE. IT'LL BE EASY TO KEEP THEM OUT," HE SAID.
EASY, RIGHT.
...FATE... CALLS...
LOOK, I DON'T WANT TO HURT ANY OF YOU, OKAY?
JUST LET'S EVERYBODY...LET'S JUST LOOK AT THE SITUATION HERE, OKAY?

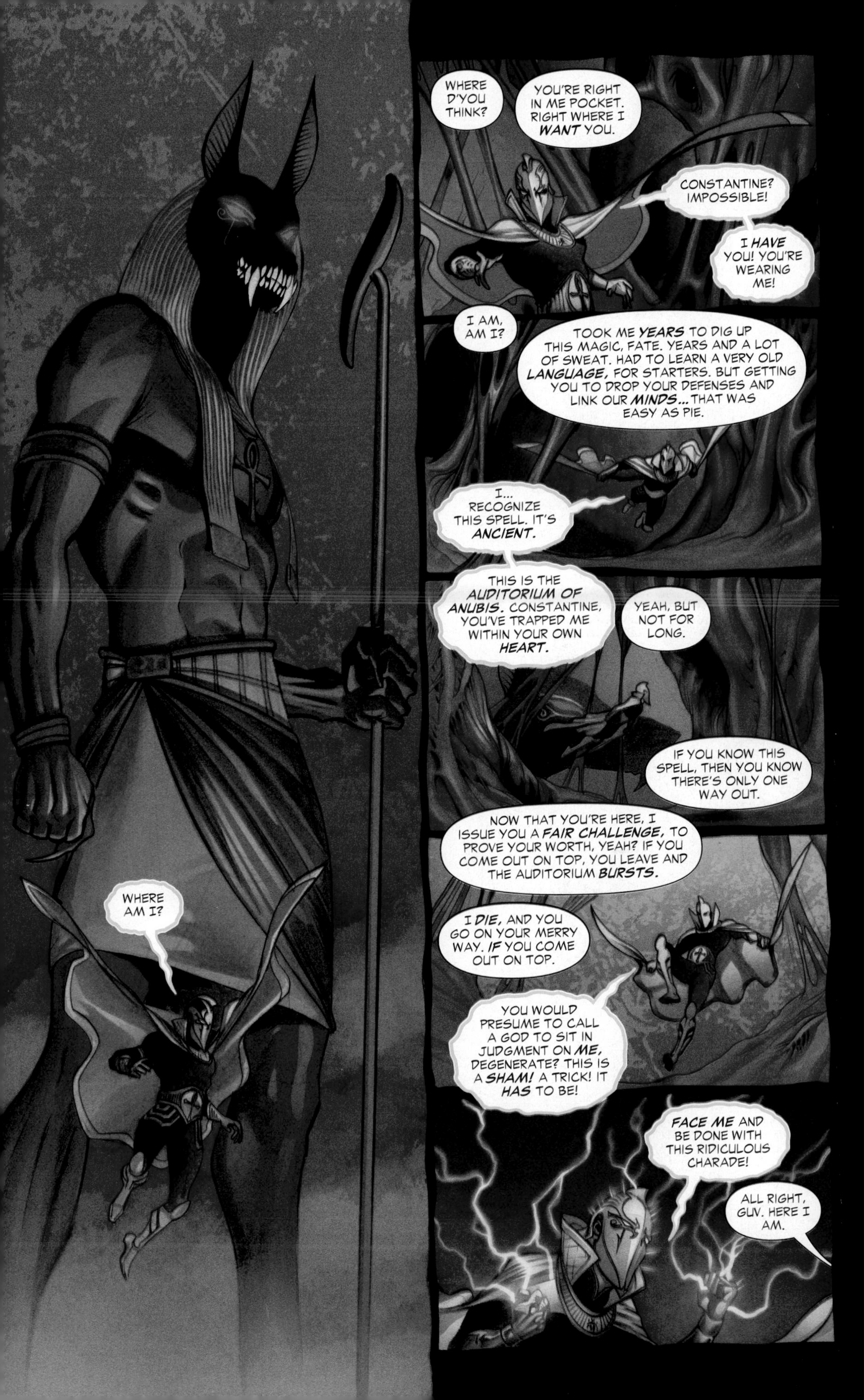
WHERE AM I?
WHERE D'YOU THINK?
YOU'RE RIGHT IN ME POCKET. RIGHT WHERE I WANT YOU.
CONSTANTINE? IMPOSSIBLE!
I HAVE YOU! YOU'RE WEARING ME!
I AM, AM I?
TOOK ME YEARS TO DIG UP THIS MAGIC, FATE. YEARS AND A LOT OF SWEAT. HAD TO LEARN A VERY OLD LANGUAGE, FOR STARTERS. BUT GETTING YOU TO DROP YOUR DEFENSES AND LINK OUR MINDS... THAT WAS EASY AS PIE.
I... RECOGNIZE THIS SPELL. IT'S ANCIENT.
THIS IS THE AUDITORIUM OF ANUBIS. CONSTANTINE, YOU'VE TRAPPED ME WITHIN YOUR OWN HEART.
YEAH, BUT NOT FOR LONG.
IF YOU KNOW THIS SPELL, THEN YOU KNOW THERE'S ONLY ONE WAY OUT.
NOW THAT YOU'RE HERE, I ISSUE YOU A FAIR CHALLENGE, TO PROVE YOUR WORTH, YEAH? IF YOU COME OUT ON TOP, YOU LEAVE AND THE AUDITORIUM BURSTS.
I DIE, AND YOU GO ON YOUR MERRY WAY. IF YOU COME OUT ON TOP.
YOU WOULD PRESUME TO CALL A GOD TO SIT IN JUDGMENT ON ME, DEGENERATE? THIS IS A SHAM! A TRICK! IT HAS TO BE!
FACE ME AND BE DONE WITH THIS RIDICULOUS CHARADE!
ALL RIGHT, GUV. HERE I AM.

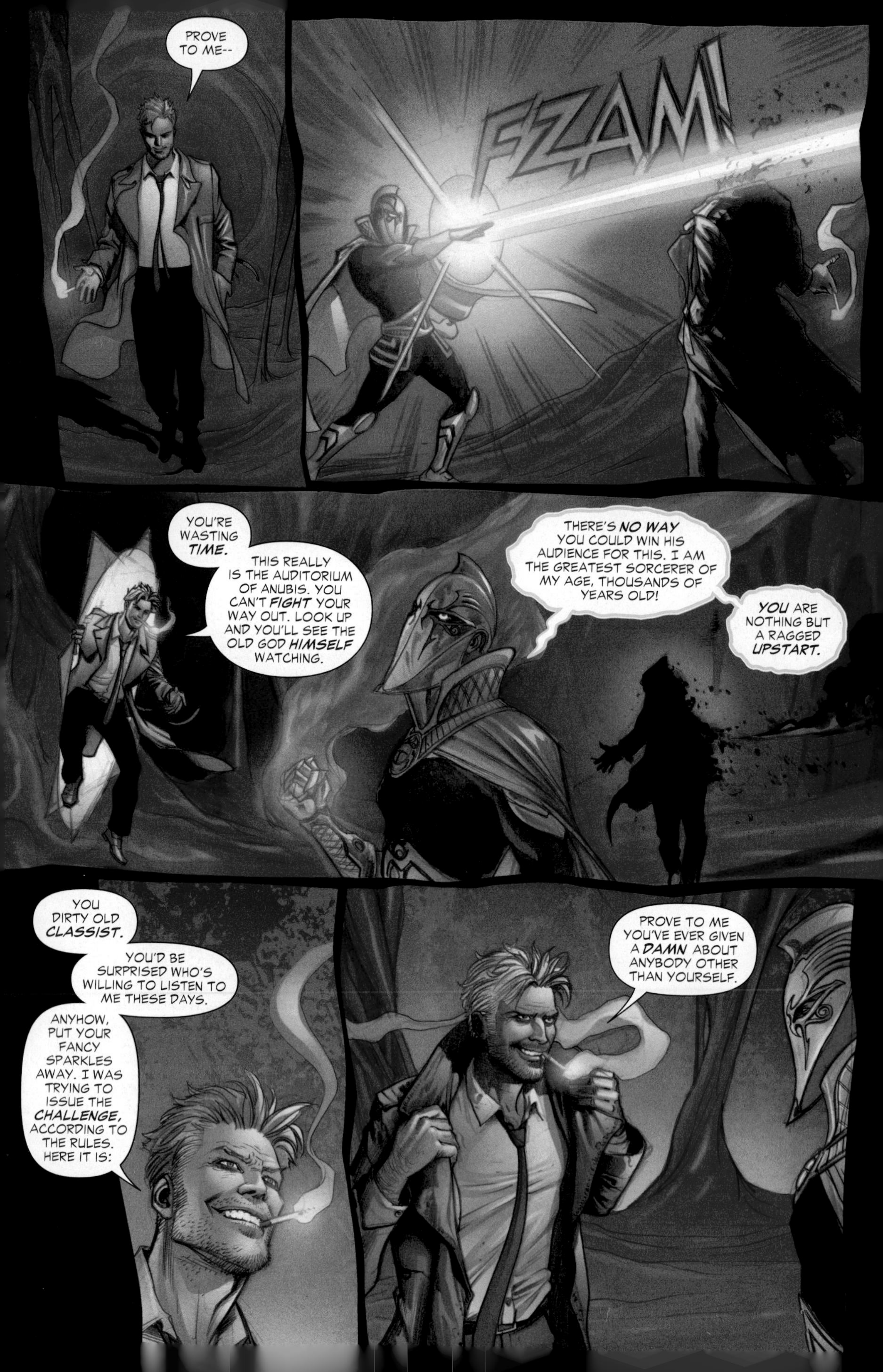
PROVE TO ME--
FZAM!
YOU'RE WASTING TIME.
THIS REALLY IS THE AUDITORIUM OF ANUBIS. YOU CAN'T FIGHT YOUR WAY OUT. LOOK UP AND YOU'LL SEE THE OLD GOD HIMSELF WATCHING.
THERE'S NO WAY YOU COULD WIN HIS AUDIENCE FOR THIS. I AM THE GREATEST SORCERER OF MY AGE, THOUSANDS OF YEARS OLD!
YOU ARE NOTHING BUT A RAGGED UPSTART.
YOU DIRTY OLD CLASSIST.
YOU'D BE SURPRISED WHO'S WILLING TO LISTEN TO ME THESE DAYS.
ANYHOW, PUT YOUR FANCY SPARKLES AWAY. I WAS TRYING TO ISSUE THE CHALLENGE, ACCORDING TO THE RULES. HERE IT IS:
PROVE TO ME YOU'VE EVER GIVEN A DAMN ABOUT ANYBODY OTHER THAN YOURSELF.

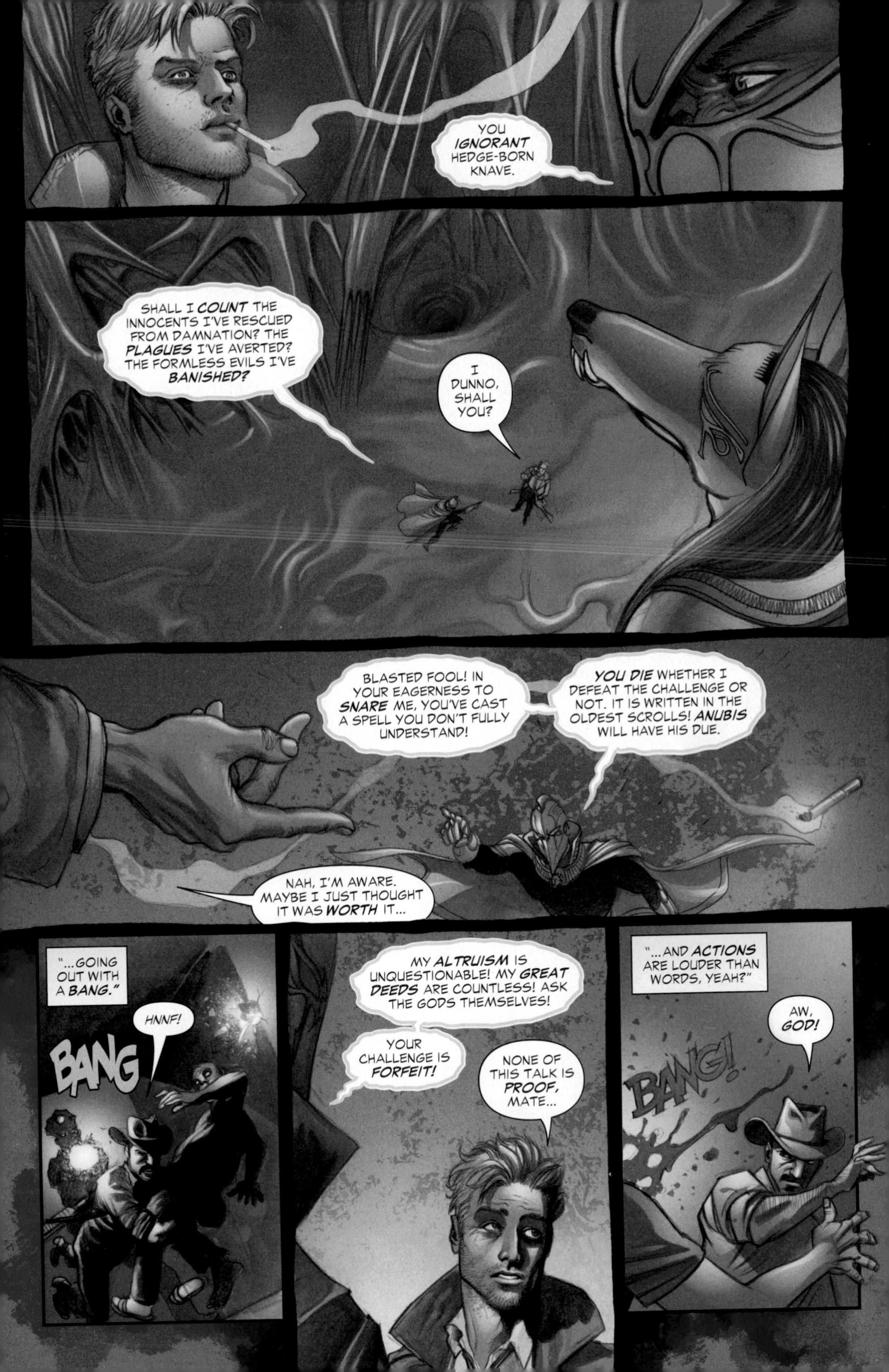

YOU IGNORANT HEDGE-BORN KNAVE.
SHALL I COUNT THE INNOCENTS I'VE RESCUED FROM DAMNATION? THE PLAGUES I'VE AVERTED? THE FORMLESS EVILS I'VE BANISHED?
I DUNNO, SHALL YOU?
BLASTED FOOL! IN YOUR EAGERNESS TO SNARE ME, YOU'VE CAST A SPELL YOU DON'T FULLY UNDERSTAND!
YOU DIE WHETHER I DEFEAT THE CHALLENGE OR NOT. IT IS WRITTEN IN THE OLDEST SCROLLS! ANUBIS WILL HAVE HIS DUE.
NAH, I'M AWARE. MAYBE I JUST THOUGHT IT WAS WORTH IT...
"...GOING OUT WITH A BANG."
HNNF!
BANG
MY ALTRUISM IS UNQUESTIONABLE! MY GREAT DEEDS ARE COUNTLESS! ASK THE GODS THEMSELVES!
YOUR CHALLENGE IS FORFEIT!
NONE OF THIS TALK IS PROOF, MATE...
"...AND ACTIONS ARE LOUDER THAN WORDS, YEAH?"
AW, GOD!
BANG!

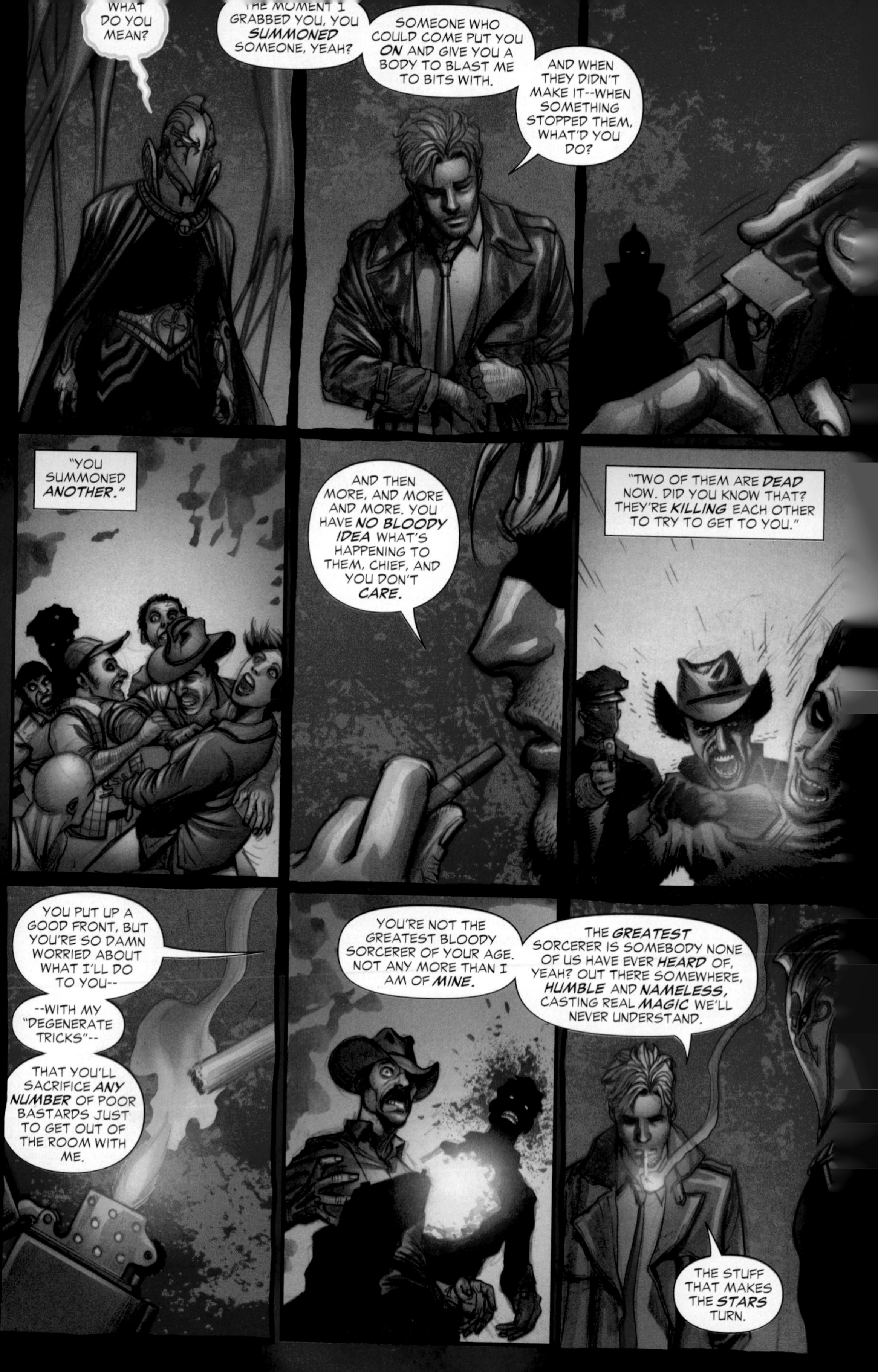
WHAT DO YOU MEAN?
THE MOMENT I GRABBED YOU, YOU SUMMONED SOMEONE, YEAH?
SOMEONE WHO COULD COME PUT YOU ON AND GIVE YOU A BODY TO BLAST ME TO BITS WITH.
AND WHEN THEY DIDN'T MAKE IT--WHEN SOMETHING STOPPED THEM, WHAT'D YOU DO?
"YOU SUMMONED ANOTHER."
AND THEN MORE, AND MORE AND MORE. YOU HAVE NO BLOODY IDEA WHAT'S HAPPENING TO THEM, CHIEF, AND YOU DON'T CARE.
"TWO OF THEM ARE DEAD NOW. DID YOU KNOW THAT? THEY'RE KILLING EACH OTHER TO TRY TO GET TO YOU."
YOU PUT UP A GOOD FRONT, BUT YOU'RE SO DAMN WORRIED ABOUT WHAT I'LL DO TO YOU--
--WITH MY "DEGENERATE TRICKS"--
THAT YOU'LL SACRIFICE ANY NUMBER OF POOR BASTARDS JUST TO GET OUT OF THE ROOM WITH ME.
YOU'RE NOT THE GREATEST BLOODY SORCERER OF YOUR AGE. NOT ANY MORE THAN I AM OF MINE.
THE GREATEST SORCERER IS SOMEBODY NONE OF US HAVE EVER HEARD OF, YEAH? OUT THERE SOMEWHERE, HUMBLE AND NAMELESS, CASTING REAL MAGIC WE'LL NEVER UNDERSTAND.
THE STUFF THAT MAKES THE STARS TURN.

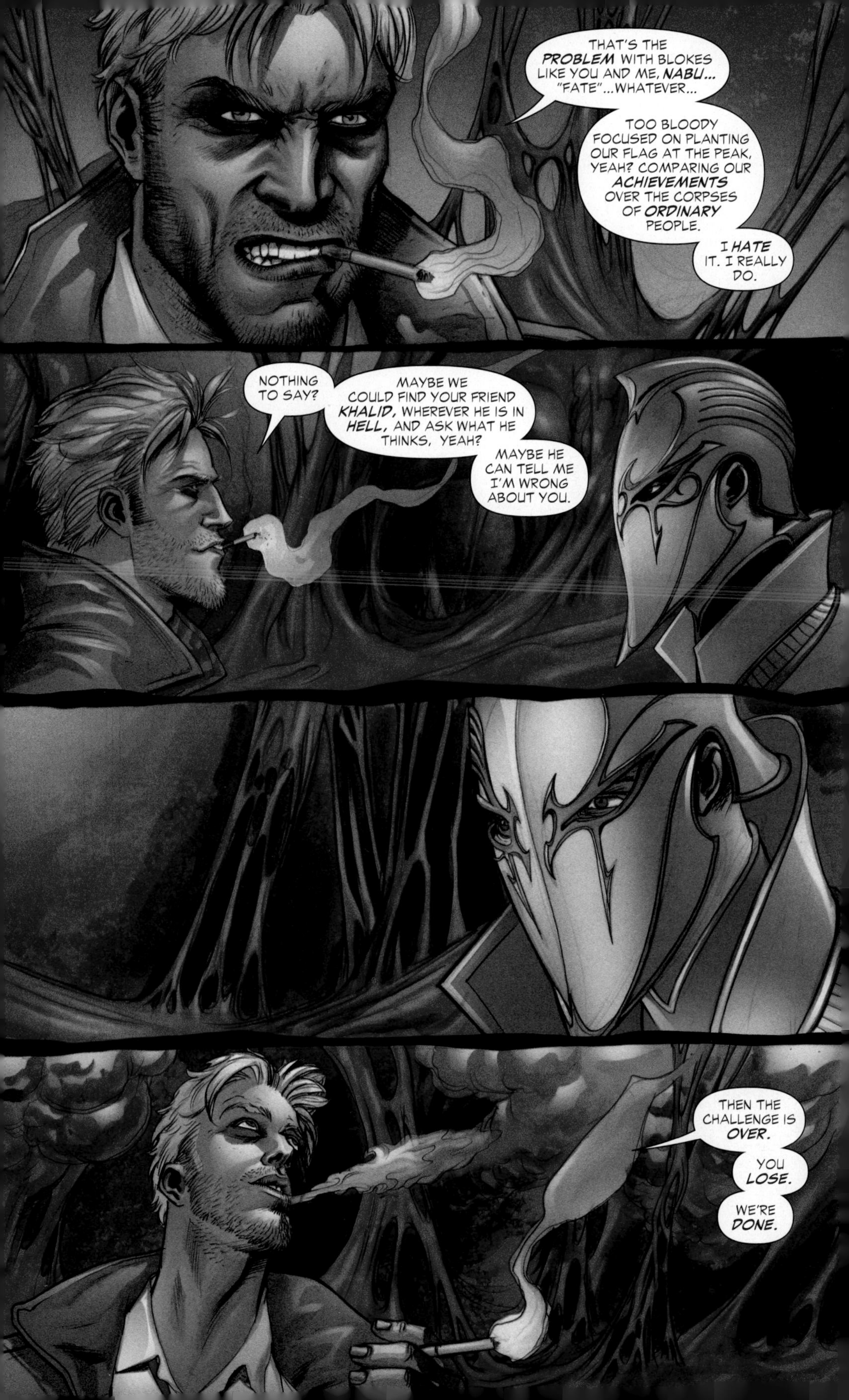
THAT'S THE PROBLEM WITH BLOKES LIKE YOU AND ME, NABU... "FATE"...WHATEVER...
TOO BLOODY FOCUSED ON PLANTING OUR FLAG AT THE PEAK, YEAH? COMPARING OUR ACHIEVEMENTS OVER THE CORPSES OF ORDINARY PEOPLE.
I HATE IT. I REALLY DO.
NOTHING TO SAY?
MAYBE WE COULD FIND YOUR FRIEND KHALID, WHEREVER HE IS IN HELL, AND ASK WHAT HE THINKS, YEAH?
MAYBE HE CAN TELL ME I'M WRONG ABOUT YOU.
THEN THE CHALLENGE IS OVER.
YOU LOSE.
WE'RE DONE.

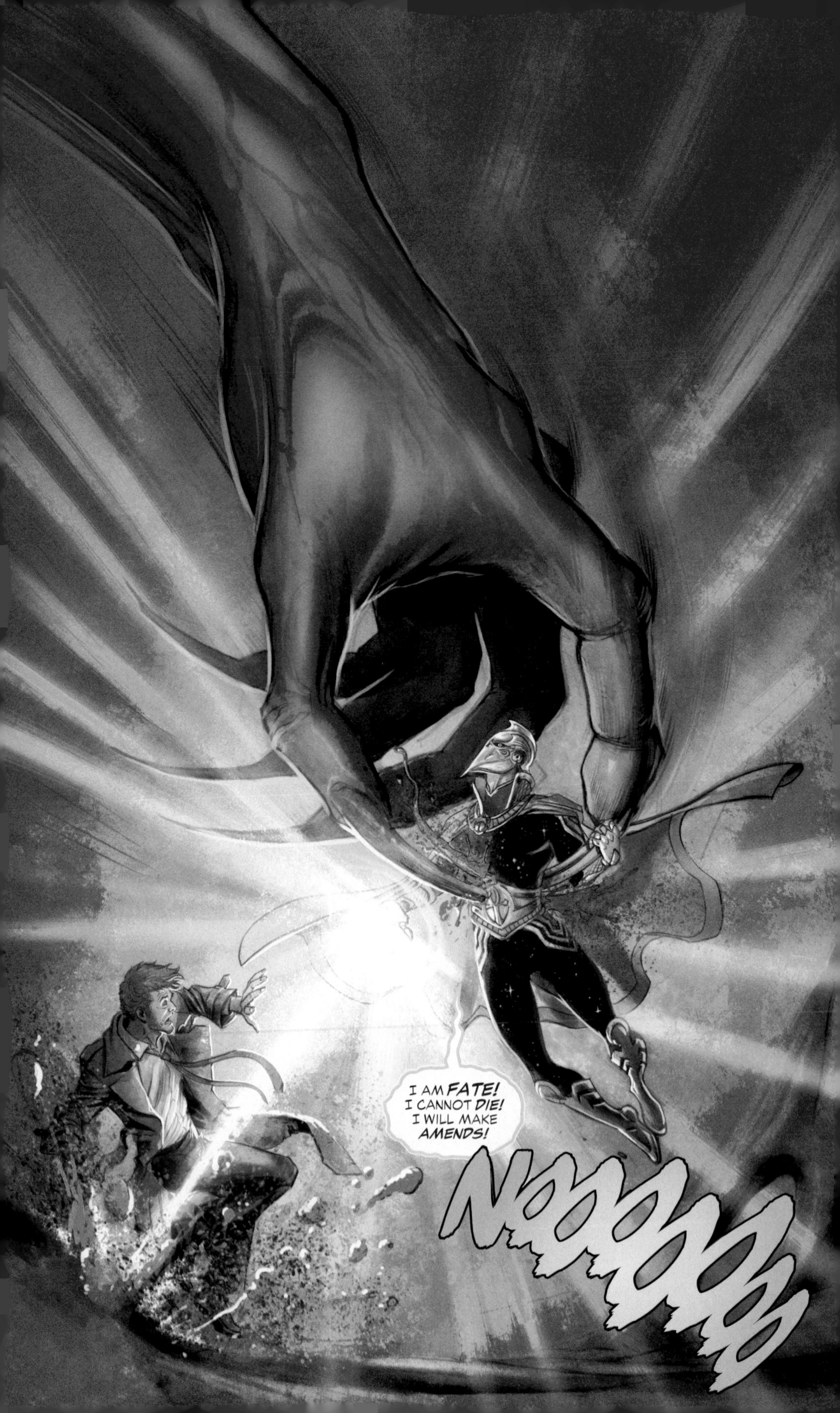
I AM FATE! I CANNOT DIE! I WILL MAKE AMENDS!
NOOOOOO

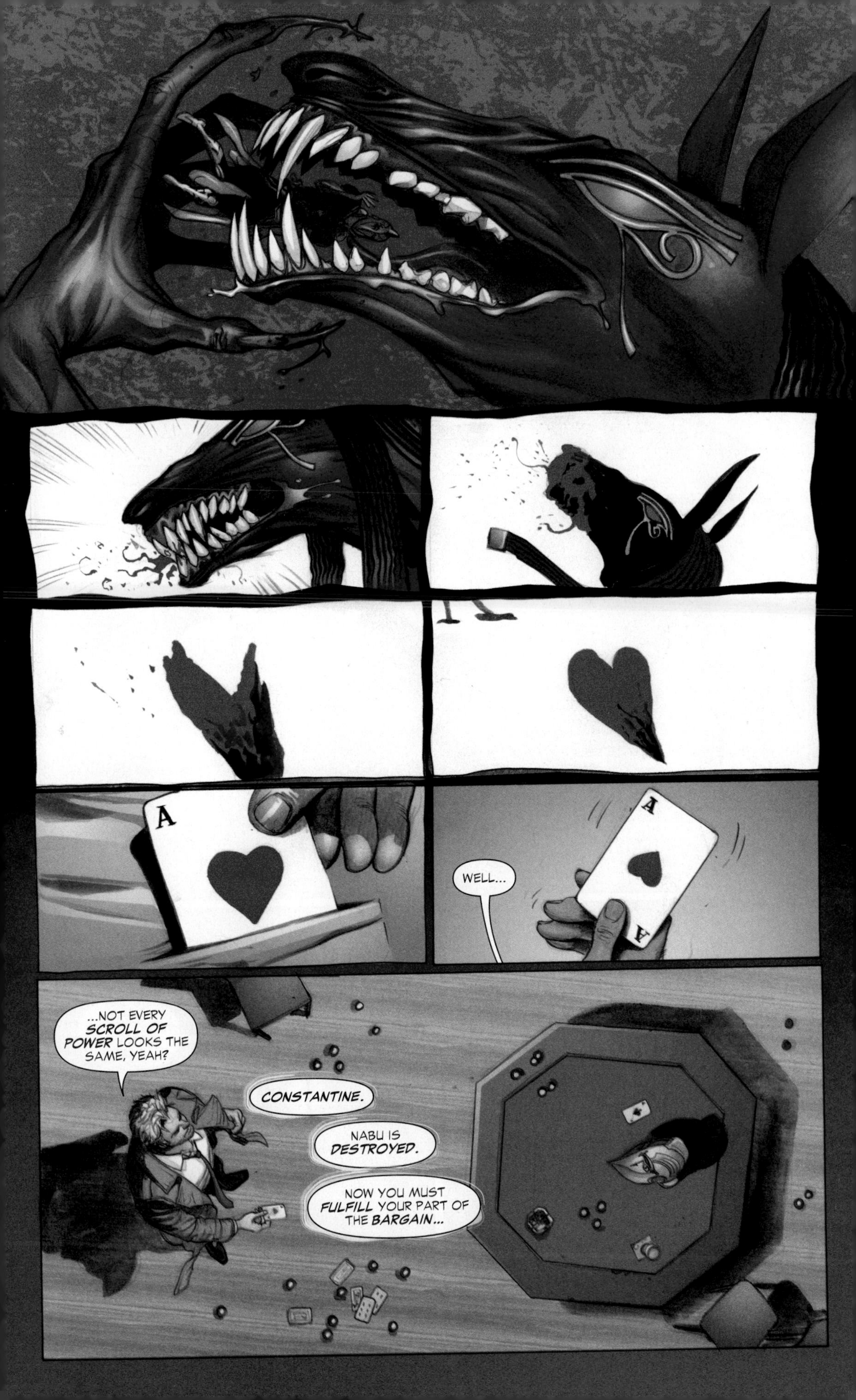
WELL...
...NOT EVERY SCROLL OF POWER LOOKS THE SAME, YEAH?
CONSTANTINE.
NABU IS DESTROYED.
NOW YOU MUST FULFILL YOUR PART OF THE BARGAIN...

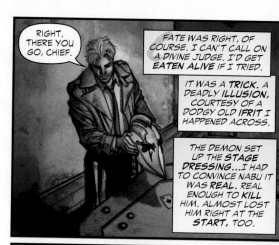

RIGHT. THERE YOU GO, CHIEF.

FATE WAS RIGHT, OF COURSE. I CAN'T CALL ON A DIVINE JUDGE. I'D GET *EATEN ALIVE* IF I TRIED.

IT WAS A *TRICK*. A DEADLY ILLUSION, COURTESY OF A DODGY OLD *IFRIT* I HAPPENED ACROSS.

THE DEMON SET UP THE *STAGE DRESSING*...I HAD TO CONVINCE NABU IT WAS *REAL*. REAL ENOUGH TO *KILL* HIM. ALMOST LOST HIM RIGHT AT THE *START*, TOO.

YOU GET IN THIS, YOU'LL BE ABLE TO *BARGAIN* WITH ANY HUMAN WHO PUTS IT ON.

CALL YOURSELF *NABU* WHEN Y'DO IT, PUT A LITTLE EGYPTIAN *FLASH* ON, AND NONE WILL BE THE WISER.

THEN THE *TRANSACTION* IS CONCLUDED.

AND I CAN ONCE AGAIN DRINK IN THE *WONDERS* OF THIS WORLD'S SMALL MIRACLES...FREE OF MY *PRISON SCROLL*.

FOR *NOW*.

BUT DON'T FORGET. *ALTRUISM*, YEAH? THAT'S THE WATCHWORD.

YOU START BEHAVING *BADLY*-- FOLLOWING OLD NABU'S LEAD...

...AND I'LL *BE BACK* FOR YOU. YOU DON'T WANT THAT.

I'M A *NASTY* PIECE OF WORK, CHIEF.

ASK *ANYBODY*.

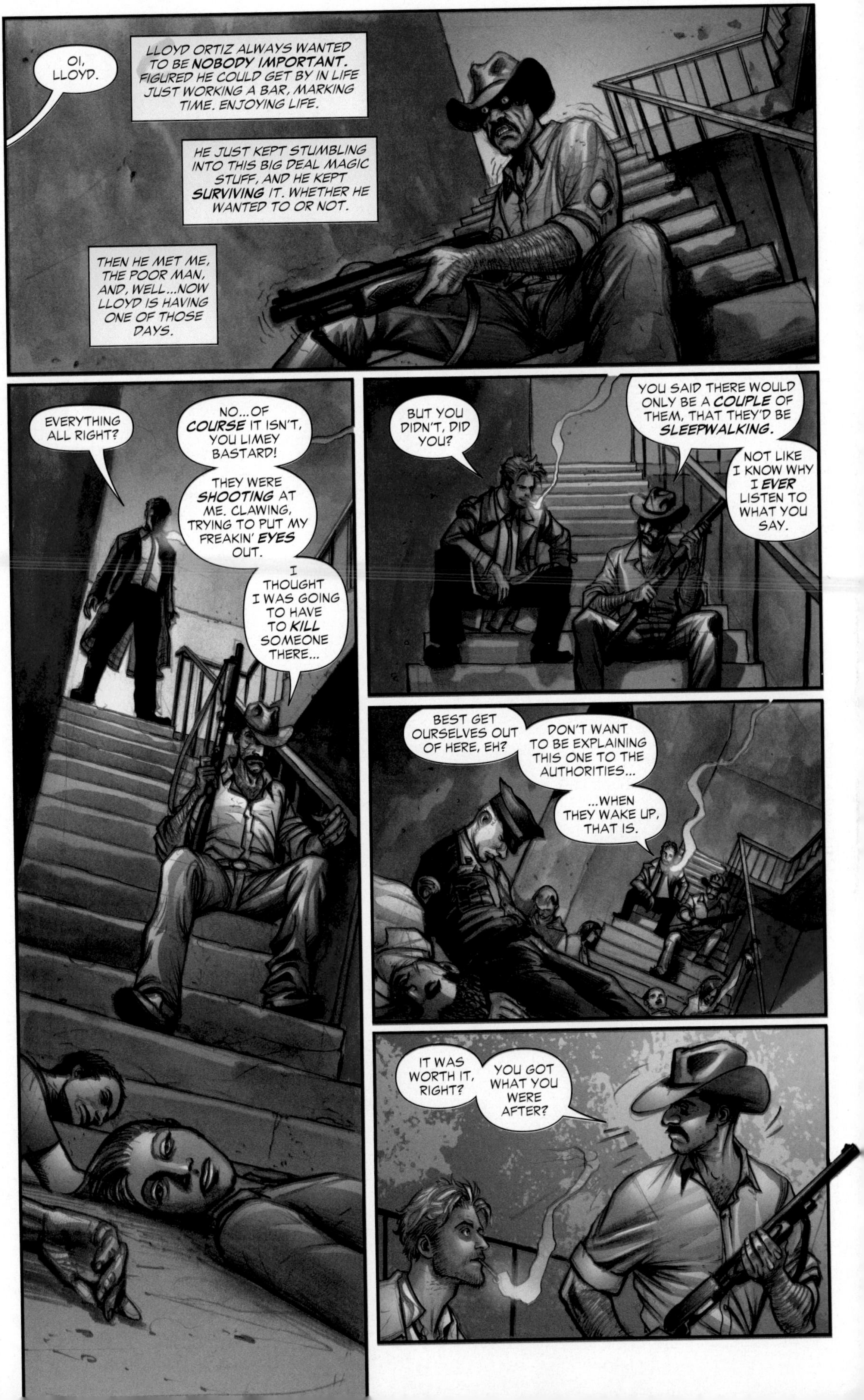
OI, LLOYD.
LLOYD ORTIZ ALWAYS WANTED TO BE NOBODY IMPORTANT. FIGURED HE COULD GET BY IN LIFE JUST WORKING A BAR, MARKING TIME. ENJOYING LIFE.
HE JUST KEPT STUMBLING INTO THIS BIG DEAL MAGIC STUFF, AND HE KEPT SURVIVING IT. WHETHER HE WANTED TO OR NOT.
THEN HE MET ME, THE POOR MAN, AND, WELL...NOW LLOYD IS HAVING ONE OF THOSE DAYS.
EVERYTHING ALL RIGHT?
NO...OF COURSE IT ISN'T, YOU LIMEY BASTARD!
THEY WERE SHOOTING AT ME. CLAWING, TRYING TO PUT MY FREAKIN' EYES OUT.
I THOUGHT I WAS GOING TO HAVE TO KILL SOMEONE THERE...
BUT YOU DIDN'T, DID YOU?
YOU SAID THERE WOULD ONLY BE A COUPLE OF THEM, THAT THEY'D BE SLEEPWALKING.
NOT LIKE I KNOW WHY I EVER LISTEN TO WHAT YOU SAY.
BEST GET OURSELVES OUT OF HERE, EH?
DON'T WANT TO BE EXPLAINING THIS ONE TO THE AUTHORITIES...
...WHEN THEY WAKE UP, THAT IS.
IT WAS WORTH IT, RIGHT?
YOU GOT WHAT YOU WERE AFTER?

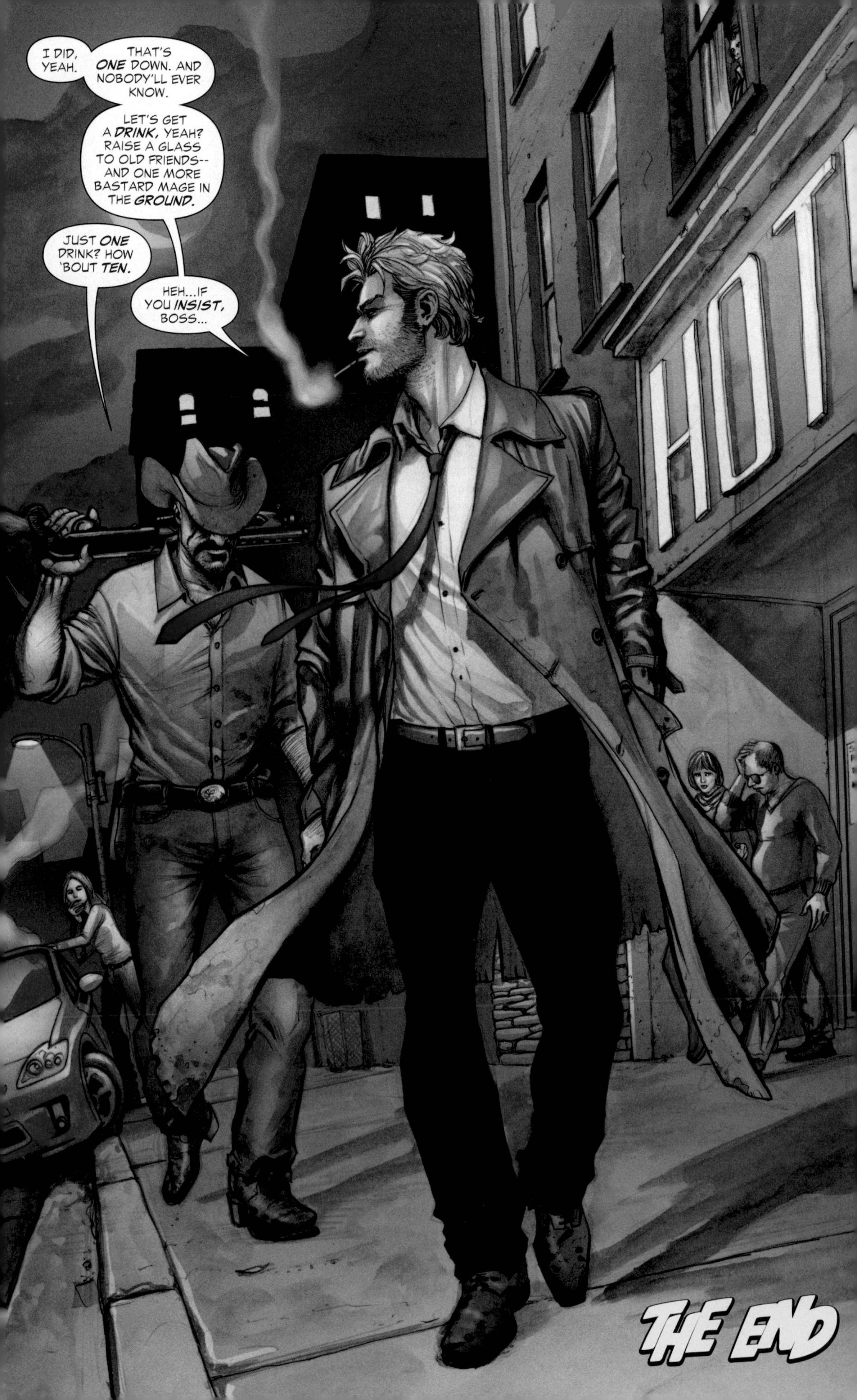
I DID, YEAH.
THAT'S ONE DOWN. AND NOBODY'LL EVER KNOW.
LET'S GET A DRINK, YEAH? RAISE A GLASS TO OLD FRIENDS-- AND ONE MORE BASTARD MAGE IN THE GROUND.
JUST ONE DRINK? HOW 'BOUT TEN.
HEH...IF YOU INSIST, BOSS...
HOT
THE END

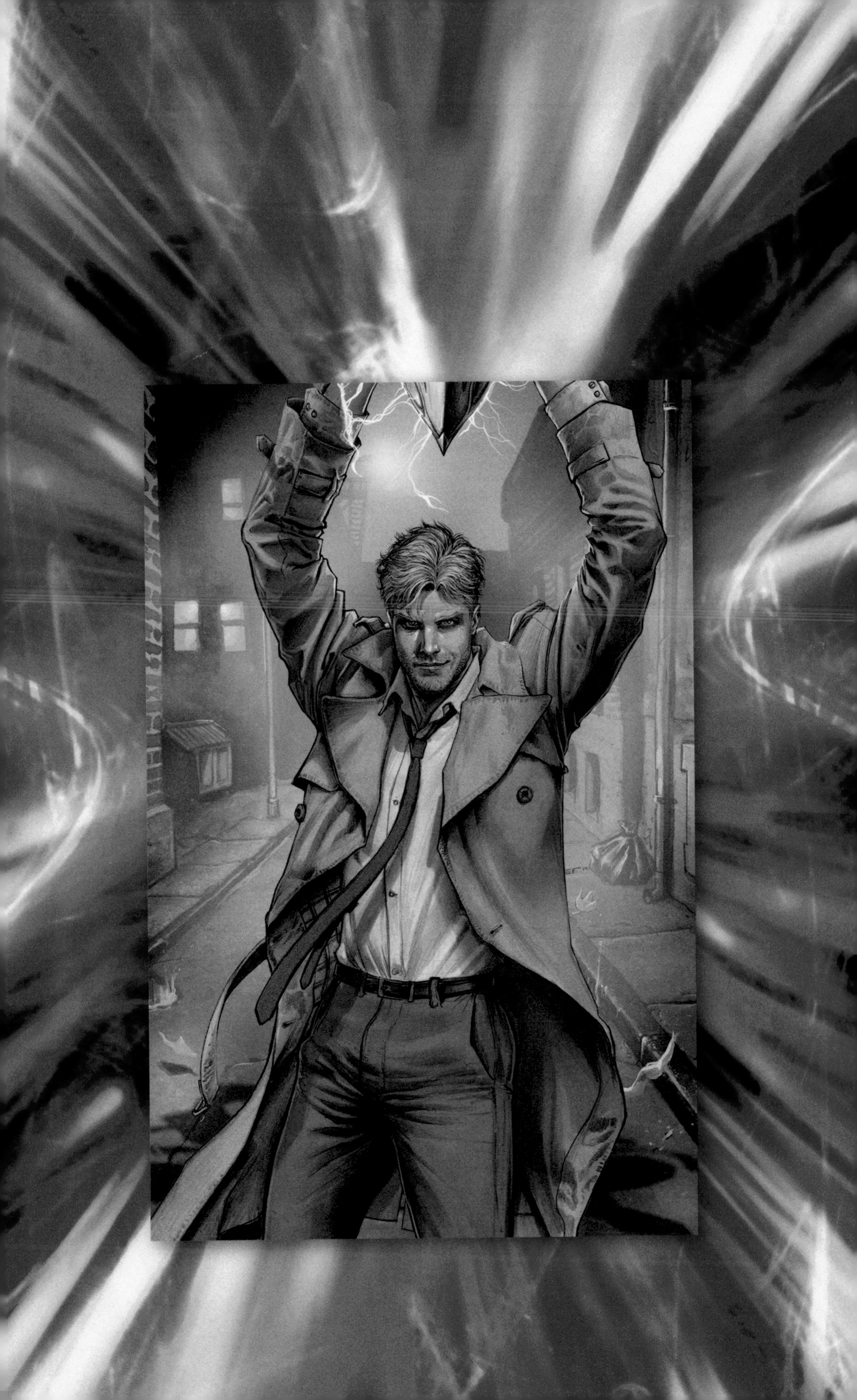

Inked pages from
CONSTANTINE FUTURES END #1

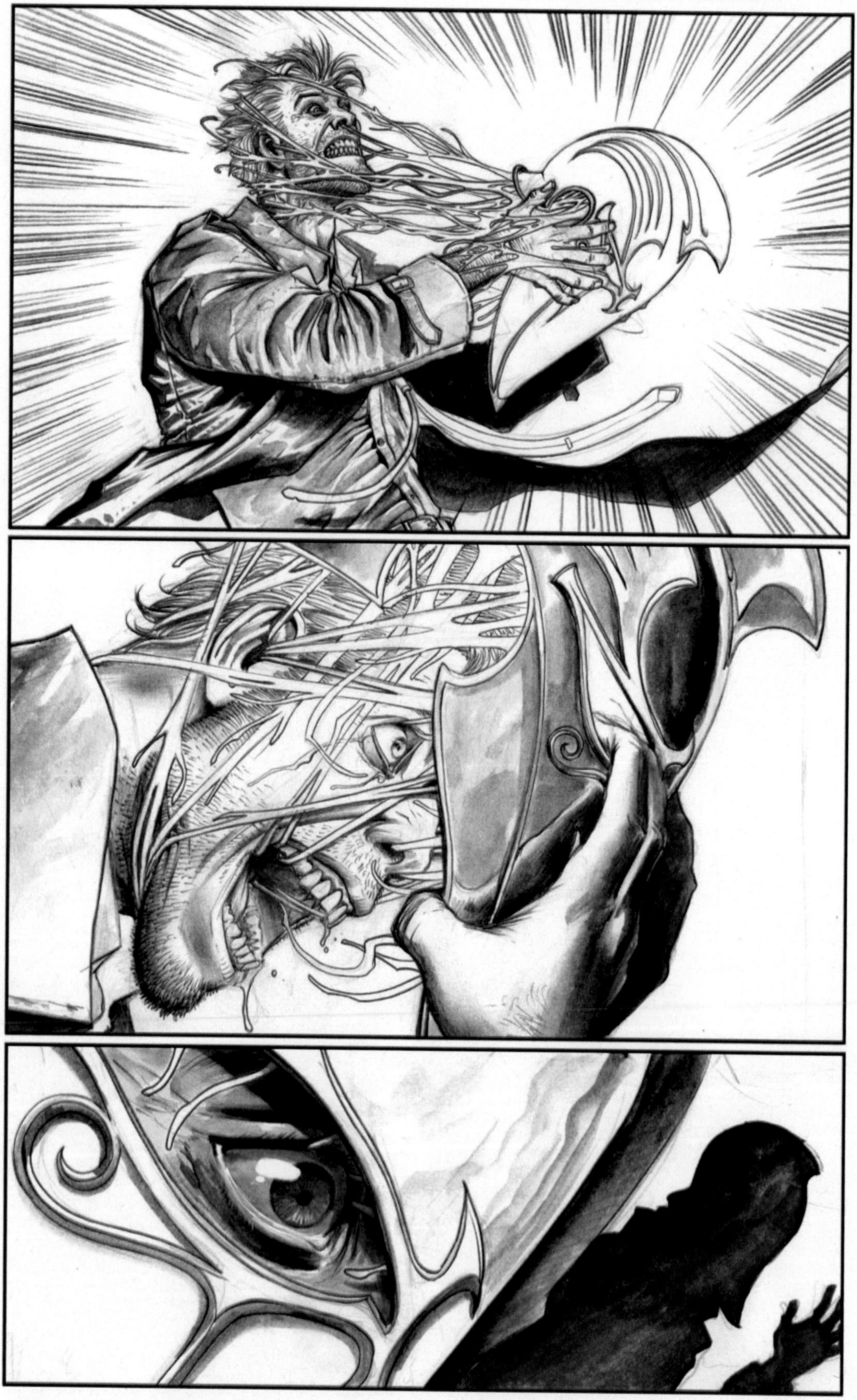

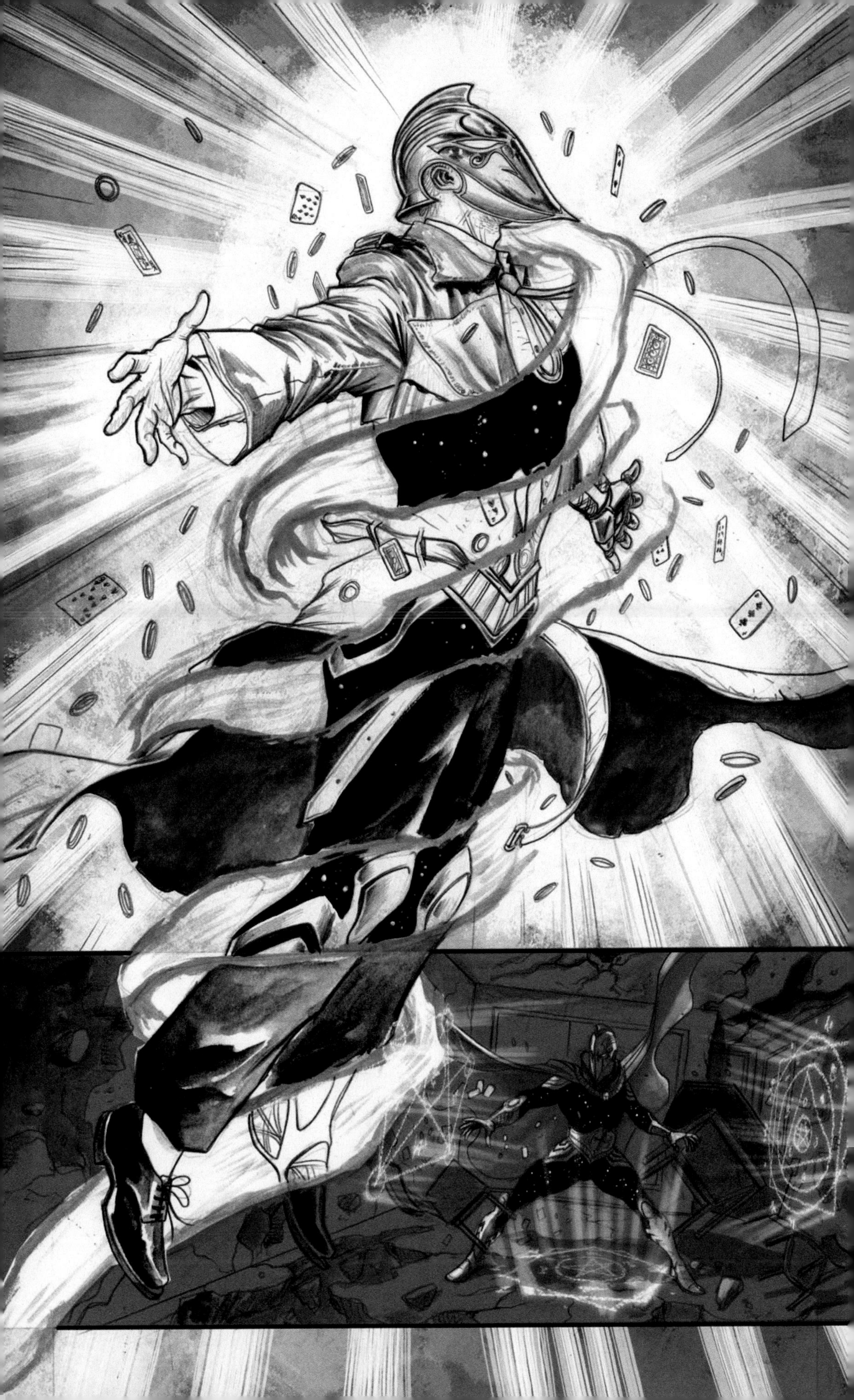

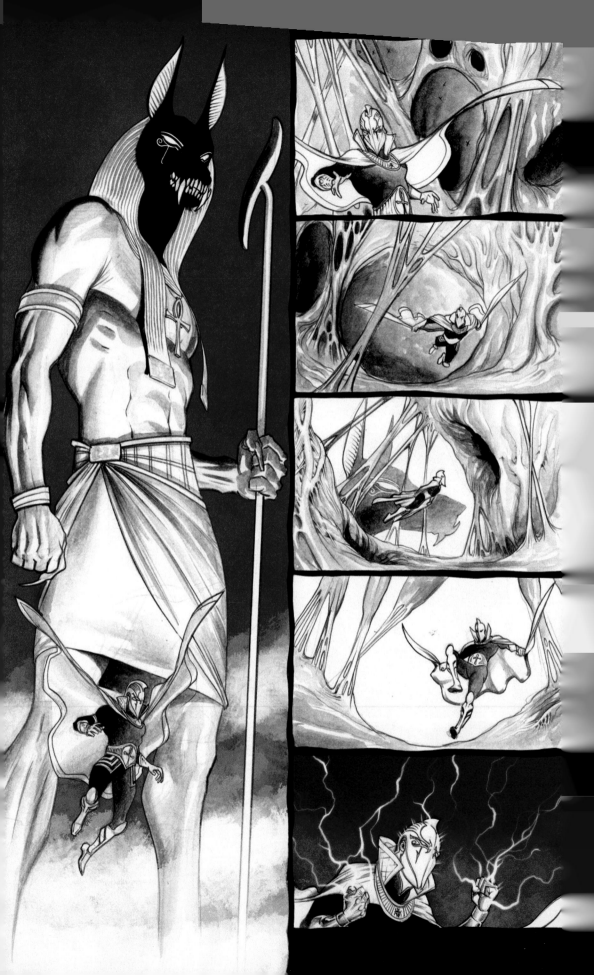

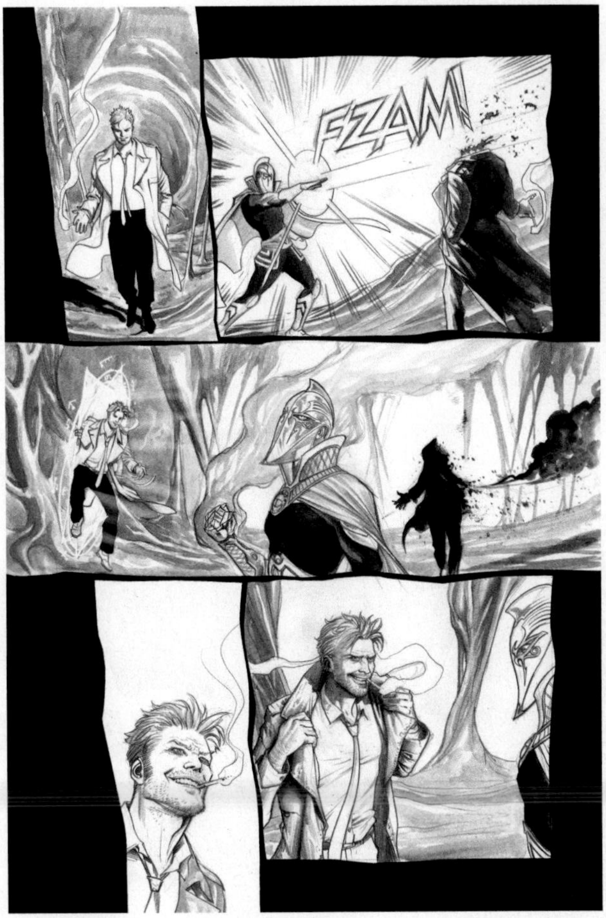
FZAM!

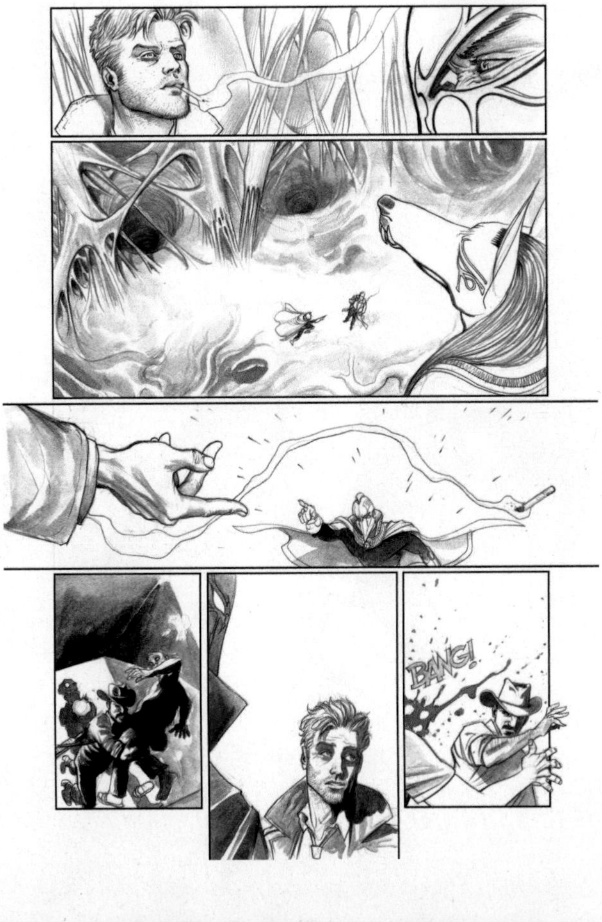
BANG!

"Worthy of the adjective, but in a good way."
—THE NEW YORK TIMES

"There are some threats that are too much for even Superman, Batman and Wonder Woman to handle. That's when you call the people who make magic their method."—CRAVE ONLINE

START AT THE BEGINNING!

JUSTICE LEAGUE DARK
VOLUME 1: IN THE DARK

JUSTICE LEAGUE
DARK VOL. 2: THE
BOOKS OF MAGIC

with JEFF LEMIRE

JUSTICE LEAGUE
DARK VOL. 3:
THE DEATH OF MAGIC

with JEFF LEMIRE

CONSTANTINE
VOL. 1: THE SPARKLE
AND THE FLAME

VOLUME 1
IN THE DARK

PETER MILLIGAN   Mikel JANIN

"If you don't love it from the very first page, you're not human."
—MTV GEEK

"ANIMAL MAN has the sensational Jeff Lemire at the helm."
—ENTERTAINMENT WEEKLY

START AT THE BEGINNING!

ANIMAL MAN
VOLUME 1: THE HUNT

ANIMAL MAN VOL. 2: ANIMAL VS. MAN

ANIMAL MAN VOL. 3: ROTWORLD: THE RED KINGDOM

ANIMAL MAN VOL. 4: SPLINTER SPECIES

VOLUME 1
THE HUNT

"TRAVEL FOREMAN'S ART IS INNOVATIVE AND EXCELLENTLY CREEPY... AS LEMIRE'S EVERYMAN HERO MAKES HIS MARK IN THE NEW DC UNIVERSE."
— USA TODAY

JEFF LEMIRE TRAVEL FOREMAN